I'VE
DONE
THAT

Brilliant Books Literary
137 Forest Park Lane Thomasville
North Carolina 27360 USA

I'VE
DONE
THAT

BRYAN W. JOHNSON

Brilliant Books Literary

DEDICATION

Dedicated to Bryan, Brandon, Lucas, Elizabeth, Niccle, and Connor. So that the children might better know and understand the father.

CONTENTS

CHILDHOOD: CALIFORNIA, TEXAS, KELLY, AND ADOPTION

I was born in San Jose, California. I was born twelve pounds, eight ounces, and was twenty-four and a half inches long. At two-feet tall it was easy to mistake me for a three-year-old in the nursery. My mother was brought to tears by the people coming in talking about the huge Indian kid taking up the nursery space. My birthday was March 17, 1969. This made me a Pisces which, if you know anything about signs, is two fish endlessly chasing one another's tails. Then you add in the year of '69, and you have the figure of two numbers endlessly chasing one another as well. Add in the mix that my mother was a Cancer whose symbol is that of the crab but whose alternate sign is that of yin[g] and yang; and you can see why my destiny is that of a confused man with great intentions, continually running in circles to get nowhere fast. That is pretty well the way things have worked thus far. I do have hope that one day the fish will catch one another, and the numbers will catch each other as well.

My birth was brought on early by my mother being hung for the third time in a month. Her husband Joe had hung her by wrapping his belt around her neck and plucking her up off of the floor with a quick jerking motion. My father, who was not my father really, was bound and determined that if he could not have my mother, nobody would. The problem is, she wasn't fooling around. She was eight months pregnant; who would she be seeing?

Joe was a mountain of a man at six-feet-seven-inches tall and almost 300 pounds. His wife would be pretty safe walking through a prison. But his mind was so drug addled that reason and common sense had left him far behind. So everything in his world was pretty gray. The world was out to get him.

It wasn't always that way. My mother says, he was a wonderful man until my uncle, who has admitted this to be true, led him into the world of Hells Angels and dope sales. I am not saying that the two are hand in hand (so get back off your scoot and nestle back into the bosom of your wench), but the evidence is strong. But whatever the case, he got pretty strung out. (As a little side note, it is not known for sure what has happened to Joe Leanard. He may have found himself at the wrong end of a gun, knife, or drag chain. No one has seen him since the '70s.)

So, there I am. Aren't I cute—all twelve pounds, eight ounces, and twenty-four and a half inches of me, with long black hair, bruised from the natural birth? I kind of looked like a three-year-old Indian that needs a diet. I was a strange wonder from the start. That was probably as normal as I was ever going to get. Guess what else? Joe and my real, real father were best friends. My real father was a married man. He and his wife were on the splits when I was conceived, so mom wasn't a home wrecker or anything, as far as I know. He believed that he was incapable of having kids at the time, but would go on to have a daughter that I have never met, with his wife whom he is still with. [They] Both men came to see me that one time, together. I believe my uncle brought them. But this isn't about the good times. There weren't many, even if I did want to tell you about them. I never saw Jim, the real, real father until I was an adult. Joe never saw me in the hospital again, and it was a while before he saw Mom again. Mom was all alone.

Mom was no innocent. Let's be clear. She was a cocktail server at the Bunny Club when she hooked up with a married man and got knocked up with his kid. His best friend had the hots for mom, so the best friend offered to take on the role of daddy as long as nobody ever found out. A good plan if he could have stayed off of the dope for a while. Jim needed someone to cover his butt so that his wife would never find out, and Joe wanted mom. Mom just needed the cover of a wedding ring. A single mother was actually frowned upon in the US of A back then. Got the picture?

We lived in San Jose in 1969. Mom soon found that she wanted to try and make it work with Joe, so she went to where he had run to. She bought a car for $200 and drove it all the way to Bryan/College Station, Texas—just her and three kids. Did I forget to mention that she already had two more kids from a prior abusive marriage? Well, she did and we all went to try and live with "Daddy" (said with sarcasm).

A funny story about mom and that car. It would seem that my mother wanted a pony. Without a truck to haul it in, she decided to take the back seat out of the car, put us three kids in the front seat with her and put the pony in the back. She drove it through the middle of town with it's head out the window like a dog and it's tail out the other side. Curious onlookers pointing and laughing at her resourceful solution to the problem the whole way. So that's where I get it from.

Joe had a very fat mom. I know little of her other than that she hated my mother and used to pin her down and sit on her while blaming all of Joe's shortcomings on her. It would be a stretch to say that mom can't piss a guy off, but really? We also had a maid. I guess she was the spirit and image of Aunt Jemima from the old syrup bottle. Mom says she just loved me. She would carry me around on her hip while she did all of the chores. This wasn't to last, however.

Don't know when for sure, but we all moved back to California. I know, at some point, Joe would lock Mom in the closet to keep her from getting away while he was at work. She would breast-feed me, and the rest of them survived on peanut butter sandwiches that he would leave in there with us. Mom, eventually tired of this, told him one night after a severe beating, "It's alright. I know I deserve that. Why don't you just fall asleep?" Joe left that night and didn't show back up for a long time.

Joe came back a time or two. He would stalk Mom a time or two, harass her at work, whatever. But then, my mother went to the right person for the job—my Aunt Kelly. (Here's where I get interested again.)

Kelly was from New Jersey. She isn't blood but don't tell her that. She was married to my grandmother on my mother's side's brother. He was a loser of the elite class. A classic drinker and partier from what I understand. He held up a liquor store, and then he abandoned Kelly somewhere back East with the notion that when he found work, he would send for her. He ended up in California where he was from in the first place. He sent word to come hither and she did. Kelly drove an old flatbed truck all the way across country with her newborn child. She relied on the kindness of truckers to get her through. The truck, as she tells the story, was on its last legs and each day she spoke sweetly to it to get another mile out of it. First one and then another, the time passed as did the miles. It made it one more day, and then did it again until she found herself on the West Coast. In Los Angeles, she had to go over the "Grapevine pass." It was steep and wound its way out of the greater Los Angeles basin. As she climbed the hill, her truck got slower and hotter. She feared it would not make the climb. Back in those days, you either made it or you didn't. There was no place to pull off. A semi-close on her tail, she worried what might happen if she were to stop. Just as the truck seemed to be on its last gasp, something happened.

The truck actually accelerated to the top. She said that the truck never had so much power before.

At the top of the hill, she stopped to give the truck a well-deserved drink of water. It was hot and deserved the rest. The trucker behind her had the same plan and pulled in right behind her. They started to talk while they waited for the vehicles to cool. "I couldn't believe the power just kicked in at the steepest point." She exclaimed with pride to the truck driver in a Jersey drawl that sounds more like she comes from the hills of Tennessee. "Oh, that," he said with a sheepish grin. He thought she was being sarcastic. "I apologize, but if you had slowed us any more, I wasn't going to make it over the hill; and I gotta be in the bay by morning."

Kelly caught on right away. She wasn't being sarcastic. She really had no idea that he had matched bumpers with her and pushed her up over the hill. So, as quick as a whip, "I Say's back to him, Thank Gawd! I thought she was possessed," she would recount the tail, speaking of her old rig gaining speed against all reason.

They laughed together and drove as company up to the bay area where both were headed. By the time she got to San Jose, her husband was dead. He had shot himself in the head while his wife and child were en route. He left them to fend for themselves in a world where women aren't expected to do things for themselves. It wasn't the greatest thing to do for your bride, but for his young bride, it may have been the only way to allow her the life she could have. Essentially, Kelly moved in as family and never left. Never asking for anything or requiring help from anyone, she never was too close to the older members of the family. It was the kids she stood for.

One hot afternoon, while Kelly was visiting, the neighbor lady was being adversarial to the children about laughing and playing. My mother and her sisters were young and this is my mother's greatest memory of her sad childhood. The neighbor called the police on the children. She complained about the noise and the constant chatter. She wanted them all arrested—small children less than ten years old in the '50s—and she wanted them hauled away.

Kelly met them on the lawn. She ran the cop off and told the old hag where to shove it in very unladylike terms. But Kelly was over the top in the ways of May West over the top. She was working for an asphalt company at the time. Still driving that same old truck as well as starting her own trucking company on the side. After she left from her visit, she visited all the stores in the neighborhood. She bought up all of the chicken guts and giblets. She then "borrowed" the asphalt mixer from work loaded with tar. In the night, she "paved" the walk and porch right up to the door. "Work I could of charged for it was so beautiful," she told me. She had infused the chicken parts into the mix as it cooled and let the hundred plus degree temps of the following days do the rest. And there wasn't a thing the old bag next door could do but "smell it rot!"

That's Kelly. (I am more her blood than any other in my family—true to the core. Why lie when the truth is so much more fun?) She was our protector. She has kept us from harm on more occasions than we can count; so when mom needed help from someone, forget the police, get to Kelly's house. And that is exactly where mom went.

Joe had followed us there. He was skulking around the shadows when Kelly came out onto the porch.

"Show yourself, you son of a bitch." Kelly blared out into the night in her Jersey hillbilly cigarette-parched, gravel twang.

She was wearing her legendarily telltale-flannel-work shirt, jeans, pocket vest, cowboy boots, and flaming red hair complimented by the gleam of her ever handy Model 1911, .45 caliber semiautomatic pistol that she still carries to this day. You see, Kelly never wanted to be John Wayne, John Wayne wanted to be Kelly. Joe knew he couldn't confront Kelly directly, and there wasn't much of a chance of getting at my mother as long as Kelly stood between them. I'm sure he must have known that Kelly knew what he had been doing to her favorite niece. He just hunkered down behind that old truck thinking he was safe. He thought he was safe, but the wind would carry thunder that night as Kelly let loose a ball of lead nearly a-half-of-an-inch in diameter. Flames coming from the barrel engulfed that bullet for the first four feet of flight with a sudden brilliant flash until all of the energy from the burning powder had been spent and darkness could once again take over. As the bullet escaped the shroud of fire and sped on its path, one can only imagine the brief thought of shock and fear mixed in the mind of the mad man. But his wait would be brief. A .45 caliber slug is slow by bullet standards at 830 feet per second. But the 230 grain weight is mammoth in projectile weights. It is known for the one-shot-knock-down and even at that slow speed, it can cross the 40 foot distance in .225 seconds—way faster than the blink of an eye.

It first penetrated the fuel tank of the truck, then exited the other side imbedding itself violently into Joe's leg, yanking his leg behind and out from under him, taking this six-foot-seven, 300-pound man, and slamming him to the ground. The shock left him bleeding and scrambling to getaway. Kelly laughed her boisterous laugh and let him go. He would not be back, and she still smiles the whole time she tells the story. It always ends with the same laugh filling the room like a contagion that fills us all.

She is proud of who she is, and at eighty plus years old, she is still not one to be trifled with. Kelly inspired my childhood as well as my adult life more than any other person, probably. She showed me how to feel safe. She loved me even though she didn't have to, and she would sing no matter the mood. Kelly plays guitar. Her friends play instruments of all kinds, and frequently, we would arrive in the middle of the night to find a room full of people sitting around playing and singing in the wee hours of the night. On these nights, I would sit by Kelly's feet with a hand on her leg and sing at the top of my lungs to whatever old country hit they were playing. I was about two years old when my memories of her become crystal clear.

Kelly smoked cigarettes that she would roll herself. She had an old cookie sheet with an antique roller in the middle of it that took up most of the pan. It had a canvas strap across the top bridging a metal framework. She would put a paper into it, fill it with her own mix of cherry pipe tobacco, and regular cigarette rolling tobacco. She would then pull a handle that looked like a credit card slider and pull it back again. Then, out would come a rolled smoke. Just a lick on the paper gum and it was ready to light. It was this smoke that my subconscious still holds as the smell of safety, and the number one reason I smoke. (My Dad is number two but that's another story.)

As of the writing of this book, Kelly is over 80 years old. I have just confirmed that for the past couple of years she has been dating a man half her age. They drive long haul truck as a team. After undergoing a knee surgery, she looks forward to returning to the road soon. I t was also told to me that prior to the shooting incident, Joe had been caught by Kelly on the hill overlooking her house with a hunting rifle. He was perched up there with his eye to the scope waiting for my mother to exit the home when Kelly spotted him. She somehow went around the hill, snuck up from behind him and put that .45 in his ear with the stern warning that if he ever came back she would shoot him. It's nice to know that there are still people out there that keep their word.

Kelly could not always be there though. Sometimes we just can't be in time to help the ones we love. Unfortunately for my mother, her lifestyle was conducive to bad men. First my older sibling's father and then Joe and then the date that would change destiny.

My mother met a man somewhere, probably her work. He seemed okay but Mom must have sensed something wrong with him; because she insisted that if they were to go on a date, he would have to allow us children to come. Three children must surely guarantee safety, in her mind at least.

He kidnapped us all. We were held for three weeks in an old farmhouse where he did unspeakable things to my mother. Each time he would pass out, Mom would tend to us kids. She says that she wanted to escape but where could she go? There were fields for as far as the eye could see; and she had a three-year- old, two-year-old, and a one-year-old. We would watch her come from the room bloody and beaten and trying to comfort us. We were in the living room with the television on. We weren't the ones needing help.

People always have told me that I could not possibly remember the details of my early childhood with the vivid detail with which I do. But I do. I was walking at eight months old and talking in clear sentences by a year. I remember the events with exacting specificity. I remember.

She came from the room late in the day. The light was falling, and her courage was waning as she took me up into her arms. The door had been left carelessly unlocked. She told my brother to take my sister's hand, and we silently fled the house out into the field. The rows were the only guides we had. Surely they must end at a road. There had to be a house or barn or some place of refuge. We continued out into the fields as the dark set in on us. My brother and sister were going as fast as there little legs would take them as mom hurried them as fast as she could. I remember the leaves passing my face and itching my skin. I remember the smell of the damp soil as we traveled in the dark, pleading in our minds for safety.

Up ahead was a light. It shown brightly but the corn was tall. We couldn't make out what it was at first, so we just did our best to get to it in hopes that it was a farm. Time passed slowly while we prayed that our captor was not somewhere behind us in the dark fields. Suddenly, the fields opened to a farmhouse area.

The whole old McDonald scene complete with rounded-top-red barn and tractors and a little house dwarfed by the massive fields.

I don't recall what happened at the house very well. I could pick out the peoples' faces in a line up if I had to, even today, but it seemed to me that they weren't very helpful. They refused to call the police. Instead, they called her a taxi and paid to have her taken into town.

Shattered and beaten, no one could blame her for what she did next. She had been abused by two husbands nearly to the point of death on several occasions. Her will constantly under attack by forces beyond her control and now this. How could she protect us when she couldn't protect herself? As we were delivered from that taxicab to the orphanage, my sister cried and my brother questioned. My mother never left the front seat while we children were leaving out the backdoor. In my memory are the films of three small children holding hands as we entered the doors of the orphanage after watching the yellow car drive off without us. My mother was still inside, not looking as she left, my sister and brother crying.

We were separated from the start. We wound up in different rooms and soon different homes. I went to my aunt's house first. I don't want to go into the horrors that happened in that house or the fact that I still to this day can't enter a house with chicken soup cooking because I was forced to eat it almost exclusively. It is important to state that it was so bad that my grandmother had me taken from that home and put elsewhere.

My grandmother hated me from an early age. I never knew why, until as an adult, I asked her to her face after she screwed me over without cause or provocation. She had called family to complain about me stealing from her when I came for a shower. Later, she had claimed that I stole a shaving kit from my uncle who lived there. (I had never owned an electric shaver. Hell, I didn't even have to shave very often. I could barely grow whiskers.) The only answer she gave for telling a child his entire life that he meant nothing to her when the other kids, especially my older brother, were her grandkids and not me, was that I looked like my grandfather—her first husband. That was a crock because although I would like looking like him, I never did. I have pictures from his youth and I look nothing like him.

But if the old bitty wanted to use that as an excuse, I let her. So, for her to save me seemed so far-fetched that I had to ask that too during the same sitting as the other question.

I was twenty-two when I asked her the question. "Grandma, everyone suspects that it was you who called Sally Plumber and had me taken from Vicky. Did you?"

"How can you ask me that?" She was shaken worse than the first question.

"Grandma, did you save me?" I just had to have one good thing to credit her with.

"Yes! Alright? I did. Now can we drop this? I don't need to be reminded that I did that to my own daughter." She was genuinely tearing up.

"Why? Why did you help me if you don't like me?"

"No child should be treated like that." Tears fell and her eyes reddened. She was touched with sorrow over the memory. "I couldn't let them..."—she stopped—"no more, (sniffs) let it go. You['re] got out."

When she was still alive, her own children got together and voted that she was dead to them. No member of the family spoke to her again until my Uncle Carrie's funeral. He died of complication of AIDS. The day he died, the world lost a treasure and a wonderful, funny, amazing human being. I then went to live with the Rice family. They had been adoptive parents to many children. They had been parents to their own two children. I knew the kids as Sissy and Jim. They were both adults before I ever arrived.

The Rices, Mama Dee and Norm, were fare and just. They treated me with a great kindness, even know their house was far from any other children, and I had no one to play with. I would play in the gravel drive or out in the pasture. I often swam in their above ground pool and actually taught myself to swim there. I never told my stepdad, later on, that he was reteaching me to swim. I let him think that he taught me to swim, but in reality, I actually took to water as if born to it.

Mama Dee was on the raised deck that Norm had built around the pool. I came to the pool side in my shorts and wanted to get into the water, but she wasn't going to let me. I was two and a half when I went to live there and should not have known how to swim. She was sixty plus years old and was not in any shape to dive in after a drowning child. "If you can swim across the pool in the deep end, you can get in." I jumped in and swam across. I was as surprised as she. It makes no sense, but I swear it is the truth. Later on in my childhood, I would be the star of preschool swim class.

The Rices were a religious zealot family. They were Nazarene and everything revolved around their faith. That was the cause of a really painful realization for me. I was with them for a couple or three years. I loved them as you would your grandparents, if yours were nice to you that is. But one day when I was three, I was on my way out to climb on the palm tree out in front of the church. All of us kids were together on the joys of climbing, it seemed. But at the halfway point, I remembered the sermon being given in the adult section that I had listened to prior to coming out. "Fire and Brimstone!" I thought to myself, *These people are nuts!* I may have even said it out loud. From that day on I never believed in God. You may notice that the times in this writing that I refer to the Almighty, I misspell it on purpose. That is out of respect for those who do believe. But I never will because the concept just does not ring true. I don't know why, but I have been cursed to live this life without a God to lean on or a Jesus to trust. I wish that I could, but I cannot.

FATHER QUEST

My father was a great man. Well, he still is. He isn't dead, he's just getting old. He is great as in "a really great guy" not as in "has lots of money" or "the captain of industry." He is and was just "a really great guy." Everyone who ever met him thought of him with respect. Sheriff's officers who worked with my mother always showed him a reverence that you never see coming from policemen. I realized the other day that my father is going to be eighty years old this December. Just that he made it this far is amazing. He did so without ever changing the oil in his car or changing a spark plug either. Even more odd about those last two things is that he instructed welding for many years. You would expect him to have been more mechanical. But he wasn't. That wasn't what made him super to me. I guess that's a good thing, because if you can't tie it to the end of a fishing line or birds don't nest in it, he can't fix it.

After I left for the military, Dad seemed to realize that the dishes weren't washing themselves, the dishwasher was broken and so he purchased another one. The wood stopped getting chopped and stacked so he got a pneumatic wood splitter. The first microwave wasn't far behind that and then, not really his fault I guess, but they got cable television. We had only been receiving one channel that somehow ran the big three networks according to what some programmer thought that we wanted to see. In the last couple of years before I left, PBS came in. So we still had one channel (except when they ran the yearly fundraiser. Ha, ha.).

Dad tried though. When we lived in Oregon, it would be subzero for long periods of time. There were times that dad and I would be under the house with my mother's hair dryer trying to unfreeze the water pipes. We lived in a mobile home—yes, there were wheels at one time—that they still live in today. But for some reason, Dad couldn't spend the $15 to buy heat tape for those stinking pipes and save himself the trouble of winter. Some nights would find him out there all alone for hours. I also remember a particular septic incident that had him up to his shoulder in sewage. Whatever it was, he did get it fixed (and a shower).

Dad was born in 1932. He left school to support his mother after his father left. He did this by going to war (Korea, 1951-1953.) He was in communications onboard a naval vessel which is funny because he really didn't communicate very well. (Okay…I thought about that last statement. He really communicated well, just with his demeanor and not his words. I always pictured his mother talking to him as a child, saying, "Baird, use your words. I know what you want and for some reason I find myself really wanting to give it to you, but use your words…Okay, but next time for sure") Then he came home to try and live out the American dream. He is related to the Cornings the "glass people" and the McCoys of the Hatfield-McCoy feud. My mother was his second wife, and I was the youngest of his three new step kids. To me, he was eight feet tall. In actuality, he stands five feet nine inches and most of my life he was about 180 pounds. He looks and kind of acts like a cross between Elvis, the Fonz, and as he aged, Tom Bosley. His voice is closer to the latter. Low and gravelly with a higher intone. (He can talk any baby to sleep with his soothing voice. Women fall all over themselves and men can't seem to resist the alpha male tone.) More of him to come, I suppose.

This is the story of me. After years of being told to write about myself, I am finally going to actually sit down and try to make a coherent story of this crazy life I've lived. If I can, I am going try and make you understand who I am and why I feel the things I feel. I am going to try and tell why I did what I did, when I did and how I did it. If at all possible, I will send everyone who reads this on a journey that will leave them with the thankful thought, *Thank Gawd I am not him.*

Major rifle manufacturers such as Winchester make thousands of rifles exactly the same. Of all of those rifles, every one but two may shoot exactly the same. It has always been that way and always will. One will be a dog. It just won't shoot straight and with every couple of loads put through it you have to tighten the screws. The other is the most fantastic rifle ever manufactured. It shoots so straight that a single hole appears at 100 yards every time no matter the ammunition used in it. I am the embodiment of both of these outcasts. It's not bad enough to be an odd duck, but I come perfectly suited to take the role of both. For instance, I can fix anything that ever breaks: toasters, cars, toys, drawers, roofs, computers, even balloons on some occasions. I even amaze myself sometimes with the outlandish miracles I come up with. At times, when I've looked at some weird piece of something or other that I can barely understand the workings of, my children will look at me and just say, "Okay, fix it."

I'm stuck. Something in my midst needs my attention, and these little hooligans expect me to fix it. So I start to look and before I know it, I have a thousand small electronic parts before me, and I can't stop working until I know that my sweet lil' minions will wake in the morning to a working watcha'call-it. And voila! It gets put back together and works as new.

On the other hand, I am the lemon as well. As of this writing, I have broken thirty-four to thirty-eight bones in my body. I guess a few less if you disallow same bones being broken more than once, but I like to count them all separately as if each break gets its own place in my memory. For instance, I have broken my ankles five times—three on one side, two on the other. I never missed a day of work with the exception of the first one, but I was in the army at that time and didn't have a choice in the matter. Also, I have the uncanny ability to train a person to do things for a very short time, only to have them fall into some outstandingly lucky happenstance that permits them to use the training I gave them to become instantly successful. I don't take from them that they do all of the work to succeed. I understand that they did it and it was their contacts or situation that got them there, but a little kickback in kind from fate would be nice. (As of the re-release of this title, the 2023 bone tally is 46 bones. 7 ankles included.)

Why me, you ask. Why should you read my story? Well the answer isn't easy. It all depends on who you are and why you need me. I have always served others and befriended people who need me. It is for that reason that I know without doubt that someone out there needs this book. Someone is just looking to hear the true and unadulterated truth of someone who has lived a life—a life full of devastation, love, heartbreak, wonder and lacking fulfillment, satisfaction, gratification and reward. Someone out there needs a man to guide them. Because of what I've done and who raised me and the world I have seen and lived, I am sure beyond a doubt that I am the last true John Wayne.

This book is full of real. Can you handle that? The stories are true and I have witnesses to prove them. The details are what happens to a man who never says die. A person who never blames society for the mistakes he makes because to do so would destroy the man and the last vestige of hope for this man's mind.

Someone once said, "It's not whether you win or lose but how you play the game." I beg to differ. Sometimes it doesn't matter how you play the game as long as you do "play the game." Put yourself out there and try. Then, every day you have to try again. Try new things. Attempt to do something. Anything. Just don't give up.

Timing and rhythm are as important in life as they are in business, as they are in breathing. Some of us have one or even two of these down but the others elude us. We must continue to continue. In my life, I have never been in the right place at the right time. I have never ignored opportunity, yet it has never really presented itself to me either. In my brief real estate career, the market was the best in US history. The problem was that the people I knew were priced right out of the market. The news we hear about people getting loans for houses they couldn't afford are only half truths. I was unable to become successful because the market was too strong. Later, I sold cars and was pretty good at it but the manager was a guy from New York who thought that it was just fine to yell and scream at the employees while customers were in the show room. I got that job just after he arrived, and so the timing could not have been worse. I am not one to be yelled at. At six-four and two hundred and twenty pounds, it was not me he was screaming at, he was yelling at others and I just couldn't be there for that. (The one time he did yell at me, I nearly went over the counter at him. He was visibly shaken.) Because timing and rhythm cannot be governed by the will of the person relying on them, a person must literally wait for the proper moment to arrive. Since we cannot see it coming, we must continue to search for it until we find ourselves in "the groove." I have never been in the groove. Just when I think that I am, I find the rug being pulled out from under me. This is demonstrated in my life. Demonstrated in how the events build and transpire.

I always strive to do the best that I can. In no place in my life has that shown more strongly than in being a father. I am not the best at getting my kids to do their homework. I don't insist on certain things that most parents do. I allow them to be themselves while teaching them what it takes to get along in the real world. Where I really shine though, is in my making sure that everything I do is for the benefit of my children and family. I don't do outrageous spending on things for myself. I never get myself something if it will take from them. I have been forced to leave them to raise themselves through my years as a single father because keeping a roof over their heads demanded it. On the weekends and the time that we had, I would make up for it—my time being their time. We had to work as a team. I would teach them the importance of giving and helping the week as well as the importance of looking out for one's self, a lesson I've never learned.

In my life, life and survival of the whole demand the sacrifice of the one and as long as I am the one, I don't really mind. As long as I can breathe in and out, my children will be safe under my protection.

MILPITAS, CALIFORNIA AS A KID

Imagine the '70s in California. Hippies thought that they were the main stream. Responsible parenting meant that there was food in the house and the electricity doesn't get shut off. Children were to be seen, not heard for the most part as it had always been. The big difference was that parents were both working for the first time in history. We're shafted out of our mother's and the June Cleaver home life. If we were hungry, we ate. Nobody was home until after six in the evening, summer, winter, spring, and fall except at my house where my mother slept all day and worked all night. We kids were to be quiet or gone and it didn't matter which as long as mom got her sleep. My parent would take trips to Lake Tahoe or Reno for the weekend and leave us to our own ways. Many times I spent the night in the house alone because my parents went on a weekend trip and my brother and sister would vanish the moment the car pulled out of the drive. Sounds like the perfect life for a kid, right? No supervision, just be in when the streetlights come on. If something happens, go to the neighbors, if they're home. But I had a different reason for not liking it.

The Rices contested my return to my mother. She had remarried and was in a respectable job as a switchboard operator for the San Jose Police Dept. My stepfather was a welding trade school instructor at a school that he was to inherit from his father and a barber every Saturday. I am not sure of the amount of time and money that it cost to get me back, but they did when I was five.

My sister took a long time to come home. I don't know why, she wasn't the most lovable child in the world. But she was the last to come home, at any rate. I really haven't much info on her time with her adoptive family in Los Gatos. All I know is that my brother was only a few blocks away.

My brother was short and skinny for his age, a small-boned boy with a narrow face and big ears. (Yes that is probably a family trait.) He had blond hair which makes his head look smaller and when his big teeth came in, they were huge. The funny caricature that you have in mind is most likely pretty accurate. His adoptive family was not really kind to him, from the way he describes it. They had a son named Ralphy who was larger than my brother. Ralphy was a bully who through his considerable weight, picked relentlessly on Mark, my brother. Whenever Mark would defend himself, the mother would take Ralphy's side. When Ralphy got hurt, it was Mark's fault even when he was nowhere in sight. And Gawd forbid Mark should win a fight with Ralphy. (I'm sick of that name just from writing it so many times.) It was, "poor little Ralphy."

When Mark came back he was damaged. It could have been in his genetics, hidden and latent anyway, but he was not a nice or good person. We had very few things in common. I had thought that all of my hard times were behind me after Sally Plumber came and took me from my aunt's house and delivered me to the Rices. I could never have known that all of that was just a warm up for things to come.

Mark was always irritable and wanting to hurt somebody, usually me. He was short for his age, I was tall. He was lightweight and thin. I was stocky and muscular. He was fast as lightning on his feet, I was medium speed. His hands were blinding fast, I was a power puncher who had yet to gain any speed or coordination.

What we did share was fearlessness. That made for some terrible fights. When we start to tell stories in a room full of people, nobody can ever top our true tales of us.

I never have gotten any good answers from him as to why, but he fully admits that he wanted me dead. No more than a week would pass without me bleeding out in some way. One fight we had took place in our entertainment room. A room made out of the garage that had a wall built in the end that left only six or eight feet of storage on the other side of what used to be a two- car garage with a high ceiling. There was a television in the wall that never worked. My parents had us share this as our bedroom, on and off. One day, Mark believed that I had snitched on him for something that he had done. I did not, but he wouldn't believe me. Mark punched me in the face twice before I knew what was happening. I reached out and wrapped my arm around his neck. He picked me up and threw me through my mother's 150-year-old, antique, desk mounted mirror. Glass shattered and we both ended up cut up. I let him go and he continued to attack, trying to kick me in the face as I scrambled across the floor, keeping just out of range. I got to my feet and swung, missing him but follow though carried my body into him and I pinned him against the wall. His arms trapped, I rolled to the right and picked him up like a battering ram. I then backed up a step and then, shifting to the left, ran forward the short distance, putting his head through the television. At that point, my father walked in the door from the house.

Both Mark and I were bloody from the battle. I could never out finesse him because I was three years younger and half the speed. He never had the strength that I had or the weight behind it. We were a good match for bad reasons. But the secret to winning, at least for me, is knowing these things both about yourself and your enemy.

Dad was pissed. He and his woven-leather belt made us forget any other injury that we might have had. Dad's choice of belt wasn't just to hold up his pants. He used a painful belt so that he would rarely have to use it, at least that is my analysis. We got ten swats apiece. Mine went pretty smooth. Dad spanked, I cried. It was the normal spanking routine. But Mark didn't stay still. He always had to fight. (It didn't help that he resented Dad from the moment that they met.) If he thought that he could get away, he was sadly mistaken. Dad had arms of iron from years of welding a lifting steel.

My daily life was pretty simple: go to school, play outside, avoid Mark. I was one of the toughest kids in the neighborhood. I didn't have to worry about bullies in my age group or even a couple of years older. I had a fighting reputation that I had formed from early on as a mechanism of self-defense. Meanwhile, Mark would set me up to have to fight his friends.

I would just be minding my own business in the park when Mark would walk-up with one of his friends. Next thing I know, I'm being told that I have to fight this kid or all of them will jump at me. So, I fought and won for the most part. Those that I didn't outright defeat would leave with a new found respect for the little brother.

We did have one code that I thought was a brotherly tradition; one that if I followed, would get me a place in Mark's heart that might make him like me. The code went like this, "If we are fighting, everybody else has to stay out of it. If anyone tries to jump in, we both turn on them." I never gave much thought to the fact that by doing that, teaching me that rule, it meant that he had free reign to kick me around to his heart's content; and I couldn't ever ask for help, even from my parents or I would be breaking the unwritten code. It was pretty brilliant on his part. It was classic abuse 101.

"Separate the victim from family and friends, and they will never be able to tell on you." Well, I didn't have any friends that could take him. I didn't want him to hate me "more" for telling

Mom and Dad, and now I couldn't ask anybody else for help either.

My sister took a neutral side in most things concerning my intended extinction. She never seemed to want to help me. Then again, according to him, she was his "full-blooded sister;" whereas, I was his "half brother." Commonly, I would be running from him as he wielded a baseball bat or carving knife. I would run out the door, around the house and in whichever door (front or back) and lock it. As I went to lock the other door, she would let him in the one I had just locked, which is pretty surprising when you think that you have him locked out, only to turn and see him gaining on you from behind. This was all too common. He knew if he fought me, I stood a chance; but if he had a weapon, I would have to run.

When we were young, I made the decision to be the good kid. I wanted my father to stay, and I felt as if a bunch of naughty kids could drive him away at any moment. I also made other conscious decisions like, not to spit when that was the age thing to do; not to swear, because I thought and still think, it makes you look like an idiot; not to get angry in a fight, because anger makes you make lousy decisions. So, as the self-proclaimed good kid it was my job not to do anything to jeopardize the house, a choice that would carry on until my adult years. Unfortunately, trying to gain my brother's love wasn't in concert with that way of thinking.

Mark seemed to have the opposite vow in place. One year, right before Christmas, Mark and I were over at his friend's house. I was tagging along, something that wasn't often to happen. The friend's neighbor had a yard full of figurines—deer, lawn gnomes, a fake stump; their yard was really nicely ornamented. For whatever reason, this night, my brother and his friend started throwing rocks. First one and then another until there wasn't a single statue left. After the porcelain massacre, I was sent home and Mark stayed out with his friend. Whatever they were doing,

I didn't want to go anyway because I hadn't wanted for them to break the statues in the first place. I hadn't thrown a rock. I hadn't said much against it either. I was seven and my brother showing interest in having me around was worth my silence, or so I thought.

The next day, the police came and got me from my parent's house. When I got to the police station, my brother and his friend were already there. I was handcuffed to the chair in an interview room for a long time, and then taken out to the booking room. At the detective's desk, I was again handcuffed. My brother and I were interviewed separately. I told the officer that I had not thrown a single stone. I told him the truth. I had picked up a stone and pretended to throw it to make my brother think that I had or he would have beaten me up to force me to. When the detective asked why he would do that, I told him, so that I couldn't tell. This matched perfectly with my brother's story that I had thrown one rock.

My parents had gone all out that year for Christmas. We knew what we had gotten due to a masterful ability to peel tape and replace it without leaving a trace. My haul was everything I had asked for and more. I got the ventriloquist dummy, Charlie McCarthy. I had wanted him for the past couple of years, a lifetime for a child. My brother got the other dummy from the set, Mortimer Snerd, Edgar Bergan's dummy duet. When we got in trouble, we had to pay restitution for all of the yard ornaments and the price of cleanup and whatever else they added to the price for the trouble of it all. This cost my parents a ton of dough, so they took every present back to the store, to include the dummies and some really neat cars, dump trucks, and other child wonderment. It was the worst Christmas, but I never questioned why. Mark was ticked, but I was just sad.

Mark and I did have a few good times. We used to go to Eastridge Shopping Mall on the city bus. From the time I was five or six, we would hop the bus to wherever we wanted to go, if we had the money, that is. If we didn't have the money, we would sometimes get a transfer pass from somebody getting off of the bus if it had time left on it or get one off of the ground. Mark or I would walk onto the bus showing the pass then switch it to the hand and pass it back to the other, who would then switch it to his other hand and show the same transfer to the driver again. Sometimes however, a pass wasn't there to be had. Those times required a little more bravery. We would either hitch hike (it's hard to resist two young boys with their little thumbs in the air.) or walk. Walking was not the chosen route and usually found us detouring our chosen target.

For two young men without a penny in their pockets, a multistory mall is a playground. But penniless only last so long when you have ingenuity. You see, Eastridge has a fountain. In that fountain, people discard their extra change in the form of wishes. Nowadays, people tend to throw pennies and nickels. Back then, people must have really wanted their wishes to come true. The fountain was rich with silver dollars, half dollars as well as quarters. Right there in the open waters of the Eastridge fountain sat the long lost treasure that fueled our dreams.

Each level of the fountain was progressively higher. People would base their likelihood of achieving their wish on where their coin landed—the higher the better, like skeeball, or so it would appear. As you sat on the edge of the fountain, coins gleamed a few here and a few there. Before the end game, we would get the larger of these when we believed we were not seen. The second level was where most prospective wish recipients would have their coins rest for all eternity, or at least until we could get our hands on it. On the second level, the change was so thick that one could reach in and pull a handful in one scoop. It was possible to get several dollars with one little handful. There were obstacles, however. First, security wasn't too fond of kids stealing the change. Secondly, there was a span of water between us and the second level. Probably why the first was so scarce of money was that most anybody who want to reach in could get it.

Mark and I got pretty good at teamwork. When we needed to, we worked together pretty well. We were always first in sack races and wheel barrel competitions. We were awesome at tricks on bicycles together. We even fought as a team well, I would fight and he would egg me on. So getting past a couple of feet of water was not even a challenge. Mark would grab me by the feet, and I would wheel barrel walk out to the second tier. I would then grab a handful of change and walk back. He, while holding my feet and allowing me to control forward and backward movement, would keep watch for the security guards. Normally, we would be on our second or third time in before the security would arrive. Running and laughing was pretty hard, but we were good at it after the first couple of times.

Ferrell's is or was an ice cream shop with the best candy selection you'll ever find. After counting our loot, usually around five to seven dollars, we would go to Ferrell's. My favorite was rock candy and the world's largest Gobstopper. I didn't like them for their taste as much as I knew I could make my candy out last Mark's candy.

The only time security ever caught us was once when I only got two dollars and seventy-five cents from the fountain. Mark was angry with me for such a small haul. He punched me in the solar plexus and doubled me over. I didn't see it coming and was at that time, just excited to have come out with a handful of money. Mark took off running without warning me of the security guard bearing down on us. I was winded and unable to breathe so I couldn't run. The guard saw what happened and stopped for a second to check on me. He was a fast-looking, skinny-black guy, but Mark had a head start and when Mark ran, there wasn't a soul going to catch him. The guard just warned me—"I don't want to see you here again."—and left in the feckless attempt to catch lightning.

Mark would also help me when it was needed. I once had a fight that I didn't have to fight. This kid from my class had told the whole school that he was going to beat me up. Well, out of self-defense, I had become the toughest kid in school. So, I couldn't allow this at all. When the bell rang, I went out the door first in an attempt to cut him off from escape, but he was so fast. I couldn't catch him. I already knew from years of playground time with this kid that I would never catch him on foot. But I had a secret plan. The next day was spent allowing him to run his mouth and taunt me. After school, however, everybody thought he had gotten away again, until out from outside the playground, came a streak of golden sneakers. The fastest kid in our school had a head start of at least seventy five yards. It took two blocks for Mark to catch him but when he did, it looked like the scene came straight from *Wild Kingdom*. The lion caught the gazelle, then guarded the prey as I caught up to them in awe of the amazing chase that had just taken place. Imagine how fast the fastest kid in school can run, and then add fear to motivate him to new heights. They were a show to behold. The funny thing was, they had the same running style.

As I came up, Mark was just panting and taunting him, saying, "Ya wanna try that again?" "My brother's going to kick your ass!" When I grabbed this kid up by the hair and stood him up, I was about twenty pounds and four inches bigger than him, he actually spit at me in defiance. Big mistake, I wasn't going to hurt him to bad. I was just going to teach him a lesson. But spitting in my face caused me not to pull my punch. You see, I never, ever, under any circumstance, punch with all of my strength. I have always felt sorry for my opponent. It is just an inner kindness. I wouldn't even hit my brother with a full punch since the only time I ever had, when I was about seven years old, I hit him in the side of the head with a full punch, closed fist and knocked him out. I was on top of him after turning his attack and hit him so hard he was concussed for a full day where he couldn't stand, so from then on I knew the damage I was capable of. In the blink of an eye, spittle just reaching my face, I found the speed I had always lacked in my fists. I slammed a full fist into his mouth. Blood flew and his lips popped like grapes. But not all of the blood was his. His teeth were luckily for him, in braces. This allowed each tooth to be supporting the other. However, I ruined them and tore my knuckles to shreds. As my fist recoiled and Marks eyes went wide, my classmate's hair pulled from my hand by my own blow leaving a handful behind and his head forcibly fired backward. The sound of his scream left me checking my memory as to whether I had kneed him in the groin. I had not, but that brief second of thought gave him a chance for escape. I took chase when all of the sudden, Mark stopped me by pulling my shirt. "Bro, he's done." He said. I looked in shock and anger at Mark's face. He was showing compassion that I had never seen from him. He was a torturer and mean little bastard, but he saw the damage. "You f——ed him up, man. You don't want to be me." It was a sign that he knew who I was. He knew that my nature was kind and sweet. He knew my strength and that he may not have seen my temper released before that. Perhaps he was aware that it was he that was creating a monster.

Mark was a torturer. Not just to me, but to any victim. I was in a fight with a black boy that was over in a flash. I don't remember why, but he started it. I rarely did start fights, I just finished them. So, anyway, this kid had an older brother who then threatened me. He was four years older and known as a tough guy. Mark in an effort to draw the older brother into a fight and out in the open, hung the little black boy by the neck. Yes, a noose and all. He strung him up in a tree on top of a hill that we all used to ride our bikes down, so that he would be found quickly and the message would get out to the older brother. I don't think Mark ever thought of the consequences of killing someone.

Hours went by and I was walking home, when I came across my father, who was in the park during work hours, and the little black boy's father. (First let me say that my father never stepped foot in the park.) He asked where my brother was, and I told him the few places that I knew of. We walked each place until we found him.

I don't know what exactly happened to Mark for that incident. The boy had lived. He had a scar to prove his injuries. It was a miracle that he lived, to be sure. But how, as a parent, how do you talk to a man whose child has just been hung by your child? I hope to never find out.

The park was a great place to hang out in the seventies. The summers were warm and the grass kept green. Rain-bird sprinkler heads would pop up and give a free cooling down. Hippies smoked their weird concoctions of weed and angel dust out of multi-hosed bongs, hookahs, and apples. You could find longhaired, freaky people to watch everywhere.

The hill in the center of the park was covered in ice plant. A sharp-pointed, triangle-sided, green ground covering that had a wetness inside when cracked open. Trails led to the top from three sides that also discerned difficulty. The back trail came from the sandbox area where there was a giant air force missile to play on and slowly rode behind the tree line, up the back of the hill to come out on the top where my brother had hung the black boy in the pine tree. From the top of the hill, there were two ways down. One to the left was somewhat steep and ended on the bottom at the paved trail. The other side of the trail was gravel where many crab apple trees were spaced out. The gravel area was a couple of acres and in the middle was an electrical substation. The paved walk went around the gravel then "figure eighted" around a larger grass area. The steeper trail ended at a grass edge that extended out about twenty feet to the paved trail intersecting the figure eight between the gravel and grass.

Oftentimes, we would put a ramp at the base of the steepest trail. We all wanted to be Evel Knievel.

On one such day when my brother was being accepting to me, I was riding on the handle bars of Mark's bike when he asked me how brave I was. "Are you brave enough to go down the jump on the bars?" I wasn't afraid of anything and would have done anything for his attention. "Let's go," was all I said.

We were on the top of the hill looking down. There was a crowd of about fifteen kids watching. Everybody, older and younger knew us. Everybody knew we would do the jump, so there wasn't any taunting, just whistles of cheer.

Halfway down, Mark decided to add a twist. We were already known, especially him, for jumping far enough to hit the paved path. Mark was well-known for jumping trash cans and people dumb enough to lay down after his home made ramps. I was well-known for being indestructible after Mark had assigned me to always be the farthest kid laying out on the ground. He didn't always clear all of us and guess who he landed on. This day his twist of venue was to leave the back of the bike. He "ghost road" the bike with me on the handlebars, over a ramp that most of the kids in the neighborhood were too scared to go over at all. The funny part comes when you know the scene a little better.

I had no idea that Mark wasn't on the bicycle. I was talking to him about how we were going to "endo" (end over end) once we cleared the ramp. I had planned on his weight in the back to give me the millisecond that I needed to step out in front of the bike and run out the wreckage. I expected then to have Mark quick on my heels running as well, as he would have to jump over the handle bars to catch up to me. Of course, all of this was idle chatter as he wasn't on the freaking bike at all. So, when I got to the point where the front bicycle tire fell off of the end of the ramp, I stepped out and on to the grass. I ran full speed for about ten steps and button hooked to the right, outrunning the tumbling bicycle. As I turned to see where Mark was, all of the kids were in hysterical laughter. The bike was on the ground as proof that it had chased me for several tumbles. Mark was at the top of the hill, on the ground, holding his stomach from laughter, rolling through the ice plant. I played it off as if we had planned it. The great thing was, I was the crazy hero and he was just an assistant. All the cool kids patted me on the back.

The most David vs. Goliath moment in our childhood came on a hot summer day that same summer. I was lying in the grass, watching the clouds, and separating them with my mind. The Milpitas summer is the best anywhere. Along came this large black guy.

I wasn't sure what to think when he told me, "Get outa' my park."

"Are you kidding, I've lived here my whole life, and I never saw a plaque with your name on it." I said in a smart alec tone.

"I'm gonna kick your..." he started as he approached.

"I'll be back with my big brother." I said as I walked proudly out of the park. We lived about six houses down. The guy in the park just laughed at me like I was a joke. I was going to get the worst eleven-year-old on the block. I knew he was in for hell's fury because Mark took great pleasure in insuring that no one was allowed to touch me without his approval.

Mark was in the kitchen making a sandwich when I came in and told him, "Hey, some black kid kicked me out of the park."

"Why don't whip him?" he asked as he spun towards me.

"He's your size," I said.

Mark swore louder than under his breath. He stormed out the front door toward the park. As I caught up to him and tried to match his stride, Mark's questions were fast and low.

"How big is he?"

"A little taller than you."

"Did you see a knife?"

"No."

"Have you seen him before?"

"No."

We were on a mission. We were on our way to destiny, and we were not to be slowed down.

As we topped the berm that encircled the park, the grass I was lying in was within feet. There, exactly where I was lying, was the guy who had told me to leave and his girlfriend. Confident that I was just blowing hot air, he laid in the grass to separate my clouds. After all, I was watching them first, I had dibs. "There he is," I spouted loudly. "That's the jerk who kicked me out of the park." Mark looked at the tall, blackman. He wasn't a kid. I had seen him as less than he was when I was full of brother pride. Now, fearful that Mark might get hurt, I saw him as the six-foot-tall, stocky adult that he was. Mark looked down at me with a face I'll never forget. The guy in my spot stood up and looked unconcerned about the children who were staring at him with ill intentions in their eyes. The look in Mark's face was somewhere between "You'll pay for this!" and "What the hell have you gotten me into?"

Mark took about one second of decision to formulate a plan. He had been a rotten bastard for a couple of years. I think it's safe to assume that he was a professional ass by now. Hurting people was the one thing he knew well, and it was about time I got him to put it to use for me. Mark shuffled his feet to get traction. I thought he was going to run away, but instead, he put his lightning speed to good use and ran directly at the man standing there. Mark crossed the distance in a blink. Before he got there, Mark jumped in the air, put both feet directly in front of himself, and planted them in the man's chest at the speed of a thunderbolt, knocking the black man off of his feet. Mark twisted in a fluid motion, in flight, landing on the guy's chest with both knees. He then straddled him and sent so many punches to the guy's face, so fast that the fight was over before it had begun. Blood was gushing from his mouth and nose. There was so much blood that you could no longer make out his thin beard, it just looked like clotted blood. In as much time as it would have taken to start breathing again, the man was screaming and crying in a voice straight out of a horror film. Mark continued his assault as the guy's girlfriend screamed and cried to leave him alone. "Please, somebody help!" she screamed, but nobody could have helped in time. Mark had his prey eaten alive before we knew what had happened.

Mark got up off of his chest and told him in his best Clint Eastwood voice, "Now you get out of *our* park." The black guy, who so bravely told an eight-year-old to leave the park because it was his, stumbled to his feet, sobbing, and screaming through blood and humiliation, and ran from the park as fast as he could. His girlfriend looked at us through her own set of tears, "Why? Why'd you do that?" I told her the short side of the story, of how I was just lying there separating the clouds and how he had forced me from the park with threats and intimidation. "I'm sorry...I'm so sorry." She left the park in the same direction he had gone—the long way across the lawn.

Mark looked at me and uttered one word, "Fu———er."

As you entered the park from our block, the berm surrounding it was covered with ice plant. A trail was worn from our block, where the park had its main entrance, to the next block over. All of the houses that ran beside it had a wooden privacy fence that stood about six feet high or so. Along the fence line were trees that the Gawds of heaven must have given for us to climb. Perfect in every way and shaded in the summer, canopy for the rains. Mark and I were in trouble. My grandmother had been over and left her cigarettes on the mantle. Mark had found them and smoked them, one by one until the pack lay there empty. We were discussing his irritating habit of letting me take the fall for his bad doings, when a group of six kids I knew from school and the neighborhood came to "speak" with me. They had heard from somebody that someone else's brother said that I...You know the story. Things said aren't always accurate among kids. These kids were smart. They had been planning this little expedition into insanity for a couple of days. They knew my brother well enough that they actually wanted us together so we could both get beat up. In their minds, that's insured victory for now without looking over your shoulder later. They had six guys, three baseball bats, and a pair of brass balls.

"Mark?" I said as I viewed the incoming problem.

"Yes." he said casually.

"I got this." I said with over confidence that denoted swagger in my voice. I didn't want my brother to see me back down from this or anything else, but in fact, I felt no fear. No intimidation. I jumped down from my perch and fell about four feet to the ground, landing on my feet and sauntering up the hill towards the group who were slowly fanning out to surround me while keeping Mark in view. They only had about twenty feet to work with and in the space were two trees with branches that left plenty of visual ability. I walked straight toward the one I perceived as the leader. He cocked back in a fantastic batter's stance as I approached. As he swung the bat, I took the entire blow under my left arm, in the ribs, as I closed the gap between him and me. I closed down my arm on the bat and jabbed him hard enough in the nose to spatter blood. He maintained his hold on the bat so I kneed him in the nuts, and he freed his grip. As he fell to the ground, I pulled the bat straight forward from under my arm and hit him in the ribs with the handle of the bat. It was well executed and the rest of the bunch started having second thoughts. I moved to my left with a sliding step and side kicked the kid that was there in the stomach. He flew backwards several feet, stopped by the fence that bordered other peoples' yards that bordered the park. He landed, still on his feet but barely able to catch his breath, and took off running. Mark watched from the tree with his arms crossed. The kid to my right cocked to swing his bat, but my Bruce Lee movie experiences had taught me to slide fast. Two side steps and I took out his face with the bottom of my shoe. He turned and ran, screaming like a big sissy. The kid who first had the bat taken from him, tried to run so I stuck my foot up his butt as far as I could to help him along his way. He screamed and ran. The others ran to keep up with them. The one boy lived on the other side of the fence and had seen us there and called the others to action. He wouldn't want to try that again and I had Mark's undying respect. At least until he chose to try and kill me again.

Not all of what we did together was bad. For instance, in the mid '70s, Marriott's Great America opened. The three of us were some of the first people to ever ride some of the rides.

My mother worked nights for San Jose Police Emergency at the time. In the summer time when school was out and kids got restless, Mom still needed to sleep. We were all pretty good about being out of the house so we didn't accidentally wake her from her peaceful slumber because Mother became an insane lunatic if woken. So much so that to this very day, I still tiptoe and climb stairs silently. Once in a while, Mom would give us five dollars each to go to the theme park. She could rest assured, so to speak, that we three would be gone for many hours. (I think I was around seven when this first started as well. Between six and eight were very productive years for me.)

When the gates first opened to the park in 1976, I think it was, the price to get in was five dollars. We all lost our minds when it went up to seven dollars and fifty cents. Now it's around sixty-five dollars to eighty-five dollars depending on season and ticket. So there were some very good times. I don't remember many things going bad on these trips other than once getting lost on the last bus of the evening and having to call Dad to pick us up from the worst part of San Jose, in the middle of the night. The funny thing about that night, the bums and hookers looked out for us. One group of ghetto bangers were looking at us funny and this overblown, transvestite prostitute saw what was going on, she/he was all, "Don't you even look at those babies. Boy, I will knock the black off yo' ass." She was backed by a lot of others who normally look the other way, but not that night. We were protected.

My brother wasn't the type to ever take the risk with faulty equipment though. If he had the chance to ride the good bike, he would take it even if it meant sacrificing me or my sister in the process.

One day, my brother and sister and I decided we were going to ride our bikes up to Sandy Wool Lake, a reservoir. My sister's bike had a problem with its handle bars. We had tried to tighten them many times, but they were completely stripped out. This caused by having them to loose in the first place. When you put pressure forward or back and they move, a motion occurs; and the strip has begun. If you catch it soon and tighten it well, then under most uses the handle bars will remain in place. But if you use them to the extreme, as my brother and I did, then no amount of tightening will help.

The reservoir was far from our house. A man-made body of water, it was located in the foothills. We had to ride for a couple of hours to get there and about half of the distance and three quarter of the time, was uphill. It was a place we all knew well. My dad loved to fish; and this was the closest spot, so if we didn't go to the ocean, we would go to Sandy Wool Lake.

As I remember, we didn't stay long. The whole idea was concocted by my brother to get the chance to go down those hills with his bicycle. I think he just brought us along so that if one of us got into trouble, then all of us would.

As we got ready for the descent, Mark chose to go last. I went second, and we sent my sister Erin first. As we started down the hill, she was already scared and really didn't want to go in the first place. My brother had pressured her into going. Really, it made sense. We had to get to the bottom anyway. All was well for the first few feet. We were picking up the male version of the desired speed, when her long, curled handlebars pushed forward, she went instantly from sitting upright to leaning all the way over the front tire. She lost control of the bike. The front tire warbled back and forth. Soon, she was on the way down. She fell to the left, the wheel turned to the right, and her head hit the ground. The back of the bike then went twisting over her with her feet still attached. My brother and I swerved to miss her. I had no brakes on the bike I was riding, so I put my foot behind the front forks between the tire and the neck—a technique that requires skill. A little too much pressure and I would go over my handlebars as well. My brother was able to skid to a stop quickly. My dad drove up the hill and stopped. "Wait! My dad?" (Any question why he seems like such a hero at times?)

My dad just so happened to be going fishing that day, all by himself, when he came across us. We piled the bikes in the car and dad took care of Erin's wounds. He drove us home in about twenty minutes. It was a much shorter ride with him driving than it was with us riding.

I learned that trick with the brakes when I was young. We never asked for bicycle parts or anything, really. If our brakes went out, we rode without brakes. If a tire blew, we had to come up with a way to patch it or we were out of luck. Most of the time, we came up with something. Those bicycle tube patch kits were in every garage in America back then. A tube was patched, albeit incorrectly most of the time, in nothing flat. Assuming that you knew where to find dad's vise grips, pliers, and screwdrivers. I had more than a couple temporary duct tape tube patches as well. The trick is to inflate the tube to size before you wrap the tape. Then let just enough air out to get the tire back on. When you inflate it, the tire pressure holds the seal. Nowadays, when the kids get a flat, we run out for a new tube. What have we become?

The first time I ever rode a bike without breaks, my brother and a couple of friends were going to the public pool. I couldn't take you the route we went now. I was a small kid trying to keep up with my older brother. But, he let me ride his bike, a twenty-six-inch-three speed. My feet wouldn't even touch the ground! Somewhere along the route was an overpass that went over, either the highway or a main road. As we topped the hill, I was feeling a little wobbly on the bike. I wasn't going to fall behind, though. When I started down the hill, I lost control of my speed (that's putting it lightly). I shot straight across the busy street at the bottom and through an intersection. I flew right into a fence that caught me like a net. Two very angry German Sheppard guard dogs tried to eat me through the wire.

When my brother got to the scene, he was laughing so hard that he couldn't talk. I may have been crying. If not, then I should have been. That was scary as hell!

A lot of our existence was like that. My parents tried the route of hiring baby sitters for us, but my brother was such a little bastard that we couldn't keep one. First, were the neighbor girls, and one at a time, they tried their hand. They were beautiful twins. They had long, straight, heavy, brown hair down to their waste. As a man, I can look back and tell you that Hugh Hefner missed out on these two. The Barbie twins may be blondes, but these girls had them beat, especially in the body department: tight, firm, and curves in just the right places. The twins had a crush on my dad and every morning when he would go out to get into his car and every evening when he would get home, in two parts, angelic harmony, we would hear, "Hi Ba-a-a-ird," as if they were singing to woo their long desired love. Mom wasn't jealous though. I think that the thought of those eighteen-year-old divas wanting her man made her so proud. She knew he had eyes for only her. I can't remember why they stopped sitting for us.

My stepsister was older than us as well. This is a story in itself, just telling what happened to chase her off; Mark had a hatred for our stepdad. He never took his name. (Back then it just required one to use it, enough that it just became your name.) I, on the other hand, was eager to have a family and some kind of security. Baird's voice alone, low and gravely enough to vibrate the room, could calm a child's fears or scare off a monster in the closet. So I gladly took his name. But when Dad had his daughter come over to sit us one night, Mark went on the warpath. It started the moment the adults were out the door. Mark first went out the bedroom window, just to show her he could escape. But he didn't leave. That would be too easy. No, he came back in the front door right in front of her. She tried to show patience, but he would have none of that. He went into the kitchen to get a knife. He waved it around for a few minutes before surrendering it to her. The entire evening went on like this. Let me remind you, there were no cell phones back then. Dad and Mom were completely unreachable.

Debbi, my step sister, kept returning him/us to our rooms. I went to her several times trying to let her understand that I wasn't a part of the whole ordeal. I don't remember where my sister was or what her take on the plan was, but she wasn't actually taking part in what Mark was doing. When Mark got a butter knife from the kitchen, Debi and I exchanged a moment of psychic energy transference. At the moment we saw this, we both had to be thinking, "You rotten little, what are you up to now?" He essentially took himself hostage.

Lacking a gun to hold himself with, Mark knelt beside the power outlet and removed the cover. He spouted some sort of demands to Debi with the threat that if she didn't comply, he was going to electrocute himself. That was the last straw. Debi didn't let him get away with anything. Meanwhile, while she was proving that she was indeed Baird's daughter, Mom and Dad got home.

Five foot-nine inches looked like twelve feet tall that night. Baird's arms were built from years of hard work. His bicep muscle was as big as my head when I was young. With a grip of iron usually reserved for steel plate that he taught California state inmates to weld on, he snatched Mark's arm in his hand.

"Is this really what you want?" Dad's voice was resolved.

My mother stood back and only lightly muttered a resistance, "Baird?"

I watched from the kitchen into the living room as Dad put Mark's finger into the socket. Mark screamed.

"You really want to die?" he inserted it into the socket again. Mark's screams and crying were that of an animal in death struggle. "Let me just help you with that." as he put Mark's finger in a third time to the 120 V electric socket, Baird was looking at the maggot bastard who had tortured his only daughter—a child without remorse or conscience who would literally do anything to cause her pain.

"BAIRD!" my mother's voice radiated a stern nature not of her character. She often screamed for other reasons, but this was more of a command. "That is enough." With that, Mark's arm was freed from the vise.

"Go to your room and don't come out and if you go out that window, don't ever come back." Mom and Dad did their best level to apologize to Debbi. It was insane what Mark had done, and we didn't see her back to baby sit again. Mark ran away out the window for the umpteenth time and didn't come back. He was arrested for something later. That's what brought him home.

I can't be too sure, time erases certain things from our knowledge while leaving other things, but I don't think that we ever had another sitter. From then on, it was all on us. With Mark constantly on runaway status and Erin not far back from him, I spent the greater part of my childhood alone. Even when Mark was home from whatever he was away for, as soon as Mom and Dad were out the door, so was he. Erin plays a very small part in my memory. I really don't remember her too much in my childhood. Certain things she was there for, but for the most part, she just seems invisible. It makes me sad to think that I missed all of the good times that we could have had, because the times I do remember mostly consist of her taking my brother's side; because they were brother and sister, and I was just the "half brother" (spoken in a snotty tone).

Erin was a skinny, gawky, knobby-kneed little girl with glasses and, like my brother, had teeth too large for her mouth. It made her thin face look like a rabbit when she smiled. She wasn't the type to beat on me. I could have easily won a fight with her. She just sided with him on everything. This included whether or not to tell for something done wrong. She also turned a blind eye to his wrongdoings which I took as being on his side as well.

My parents believe in spankings too. So when the three of us were lined up and Mom and Dad had to find out who did something wrong, it was kind of like playing pin the tail on the donkey without the blindfold. Mark did it. The mistake they made was telling us that if someone didn't fess up, we would all get a spanking. Mark didn't care if we all suffered together as long as he didn't have to be the only one spanked. He would literally allow all of us to be punished for his crime. I think, sometimes that he knew that I was softhearted from the start. I could never let someone suffer who was innocent. He would tell us we were all going to get a spanking. Then he would say, "She won't spank you. You're the baby." When it broke right down to it, Mark watched us squirm until he knew I would break. I told my mother I had done it.

The first time, my mother questioned my admitting that I had done whatever had been done. She told me how wrong it was and I got a spanking for putting my brother and sister through whatever they had gone through by sitting and waiting to be punished for my crime. When this became a regular occurrence though, she got wise to the ploy. I had been getting spanked for things I had not been doing and she knew it. So when I went into her room and admitted to something that she knew Mark had done, the cat was out of the bag. "You sit on the bed and act like you're getting a spanking. Don't let the other kids know. This is our little secret." Mom wasn't going to spank me for his bad behavior any more.

"You know better, don't you?" she asked with her normally upset tone.

"Yes Mom," I said in a sad, scared tone.

"Bend over the bed."

"Whack!" she swatted the bed with the belt.

"Aahhh!" I screamed and pretended to cry.

"Whack!" again she swatted the bed and again I pretended to cry.

We hugged afterward as I pretended to weep. My mother understood that I wasn't going to watch Erin suffer for what he had done. Mark, unfortunately knew this as well. Mom left the room to take the scene in the kitchen, to see if she could see any remorse in him. None. He was glad to be out of trouble and didn't care, one way or the other if I was taking his punishment.

My family moved from Milpitas in 1979. We were going to be Oregonians. The move was made to keep my brother from trouble. That didn't really pan out so well.

MILPITAS BEES

Milpitas had many hidden treasures. Many trees to climb, brick highway, sound barriers to walk, parks to play in, and a canal that ran close enough for us to find. The canal had bullfrogs, crawdad, and minnows galore. But the greatest part for adventuresome children was the tunnels. When a young boy is wet and laughing and wants further adventure, the mystery of a tunnel is undeniable. The largest, most fun tunnel had a downward, slime-covered slide into the water. The muck and mud had been eroded through the years and we found the stinking waters to be cooling in the summer sun. Rarely could we walk past the canal without going down into it.

Saturdays, my father worked as a barber in the Sierra shopping center, named after the mountain range to the east of the bay area. Every week, we three children would walk out of our neighborhood, called "The Pines." We would cross the road and follow the sidewalk past the correctional facility and the rest area until we got to the shopping center that housed Dad's work. Across from his barber shop was the Sierra/Nevada movie theaters. After we collected our allowance from our Dad, we would often go see a movie.

The scene stayed the same until we moved to Oregon in 1979. The characters just changed from time to time. For instance, if my brother was either incarcerated or run away from home, obviously he would not accompany us. If my sister was runaway, she would not come either. I am not sure where my sister was that Saturday, as I have mentioned before, she was mostly invisible in my youth, but Mark was a runaway again. I walked all by myself. I don't recall where my parents were either. They may have been out shopping for my birthday gift, because this happened on my eighth birthday. *Enter the Dragon* was playing at the theater, and I was in heaven getting to see my idol.

I purchased my ticket at the door and used the remaining money for popcorn and a soda. I found my way to the seat and waited in the dimly lit theater for the movie to start. I was early for the show as usual, so I watched as the theater was packed to capacity. I watched as several boys were caught trying to sneak in the back way and as they were being dragged out the front by the security, another group was let in by a group of girls. Several people in the crowd then took the security role and kept them as someone else went out to get an usher to escort them out. So far the movie was great, and the curtains were still drawn with the lights still up.

As the lights dimmed and the curtains pulled back, I was giddy in my seat. The opening scene had every voice fall silent. Nobody knew what to expect. Bruce Lee was like no artist anybody had ever seen. Just then, the movie froze and the lights went up. "Bryan Johnson, please come to the box office. Bryan Johnson, please come to the box office." Over the loudspeaker, they were blaring out my name. "No way!" I got up from my seat and went up front. I was afraid that they had somehow decided to kick me out. Was this a rated "R" movie? Did they decide it was too graphic for my young mind? Who did they think that they were? My day to day life was worse than any movie could portray. It was a little confusing for me when I came out to the box office, and they told me that I was needed for a family emergency. I didn't see my parents. Where was Mom? Was Dad okay? Why am I leaving a movie that I had dreamed of to come out to the lobby?

I had a front-row seat and I was sure that my seat would be taken before I got back into the theater. "I think your Dad went back out to the car," the lady at the counter told me.

"Can I get a rain check?" I asked her.

"Sure." she said as she wrote out a complimentary admission ticket for me.

My parents were out in the car waiting. They had come in to the box office and had me paged for a family emergency. "Mark has had an accident," Mom laid out a confusing story of what sounded like a nightmare.

"He's in the hospital. Dad and I are going to see him."

They dropped me off out in front of the house and drove away. I walked into the house to find the kitchen wall plastered with green frosting like paint from a leperachons hiney. The floor was covered with frosting; and there were half-eaten steaks, the likes of which one doesn't often see, in the sink on the plates. My first thought was that someone had obviously started my party without me. And it obviously got way out of hand.

My brother had brought a friend over to the house. I don't have any idea how he would know the house was empty, but they had fired up the BBQ grill and snatched the best, two-inch-thick steaks out of the freezer. The two boys had taken Dad's gin from the cupboard and guzzled it out of thirty-two ounces plastic cups. During their little drunken exercise, they had smeared the entire kitchen with my birthday cake. I had not seen it yet. I will never get to know what it looked like, I guess. But my birthday is on St. Patrick's Day so the walls were green. So was the floor and parts of the ceiling had chocolate cake stuck to it like large spit balls in the junior high boys' locker room. Mark then filled his mouth with lighter fluid that my dad had in the cupboard for filling his Zippo lighter. Mark would spit the fluid out in a mist while holding up a burning piece of newspaper. The imitation of Gene Simons would have been more flattering had he known that the flame would follow the fluid back to his lips. On the third try, he accidentally caught his face on fire. This caused him to swallow the entire remaining mouth full of lighter fluid. The poisonous fluid mixed quickly with the alcohol already consumed. He passed out on the floor quickly thereafter, and his friend wasn't really all that much help. He, in his drunken state, decided to leave. Meanwhile, Mark started to drown in his own vomit as his body fights to reject both the gin and the lighter fluid. As far as I can remember the story, Mom and Dad returned home to find Mark passed out on the floor, mouth and nose submerged in vomit. For some reason, after the ambulance took Mark to the hospital, I was gathered up from the movie just to come sit in the mess that he had created of the cake I would never see.

One often wonders why people do the things that they do. The drinking and carrying on with the Gene Simmons impersonation and the smearing of the cake under the influence of all of that, I can understand. But why come get me from the movie? My parents would often leave town and leave us kids on our own from the time that I was five or six; so why wouldn't they just let me finish the movie, come home to find the same scene that awaited me anyways, and then explain it when they got home? I would have walked in the door and instantly known Mark had done in my doomed birthday cake and passed it off as another act of a psychopath. No harm, no foul. But why make me miss the movie?

I didn't get to see the movie for another couple of weeks. Mark came home from the hospital, and we were one big messed up family again. Mark was completely unapologetic for ruining my party. I never received a present that year due to Mark's selfish act of stealing the attention away from me in what could be thought of as the most dangerous act of sly maneuvering in history, if not for the way he took the steam out of my 40th birthday. It is more dangerous and even slyer. (I'll tell you about it later.)

For a while, we had the garage as a family room, funny name because it was still primarily a place for me and Mark. I had a weight set that consisted of about fifty pounds of plastic weights and a bar with collars. We had a bowling ball that I can't, for the life of me, remember where it came from. We had a bumper pool table and enough space to get into a lot of other things. Also in here was kept the smelly aquarium of my turtle "two-ton Tilly." One day Mark came into the family room and started asking me where things were. I was always the one with the knowledge of how to, and where, and what. So he wanted a broomstick. There just so happened to be one in the room. He needed a chain. Well, the dog has a thin chain choke collar that he doesn't need. Heck, he's a police dog. He never needs to be choked. He answers all commands as if issued by Gawd himself. He wanted screws. There was a couple on the wall that held up a display which had never had a single thing displayed on it. He wanted a saw. Mom had a great, saw-toothed-bread knife. It had always come in handy for cutting.

Mark had me measure the two cuts to be made on the broomstick and cut them. Mom would never notice the shorter broom. Then he had me measure the chain across my hand and cut it to that length. "Is this for you or me?" I was thinking. He then had me screw the chain piece between the sticks we had cut. All the while, Mark was showing off to his friends that we're there, how I would do what I was told. I didn't want to make him mad by showing what a liar he was; so I just did what he asked, besides, I was interested in what I was making.

I made all this and did the cutting and screwing and foraging for unique items, but it wasn't something I recognized. It was a secret thing he called the "choco sticks." As of this time, I had not gotten to see Bruce Lee swing a pair. Sure, I had heard the name before, but I was just pretending to know what they were, same with the name "nun-chuck." Later, in Oregon, everybody would call them that.

Mark showed me a couple of moves that he had seen. He had a friend with more experience that would show him some moves. I, on the other hand, had to try and copy what Mark would clumsily try to learn from memories of what he had been taught. Nobody could have seen what would come of that. I practiced day after day. I had my share of bruised elbows. I shot those things across the room as I lost grip on them several thousand times, I'm sure. But I loved them. I soon was able to copy any move I would see. I was inventing different styles. I got fast, fast. Soon, Mark was showing me off to his friends and having me put on shows for his buddies. I was around eight when I mastered them. I was seven when I first tried them out. Right out of the gate, I was the best. Natural. Amazing in my flow. I have only gotten better. If I was in feudal Japan or China back in the days of the emperor, perhaps this skill would have gotten me something. Someone would have come up from the royal house to gain my services as a guard for the emperor. But as it was, I was a kid in modern America, in the '70s and there wasn't much use for skills of that nature. I may have been able to be in the movies, I was a cute kid, but no one ever came to me to offer the part. I just loved these scenarios while I practices over and over for years.

This little hobby did show me a skill that I have used extensively in life. I can copy any move, fighting or other, that I ever see. This made me one of the most formidable fighters you'll ever meet. In my adult life, I have yet to see a man that I would say, "I can't beat him." On screen or off, there was only one Bruce Lee; and I believe he's dead, so I am pretty sure I can take the rest. Also, it keeps me able to put together anything I see taken apart. I credit the ability to copy with giving me the mechanical skills that I have. If it's broken I can fix it. Period.

Remember the canal. The water was rarely flowing through the canals. They may have been for drainage or sewer, I don't know. But they were great fun. The main tunnel passed under an intersection at the Ford Motor Plant. The intersection was five lanes wide if you include the turn lanes. It y'd in the middle and you could follow it in either direction. The tunnel was about four feet high, which was perfect for young guys playing guns or hide and seek. The best tunnel came out under the rail tracks and was a great ambush point because as it came out, you were still under the tracks and could hide beside the opening where it was still shaded enough not to give you away.

One sunny day, when we had neglected our tunnels for the winter, the time came to reinvestigate the super-secret fort of tunnels. We walked the tunnel under the street and to the other side. Mark and I came out on the Ford side under the tracks. A couple of bees buzzed us. We swatted away at them with our hands and continued our investigation. Just then, Mark discovered the hive in the railroad ties just outside of the entrance. It was a huge nest within the ties. Bees swarmed in and out of the nest with little regard to us as long as we stood still. I had my face way too close to the nest when Mark thought that it would be funny to throw a rock at them. Speed was needed and fast. I am not sure if there is a record for the fastest escape from a bees nest, but I was in the running that day. It may be the only time in my life that I outran my brother. I had stings on my face and hands and a couple on my back before I could get across the intersection, with cars screeching to a halt all around me. Horns were honking and people cussing, and I was bookin'! Those stings hurt and the only water I knew of within distance was the stagnant canal water across the street; and to the best of my knowledge, there was probably only enough water in the hole for one. I leaped from the roadway, over the cement edge, cleared the slimy moss slide of cement, and landed in the pool that was formed where the water dropped from the tunnel. If I didn't make the record for bee escapes, I surely made some sort of record for blindly jumping into a 3x3 pool from a blind jump over a cement barricade. Of that, I have no doubt. I have always been able to hold my breath longer than anyone else I have ever known. I may have broken that record as well, had it not been for the intrusion in my stagnant pool of solitude of Mark. He wasn't far behind and I don't have any way of telling you what route he took or if he flew over the edge as I did, but he was in the water with me in no time.

We visited the bee hive a couple of more times before we moved. But the tunnels were never the same. We still caught the crawdads in the water and a few bullfrogs did make it back to our house to starve to death in our terrarium. But the tunnels now belonged to the bees.

SANTA CRUZ BEACH BOARDWALK

Santa Cruz Beach Boardwalk was our favorite destination as kids. It didn't matter if we were given money for the rides or not. (We rarely were.) The beach was best there, the pier had stores on it to shop for trinkets, and the seals could be seen through the holes built into the pier for viewing. Everybody there seemed to be nice. Maybe because it was such a great place to be or maybe that's just the way you see things as a kid in your happy place.

My mother often played with us on the beach. She and Dad would fish for the better part of the morning until she started to show him up with either bigger or more fish. Then he would say something like, "you wanna go check on those kids?" That was her cue. That's how he told her that it was time for her stop showing him up. He had all of the years of experience and all the best equipment. He would bait her hook, cast out for her, and she would stare at him lovingly as he worked his magic with his own gear. Mom wasn't a fisherwoman, she was just the luckiest woman alive when it comes to charming a fish onto the hook. She didn't try or even care most of the time and perhaps that's why she did, or does, so well.

Mark, Erin, and I would take to the beach. At times, there would be surfers out in the low to moderate waves that Santa Cruz has to offer. The waves, relentlessly called to the avid bodysurfer within me. The sun shown for the most part, all summer once the fog burned off each morning. Seaweed washed up on shore and made for great whips for chasing one another around on the beach. We rarely stayed together. The beach was an extension of our home and my well-being. Each of us had our own favorite things to do.

Mom usually came down and found me on the occasions when she would want to play—rafts, inner tubes, what have you. We would inflate, or rather I would inflate them. I had lungs of steel and would almost always end up doing all of the blowing up of toys. Then we would head to the water with Mom.

One time in particular comes to mind when I think of all of the great ocean times we had. I actually have it in a song I wrote that gets the most plays of all of my YouTube videos. We had spent the morning looking for an inner tube around where we lived in Milpitas. We found a giant tractor inner tube and headed home to get Dad who was getting the poles and such ready for the day. It takes place at Santa Cruz on a hot summer day. My mother and brother and sister and I are all in for tube surfing, so we all headed out into the water just past the breaking point of the waves. We were about forty yards from the pier where the waves seem to be the biggest. My mother was the first on the tube. It took me and my brother both to hold the tube for her to get on. She was still young and thin enough that we had only the trouble of balance to deal with. Then we got my sister on. She had worse balance than my mother, and if memory serves, caused my mother to end up back in the water in a comedy of errors that still makes me giggle under my breath as I type. We would get mom situated on the tube. One of us would hold on to the front of the tube that was rising in the air from being off balanced as mom sat on the other side with her legs in the middle. Then the other would help in any way possible to get Erin in the tube. Erin would sit on the opposite side as my mother and counter balance the tube to the tune of about fifty pounds. Mark would then attempt to climb on and Erin would lose her balance and fall through the center, Mark would lose his grip on the slippery rubber surface and the tube would flip over with Mom's feet sticking straight up out of the center. Her feet would disappear from view, I would have to recapture the tube before the ocean claimed it. Then, everybody would come to the surface and laugh and try again. After a couple of tries, we would find our way.

The ocean is a cruel mistress and has a great sense of humor. After all of that, we were already half out of breath. Our arms were tired and our tummies tense from laughter, and then came the time to ride the waves. We would paddle from both sides of the tube. Mostly, we would achieve circles, but eventually we would get to the point where a wave would take us. The weight ratio is probably key to our journey from here on; it went Mom, me, Mark, Erin. Being that I was the last on to the giant truck inner tube, I was destined to sit next to Mom. So, all of the weight was on one side of the tube. As we were pulled by the current of the wave, coming to crest over the shallowing beach waters, our side was spun toward the shore. As the wave carried us in and the inner tube accelerated, we all squealed with delight. As the wave crested and rolled out from under us, my mother and I dropped like a rock, jettisoning Mark and Erin into the air. They launched, we fell. Our legs were intertwined in the center of the tube. The wave was large and powerful and rolled us under and over and under again. The image of a doll in a front load washer comes to mind. My mother, being taller, was bashed against the sand on the bottom again and again as we tumbled. When we finally came in far enough to gain control of the tube, my mother still had a single foot caught in the middle. I wrestled the tube off of her foot which wasn't easy. Mom was crying from the abuse the ocean had just dealt her and possibly because she had sand and water up her nose. She used to have a joke about beach sand. "Get sand in you schlitz," she would say. This day, sand was effectively in every schlitz we had. Mark and Erin and I were in hysterical laughter, having just survived an amazing ride and a tremendous tumble. It took a minute to realize that we were not joined in our hilarity by Mom. I was in possession of the inner tube when I heard the voice of a man. "Ma'am, Ma'am," he yelled in a panic. He was wading in our direction holding up something for us to see. "Lady!" he yelled once again. He was obviously trying to get my mother's attention to whatever he was holding up. He waved it in the air in his hand, and as he did, some of it came out of his grip. It was waving like a flag in the wind as he yelled, "Your swim suit!"

WE MOVED WHERE?

Just before Christmas 1979, my parents moved us to Bend, Oregon. We had gone there on vacation with a couple that my father worked with, the prior summer. Mom must have fallen in love with the trees and mountains.

My brother had been in so much trouble, for so long that my mother thought that a move to the country would fix him. It didn't. He just found the kids in the central Oregon area that would be bad with him. He still spent the largest portion of his youth incarcerated for one reason or another. He still found the drugs and parties.

Our move was a three-staged process. First step was a motel. We had no internet in 1979, so you actually had to go to a town and find a place to live. We stayed in the Pines Motel, a small cabin with kitchenette, fireplace, and beds just off the highway. We kids shared an adjoining cabin with our parents. We also had two Airedale dogs with us, Molly, and Charlie (can't quite remember if that was his name, it was something like that). Charlie was a puppy of about six months. Molly was a full-grown female and my mother had planned on breeding them. The motel was on a large property with a grass area and a picnic table and lava rock sticking out of the ground.

The motel was a really neat experience. It snowed the first days we arrived. My parents were fun and helped us build our first snowman. Dad decided he needed a penis and so we were "forced" to build a female so that he would not be lonely. A snowman in the condition that Dad had built him would get very frustrated if he didn't have a female to "keep him company." Christmas came and we enjoyed a wonderful holiday with our parents in the hotel. My mother introduced us to chestnuts, and I can still remember the smell of them actually roasting on the fire. I received a train set and my brother a slot car track. My sister must have gotten a girl toy, but I cannot remember what it was. We didn't get much, but we didn't have room for much.

One day, while we were playing in the snow and our parents were out house hunting, our puppy disappeared. We looked high and low until I looked in the back of a pickup truck. There was a black garbage bag in the bed of the truck that I felt so strongly about, that I looked inside. I found him there. He had been hit on the highway and the man in the truck was kind enough to get him and bring him back after recognizing that he had seen him there, a country thing to do. He tried to hide the corpse from us so that we children could avoid the death. Perhaps it was better that we saw him. I learned a lesson at that moment. Responsibility matters. Even when you think nothing could go wrong, things do.

Second step was the property we moved to just outside of Bend in the small Village of Tumalo. If you've ever wondered if hillbillies live in the west, Tumalo was your answer. The property was great, however. We rented the property and had a coral, barn, and double-wide-mobile home. I had never even seen a mobile home before. I thought that we were living in an RV. It sounded like an RV when people talked about it having wheels.

We walked in the front door, the very first time to find a television sitting in the front room, a statue of a beautiful silver Persian, and…"Oh My Gawd! It moved." My father had picked up a cat to surprise my mother, and she just about gave us all a heart attack when she came to life right in front of us. I swear I heard her snickering. My mother told me, as I set my things aside, "See what you can do to find us some channels." So I looked and looked for the crazy tuner and finally realized that it was a heat-sensitive-touch system—up channel and down channel. But in order to tune it, one had to adjust each channel with a little knob that had three settings, like a watch. Pull, turn, pull out again, turn, push two clicks, turn. It was so very complicated especially when you are unaware that there is only one channel to find. I searched all day. I only got the one channel. "We are not in California anymore."

My brother and I had a couple of old BB guns that my mother had convinced my grandmother into giving us before we left California. We would play out at the barn and in the field with those guns for hours. Snow fall was still new enough to us that we rarely let it stop us from leaving the house. Soon, however, my brother became a ghost in my life as he found other things to do. One day my brother and I were out in the field when we spotted the neighbor's house across the street, was on fire. We ran across the highway and, with snow in hand, I flew up the roof. Mark went to the door and pounded like a mad man. We knew that there were four male children and their parents living in the tiny cement building. As they answered the door, Mark came up with me as they handed us glasses and pots of water. The hoses were frozen solid and would be of no use to us.

We doused the flames and smolder and accepted the gracious thanks of the poor farmer and his family. We never asked for more than a thank-you from them, as no one should. We were just happy to have been there for them at the right time. The whole family was still asleep when it happened and could have died in that fire. The four boys slept in what would amount to a four by eight hallway and the parents a six by eight room. The kitchen must have been about eight foot square. That was all there was to the house, and it would have consumed them fairly quickly.

This is also where our first horse was bought and where she would give birth to her first foal. The horse was Black Butte. We were told that she was John Wayne's stand-in horse in *True Grit*. I don't know if it was true. She was exceptionally well-trained and beautiful black with a star of white on her forehead. Mindy is what we named her filly. She was a pinto-colored horse with red where the black should be. I know there is a better name for the color but time and distance from horses allows me to forget more than most will ever know about them.

I went to Tumalo elementary for the first part of my fifth-grade year. When my parents were introducing me to the principal, he warned us not to tell people where I was from. So I accepted that Californians could be unwelcome as we went to the class. He called the teacher from out of the room. "Mrs. Rottoncrotch this is your new student. Let's not mention that he is from California." The principal told her.

She then took me by the hand and led me to the door, in front of my parents and the principal, opened the door and, "Class, this is Bryan. He's from Califoooorrrniiiaa." Her tone was snotty and disrespectful and I was going to have to put up with her every day. I fought every day. For the first week or two, I stood my ground.

I gave more than I got. But you can only fight for so long against so many. I learned to run. I had to. If someone started to catch me, I turned, grabbed, rolled, beat on them, and back to my feet to run some more. I swear the game never got old to them. They spit in my lunch and threw things at me. Our class had three grades and fifth was in the middle, so the age groups were all about the same as mine; as big and tough and strong as I was, as good a fighter, and as much pain as I caused them, nothing stops the inbred when they have direction.

I hid on the roof before the bus came. I learned very quickly, to round the corner and scale the wall where they couldn't see me. I tried to hide in the closet one day so that I wouldn't have to go out to recess; but the teacher grabbed me by my coat and as I pleaded with her and told her of the danger I was in, she threw me out of the door saying "don't let me catch you hiding in the closet again!" at the top of her lungs so that all of the others heard her.

The principal was never called for a single fight. The only teacher to ever step in was when I had two of the bigger boys crying on the ground, and I was told to stop making trouble. The moment he turned around, two more jumped in, and as I beat them down the same teacher took me to his class to sit out the remainder of recess. He kept telling me how my parents had made a mistake moving here and how I should go back to California. A teacher said this. He was no better than the kids, no better than my own teacher. I never told my parents. Although my father took notice of my bruises once in a while, I sent many more bloody noses and busted lips home than I ever got.

Third was Bend. The schools in Bend had a few more Californians. There were still many jerks, and I still fought many days of the month. But the numbers weren't so readily on their side. We had a six acre parcel with another mobile. I remember the first thought in my head as we drove up to the property, "Wow. That roof is shiny."

Here is where we would live—down a two-mile dirt road, trees and dirt and crickets and grasshoppers and chipmunks and squirrels. Bats at night that flew around our twenty-five-foot lamp pole, mounted on top of the largest double-wide manufactured in 1978.

Loneliness and the trees I grew up almost always alone. Some would think that to be alone all the time is a dream come true. However, to actually live that life is less desirable than one might think. By nature, as a child, I was loving and tender and sensitive. I would try and console anyone who was in sadness from a very young age. Birth I imagine, since I cannot remember a time when that was not the case. If someone was crying, especially my mother, I would cry right along with them. Any streak of mean or tough that I ever had was brought on by my brother or the kids at school who hone in on what they perceive as weakness. Little did they know that it was a strength. I was strong enough to care. I was strong enough to lend my strength to those who needed it most. As I grew and persevered, toughness took the place of that kindness, I never let go of that. Even as I shaped it to benefit others in a violent way, defending people too weak to defend themselves, I always try to remain true to my soul.

Since I was little, my parents worked. My brother had gotten rid of sitters before they had even gotten the hang of watching us. My brother and sister were perpetual runaways. So I was all alone after school, when my folks left town, when I went out to play, whatever. So when we moved to Oregon, it got worse. We first moved to a small town of Tumalo that was populated with hicks that hated just for the sake of hating. Then, Bend where the house was out in the woods. Our only neighbors were an old couple who had once owned all the land in the area and whose children were adults. We had one other family within a half mile, but they were not friendly, and their daughter was my older sister's age. I never knew what it was that made them treat us badly, but it didn't really matter I guess, anyway.

I used to be the most creative kid. I only had a few toys. My parents had bought me stuff for Christmas and birthdays, but I usually had to ask for clothes or other needs rather than the common toys. I always saw us as poor. I believe that my mother thought that if she didn't spend Dad's money on us kids, he was more likely to stick around. Not a realistic fear, him leaving. To this day, I as her child and favorite son, cannot say a negative word about her or her actions, or my Dad will blow a gasket. So I had to either make do with what I had around me: ink pens, fishing hooks, sewing string, ant hills, trees; or, if I was lucky enough to get a toy soldier from a friend or a five finger discount at the store on rare occasion.

I learned from experimentation how to create launchers for grappling hooks out of ink pens. A three-pronged-fishing hook on string launched from an ink pen tube would allow G.I. Joe and the A-team to climb the treacherous woodpile of doom. Every piece of anything becomes part of the game. I made cannons out of clothes pins that would launch popcorn kernels. Land mines out of paper clips that would actually spring when stepped on.

I was so lonely that the dangerous became the norm. I was watching the squirrels in the trees as the cat tried hard to catch them. She would climb the tree, and the squirrel would leap to the next tree and bark at the cat. So, I climbed up to the top of the tree, swayed in the wind, and questioned my sanity as I flew from one tree top to the other. More than once, I misjudged the distance from tree to tree and fell a great distance before catching limbs to stop my plummet. Pretty soon I was so overconfident that I forgot how scary it was to people who didn't have missing marbles.

I was up in the top of the trees one day when my parents came up the drive. The wood was in and the chores done. It was summer and the sun was up much longer, so when my parents came home at 6:30, I was out playing.

The car stopped and they gathered their stuff. After a minute or so, they got out and shut the doors. I yelled down to them, not thinking of what it must look like to see me in the tops of the trees, after all, the only TV we got was from an antenna that my mother had sent me up a tree to install when I was ten, so for sure she would think that the sight of me in the tree was pretty cool. "Hi, Mom!" I said it loudly. She and Dad looked around for me. "Up Here!" They looked ahead of themselves at the larger Ponderosa pines in the front of the house. "Behind you, watch!" They turned around to see me up in the top of the much thinner trees. I waved and Dad began to ask something but by that time I was in flight. I caught the other tree, swooping around and back to the other using just my arms. I sprang from tree to tree and finally touched down. My mother's face was pale as she feigned a smile and turned to walk, a little unsteady toward the house. "That's not exactly the reaction I expected." I spoke softly to Dad as we stood side by side watching her walk into the house. "I better go check on her." was all Dad said as he left my side and walked into the house behind her.

One day I discovered that at my school there were trees dangerously close to out of my range. I couldn't help myself, I had to know. I climbed the outside pine to the very top, looked ahead at my distance, and leaped from that to the next at around sixty feet in the air. I hadn't noticed the entire student body, out waiting for the buses, was watching. I jumped from tree to tree losing altitude as I went. I zigged and zagged back and forth between a grove of six or eight trees, swinging around the trunk and reversing direction and making my way back and forth until my last swing landed me on the ground. A loud applause went out from the crowd of unruly teens and preteens. The principal gestured me over with his pointer finger. "After I change my shorts, I don't want to ever see you do that again," he said in the most serious voice that he could muster.

At home, I had made my best attempt at a Spiderman costume.

It didn't help me climb but the imagination thing was there. Several times I would get out of the trees and out of the costume just in time to beat my parents as they drove in from work.

I had chores to do when I was a kid. We didn't have an ax, we had a sledge, and a wedge and I had to split wood every night to feed the fire. We had a woodstove and we always used it as a primary source of heat. I also had to have the kitchen, dining room, and living room clean. I had to vacuum or mop or whatever needed done. I had to take out the trash as well. If the burning barrel was full, I had to light it up. After we ate dinner, I had to do the kitchen a second time, every night. Since I rode my bike to school in all weather and tried to make life interesting by riding all over town before coming home and my nearest friend was around five miles from my house as well, sometimes I would get home with minutes to spare. But guess what? You could count the times that I wasn't finished with all of my chores before my parents got home, on one hand. I never once had to be told to do any of it.

My parents were so spoiled that after I went to the army, they bought a hydraulic wood splitter, a microwave, a dishwasher (ours had been broken for a couple of years), and started eating frozen dinners. They stopped using the dining room table and it piled high with stuff. My mother's house was in constant disarray.

The neat thing about being in the woods was that I could shoot my BB gun anywhere I wanted. I could launch arrows from my bow in any direction, and they were sure to fall harmless to the ground. I shot my Dad's shotgun out in the front yard as well as his .357 and never had to worry about offending the neighbors. I spent hours and hours hunting and fighting invisible enemies. We had a natural rock fort that nature put there just for my pleasure. I would have a fort one day to defend and a castle the next. Indians were invading and then the Hun. Life can get a bit hazed over between reality and fiction for a young man with all the tools to entertain and no one to share them with. I never have to wonder if that is why I cherished my friends so much. To have someone to call a friend was a treat.

My loneliness was the inspiration for a lot of my better and not so great inventions as well. I once found an old bicycle pump. It gave me a strange idea. Follow with me here. I took the hose off of the pump. Then I got a one quart propane tank. In the end of the hose was a metal +. I put a nail in the end of the hose with the head toward the + and the point, which I had dulled, into the valve of the propane tank. I strapped them together flexibly with an inner tube from a mountain bike tire. My mother's discarded overnight bag strap completed the set up. Lighting it required a gentle touch. Then squeeze the tube and presto, a six foot flame. Well, that was a pretty cool toy, so I took it to school.

I always wore a very large coat that my friends referred to as my house. I was capable of hiding just about anything in that coat. I weaved a strap over my shoulder and put the hose inside my sleeve. The tank under my arm looked like a gun. At lunch, I took it out back of the school between the school and the football field and showed the bad kids my invention. It went over very well. Blast after blast of flames shooting into the air. It looked like a professional wrestling event or a reenactment of Ray Bradbury's *Fahrenheit 451*. That is until it burst into flames inside my jacket.

Propane stays liquid at temperatures below -50 Fahrenheit. Rubber inner tubes become brittle well above that temperature, so what happened was that the rubber inner tube that I had used as a flexible squeeze trigger had frozen and cracked. The flames leaped from the end of the hose when I fired the trigger as gas squirted out of the crack in the rubber. When the flames jumped to the inside of my jacket, I came to an eerie knowledge. I was strapped to a bomb, and I couldn't take it off. The entire strap was under my coat and the flaming hose and nozzle were inside my sleeve. To make matters worse, the nail had jammed in the valve and the entire force of the spray was stuck on full blast.

Thinking fast, I put both hands between the propane tank and me and shoved hard. Both ends of the strap broke and the cylinder disconnected from the hose. The propane canister spun away as if in slow motion as it landed in a large sage bush. "Oh no!" I ran over to the bush and kicked at the canister which then flew ten feet, landing squarely into another sage brush bush, igniting it instantly. Fifteen teenage kids were stomping out bushes and having a great time. The fire was extinguished in no time and we had it all under control. Just then, I notice a figure watching us that had missed my notice—the principal.

Brian Lock (name changed) was the vice principal in my first grade school in Bend. When I went on to Jr. High, he did as well. He became Principle of that school the second year I was there. When I went on to high school, so did he. He was the principal there too. And he hated me.

It may have been because I was from California, or it could have been because I was tall and he is just north of midget, I am not sure. But the fact that he didn't like me was clear. When I got attacked on the bus by three guys, I got in trouble for winning while they were sent to class. When the resident giant picked a fight with me in sub-zero weather in junior high and subsequently got humiliated as well as banged and bruised up from hitting the ground so many times, I got in trouble. (Hey, I took it easy on him.) When any fight, for any reason, by anybody happened on school grounds, I got called into the office. Commonly, I got a swat for withholding information, even when I wasn't involved in any way.

No joke, one day he called me in from class. I asked, "Why am I here this time?" He looked at me. "I don't remember doing anything." He just watched me squirm. "Are you alright?" I asked. "Just know that I am watching you. Go back to class." His little, two-part, dusty orange mustache just covered his lip line. I thought of how silly it made him look and how much better he would fit in with the cast of *The Wizard of Oz* than in a school with children who were taller than him.

So there he stood. Watching the entire scene with disinterest? I saw it in his eyes. He looked as if saying "this is just too much to take in." I picked up the now cooled canister from the bushes. Somewhere in the fray of battle, the nail had come dislodged. I walked toward him, knowing what was to come. Then he spoke. "You better not bring that back to school." And he stepped past me.

I walked to my locker and put the stuff inside. I went to class. No call to the office. I was sure that at some time I would hear about it. Surely my parents would be called and I would have to answer when I got home. Nope. Nothing at all came of it, nothing but a sincere respect for the power of fire, explosives and creativity that I carry on to this day. Now when I play, I never strap myself to the bomb.

I tended to be hyper when I got around friends. I learned early on that I was the creative genius of my friends. I didn't always share my designs or ideas, but when I did, we had a blast. For instance, we had a science teacher that we called the Walrus. Walrus was flat and boring to listen to, and he looked to be the identical twin to our vice principal with the exception that his mustache was three times as long. When describing dissolving solids, he once said "with heat added, the solids dissolve more thoroughly. Then we stir and the dissolution becomes more rapid and more solid may be added. If I stir the other direction, it will not unstir." I made a plan when the school year started to come up with an actual science question that he could not answer, every day. Mind you, we didn't have the internet. Finding questions was a very hard thing to do. I actually had to go to the library and watch Public Broadcasting Service (PBS). It was sometimes a torture. I did learn a lot of things that way, however.

One day, Walrus gave a pop quiz. I aced the quiz but pretended to be bent out of shape about how he had betrayed our trust as students and how in any civilized society, tests of this nature would be given open book. When I left the class, I made a plan. After school, while he was grading papers or picking his mustache clean or whatever he did after school, we would steal his car. Not just a theft, more of a move. Before the end of school that day, I took a screwdriver from shop class and removed the center divider from the double doors at the farthest hallway from the office. I then recruited three of my friends. None of us were thieves, so we couldn't get in the car without damaging it, and we didn't mean him any harm, so we carried his Le Car into the hall, down three steps and half way to the end. When we were tired, it was far enough. We left it sideways. The bumpers on the front had about an inch from the wall and the same in the back.

I then returned the center post, the screw driver and left for the day. The car was still there the next day. That started a rampage. Every day, someone's car was turned sideways in the lot, between two other cars.

I wrestled in school. I went to state championships twice and was on my way the third time when I was pulled out of wrestling by my Dad. That added to my list of things to do before I got home to do my chores before my parents got home. I rode my bike to and from practice. My parents never came to the practices or meets except the one, of course. But I have already written on that one I think.

STONES IN CAVES

Have you ever had someone do something so stupid to you that it begged the question "What, are you retarded?"

Outside of Bend, Oregon are a series of caverns that were formed by air bubbles in the volcanic rock. As the molten rock cooled, air bubbles were trapped under the surface that eventually became solid. The millennia of erosion caused by ice age retreat, snow melt, and rain run-off have finally exposed them to the surface where me and my family were able to come enjoy discovering these holes in the earth.

We had been to them on a few occasions. My mother usually took me and my brother. My sister had gone on occasion as well. But over the last year or so before this incident, I had ridden my bicycle out the twenty or so miles of dirt road to the caverns, by myself or once with a single friend whom I could get to ride out that far with me. (He wasn't all there, if you know what I mean. So he was the only one crazy enough to follow me on my adventures. But he isn't in this tale.) I had been several times without my family. This left me to be the real expert on hidden tunnels or the closest to having mentally mapped out the caves that we had to offer.

The summer sun gave my mother the idea that day. She took me and my brother and the neighbor's two grandsons to the caves for the afternoon. The caves always maintained a steady temperature throughout the year. The idea was good and we were all very happy to go. Mom was renowned for over packing lunches and crowding coolers with great munchies, so the kids who were visiting their grandparents next door were happy to come as well. So the five of us set out to go exploring.

My mother had a 1970 Buick Electra limited. It boasted a 455 cubic inch engine. It was ten feet between the wheels. Four doors and bench seats made for a great travel vehicle. If you had a crowd to haul, four thin people could easily sit in front and back. There was no center console or hub to get in the way. One could slide in close for a romantic drive with their spouse or lover; or, if it was a long trip, one small child on the floor on either side in the back, using the drive line hump, which always stayed warm, as a pillow and the larger kid or two on the seat could lay out completely like a bed. The seat was wide enough for two to spoon. But for our story, it allowed for three in back, two teens and a younger, and me in the front seat while Mom drove us out to the caves.

My mother wasn't aware at the time, but she was suffering from a brain tumor. It had been misdiagnosed from the time when I was a child. She was tired more times than she should be, and while she was relatively young, she started to put on weight. She dieted and starved herself and tried all of the fads to curb the weight gain, but none of them had any effect. She had gone from model skinny to overweight in a short couple of years while maintaining an active lifestyle. She was diagnosed with gestational diabetes when she was pregnant with me, but it never went away. That should have been a hint that something was far more wrong than they were giving credit for. She would not find out about the tumor for many years. Sometime after my first marriage, I was told of it and I don't know how long before that she found out about it. So Mom hadn't any energy that day. She chose to stay in the car and wait for us.

The cave was one of the smaller ones in the area and only took a short time to get into if you knew your way around. My brother and the two boys with us were relying on me to take them into the cave and show them the way around. This cave was called wind cave. The opening resembled an amphitheater. It was well- opened and looked like a half clamshell buried halfway in the ground. The entire entrance was strewn with larger than a ton boulders that had fallen from the roof over the many millions of years since it had formed from the flowing lava. One had to know where to find the actual entrance into the main cavern. I often thought of how lucky the first guys to find this place had to have been to find the actual entrance. From the surface, it looked as if all this cave had to offer was the amphitheater. A fellow with the gumption to look further would find a door to another world. The route required one to jump from boulder to boulder.

Toward the dark in the back, jumping from stone to stone, slightly off from center, was a doorway literally the size, shape, and thickness of a door. The stone wall thinned as it came to the small opening. Looking down from the perch atop a boulder, directly into the opening, one could still miss it because of the angle. When looking at the doorway from either side, one is looking downward, looking into stones and dirt that allow no transfer of light. But, once you get through the door and into the other side, you must mount another stone and then all becomes obvious. From the shadowed cover to the outside of the room, a light is shown from the roof, sixty-five feet above, directly in the center, from a hole that is about twenty feet in diameter. The ground beneath the hole is sandy and has had a fire ring formed by teens wishing to party out of view of the adults who would stop them. Surrounded by giant stone, a perfect area for a large crowd to mingle, fight and tell BS stories. There are areas to try and get your best girl to be your even better girl and the whole scene is perfect for teen fun with one exception. It is twenty miles from the main road, down a dirt and gravel road. Other than that, though, it's perfect.

I guided the others into the cave without the aid of a flashlight. We had only brought two and I was perfectly fine without one. I had been here so many times that I could nearly close my eyes and find my way. That is a good thing, because once you got to the doorway, you might as well have had your eyes closed, it was so dark. After we got through the door, my brother and his friends went through; and I remembered something that I wanted to look at outside before I continued. They took the lights and I went about my merry little way.

I checked out what it was that I wanted to look at. It took a few minutes. I then went to the car to check on my mother and make sure that she hadn't changed her mind about coming in with us. She had not, so I went back down to the opening and went in. My gazelle like legs helped me to leap from place to place with blinding speed. I had ridden my bicycle so many miles for so long that no amount of leaps, jumps, or bounds would tire me out. I imagine that I looked much like a flea bouncing from rock to rock.

Sometime after I left, my brother decided that he was going to try and scare me when I came in. I am not sure what he was thinking. I wasn't the one to try and scare, but he tried. Mark picked up a large lava rock. I think it was about the size of a softball or larger still. He waited to hear me coming in over the rocks, and he threw it in my direction. His idea was that the sound would elicit a scream of panic or at least a swear word from me. That isn't at all what he got. What he got to hear was the dull thud of a rock connecting on the top of a human skull, the sounds of a body falling near limp into a crevasse, and the scramble of that same body trying to surmount seven foot boulders to extricate itself from the area.

He threw the stone as high as he could toward me. It lobbed through the air in a great arc and landed dead on top of my head. I had just leaped from one stone in a path to another when the impact drove me between the rocks and down into a space between. Without a full understanding of what had just happened, I climbed back out by putting one foot and one hand against each wall and stepping up a little at a time. My memory of the event was that I had been hit and taken a minute to crawl out. My brother's recollection is of how fast I responded that I was heading out because a rock had fallen from the ceiling and had hit me in the head. "Meet me at the car!" I shouted to them, turning to go. Either way, I left the cave.

I scrambled for the doorway, dazed, and bleeding. My head ached and my knees were week. Blood streamed into my eyes, and I could feel the flap on top of my head where there shouldn't be one. The world turns all the time, we just don't always feel it. I felt it as I tried not to pass out on my way to safety. By the time I hit the doorway, I was blinded. I closed my eyes and kept them that way. Vision would return. It didn't worry me so much as I thought about the safety of my brother and his friends. I worried that the cave would come in and they may be trapped.

I fell between two stones just out of reach of daylight. Again, I scrambled out of the in-between. I was a bit more careful this time to try and make each step count. My equilibrium was shot and up and down felt a little bit confused. Even as I felt the light on my face, I only opened my eyes for brief peaks. It was no good, my eyes were polluted with my own blood. I felt my way to the car using familiar footing as braille.

My mother was none too thrilled when I arrived at the car. She has a queasy stomach when it comes to blood, and I was definitely over her limit to handle. We attempted to stop the bleeding with towels and napkins. She found them throughout the car, and I dabbed, blotted, and soaked up the blood. Discarded napkins littered the floorboard and I was unable to keep the seat as clean as I would have liked. She was a real trooper, considering that a bloody nose was enough to make her pass out on any normal occasion. We had a ready supply of juices and water and luckily, ice from the cooler. My mother had over planned us into a great situation. (If it were nowadays, I would have sewn my own head shut on the spot.) We sopped up blood into everything we had. All the while discussing where the others had gotten off to and why they had not emerged from the cave yet.

We came to the conclusion that the boys were lost. I would have to go get them if I was going to get out to the hospital for the stitches that we assumed would be needed to stop the ever flowing gush of Bryan fluid that now had the front seat of the Buick looking like it had been used for the final scene of Bonnie and Clyde.

I was dizzy. My knees were "jello" but at least I was able to see after my mother cleaned out my eyes with the water formed from melted ice in the cooler. I had one hand on my head holding a sweat sock filled with a ziplock bag of ice. I had wounds all over me from falling into the spaces between. I was bruised, battered, and frankly, pretty pissed off that I had to get these guys who should be capable of finding their own way out. But I went for them anyway.

We could yell all we wanted, and they would never hear a word of it. The design of the cave made for excellent acoustics as long as you were on the outside of the hole. Inside was actually shielded from sound by the same forces that reflected sound outward. So, as I got closer, I listened. When I got to the entrance, I heard the yells from inside the main cavern as the boys had fanned out all along the side to try and locate the hole. I peered through, and the sounds of them trying to get my attention were overwhelming. They were all calling out at the same time. I waited for a lull in the action. "Yoouu Hooooo! Are you guys coming or are ya just going to let me bleed to death out here?"

The boys fanned there flashlights in all directions to try and locate where my voice was coming from. The echo disguised the location of my silly call. But after a few moments, I was able to get them to look in the right location. After I guided them out to the hole, I again leaped and bounded my way to the car, requiring me and my mother to have to wait for a few minutes for them to catch up.

The teen neighbor let the cat out of the bag as to what actually happened. I don't think that my brother was ever going to tell the truth. The other kid remarked, "That rock was huge."

"What rock?" my mother asked as we drove the dirt of China Hat Road.

"The one Mark threw!" he said as if we knew what had happened. "I can't believe you got up." We did determine that it was an accident, that his intention was to startle me, but it sucked that he wouldn't have told me if he hadn't been snitched out.

The bleeding was slowed by the ice, and we were able to get it under control. We chose to avoid the hospital and instead went home where I could get into a bath and wash the blood off to allow a better look. My mother left it up to me as to whether we went to the hospital or not. I chose not to but kept it in reserve depending on the injuries final outcome.

I chose not to exact more financial burden by going into the emergency room. I just got cleaned up and accepted mommy coddling. After all, Mom made me French onion soup with the French bread on top, covered with cheese and baked crispy. (Oh my GAWD Mom can cook.)

My dad looked at it when he got home. Funny the difference between Mom's and Dad's, Dad just looked, adjusted his glasses, and looked again. He then pulled the flap back far enough to see under it and said, "Hmmm. Looks pretty good." To which I replied, "Got a stapler?"

SUMMER IS A GREAT TIME TO FLY

Summer in central Oregon has its privileges that a lot of city people will never know. Alone or with friends or on the rare occasion that a brother is being kind; camping, swimming, and just getting lost are the best way to grow up, or not. There is no prerequisite that any country boy ever has to grow up. If you have a 4x4 truck, there is never a problem to find rocks or mud to get stuck in. Gun nuts can shoot almost anywhere they want. I grew up with all of this at my command and almost no supervision.

One summer that just wasn't enough. I had ridden my bike all over the county for years. I had been to the caves so many times that all I had to do was close my eyes to relive the experience. I could jump in a river or lake or stream any time and would. Rope swings, secret mountain bike trails, abandoned mills, I knew them all. Bridge diving, river rapids, secret forts, no one knew them better. No, central Oregon had to have an adventure that I had yet to try.

I was working for old man Callious cutting wood, pulling weeds, listening to stories, and just being the friend to a ninety-year-old-war vet. I made a few dollars here and there and had been saving my money for a while, from cans and bottles collected from dumpsters and trash cans collected and cashed in as I rode through town. I had been inside of the ice cave a few months before when the idea first hit me.

My friend and I had ridden out to the furthest cave. Arnold Ice Cave is a cave that was once used to supply Bend with fresh ice for the refrigeration needs of stores as well as its citizens. I read recently that the name was an accident. It was from the sign that once shown the way to Arnold ranch and ice caves. Someone said them together and the rest is history. The entrance is about as far as anyone gets to see there, due to a steep descent into the black unknown on a few feet thick of permanent ice. I wanted to know what was past that. My friend and I took every last bit of rope we could find and set out to delve into the mysterious unknown.

Stories abound about anything that people are afraid of. Most were under the impression that a poor spelunker or two had met their untimely death when there ropes either gave way or were cut or perhaps the ropes were too short and the intrepid explorers found it too much to resist the urge to abandon their gear for a deeper look, only to slide to the bowels of the earth, never to be seen again. Any story like this made me need to explore it even more.

We went as far as the ropes would allow. In retrospect, it was probably only a little over a hundred feet, but we were sure nobody had been that far before. My buddy insisted we leave when I untied from the rope and instantly slid twenty feet into the black. Luckily, we got saved by an outcropping. My light did not reach the end, and I have no idea how I could have gotten out if I had gone all the way. I did wish that we had found the bones of those lost cavers though.

That experience cemented my need to do more. I thought the process out loud with my friend as a sounding board. I said, "If we fell to the bottom, we would have a hard time getting home. Right?" I didn't need him to answer and he knew I didn't expect him to. He was a friend for sure and would follow me to the ends of the earth. "Okay! Think about this. If we were up in the air and fell, we would already be where we started. Right?"

Rob's face contorted in a smile/what the hell look. He was right, you know? Most people would never follow me into this line of thinking. He knew I was always serious even when I joked about something so hair brained. He knew what most people didn't. The wilder it sounds, the less likely it could be done; the more dangerous, the more likely it was that I would do it and it would work. I wasn't the kind to give up on anything, to many head injuries I think.

We planned to find a way that year. So when he went to Portland for the rest of the summer, our plans not only didn't get canceled, he would never have understood if they had. It was my goal now. I would find a way to fly over my parent's house, and hopefully, not fall out of the sky. Sounds easy, right?

I did everything I could think of to come up with money for—I wasn't sure what for. I wanted to get an ultralight airplane. I had imagination dreams of showing up in Portland at my friend's school to take him for a ride. I knew that one needed no licensing to fly one, and the thought of being able to fly anywhere I wanted at any time was quite appealing. I could park it in the backyard. I had a yard big enough for a fleet of ultralight aircraft and a runway built in as our back drive. I also knew that our horses wouldn't mind the engine noise. They never minded motorcycles or lawn mowers. But I didn't know where to get one. Plus, my meager funds would be hard to save at that level.

By the time fate finally played its hand, I had saved $550. It was a king's ransom for a boy like me. I had saved every penny found in every parking lot of every market, store, and mall in the Bend area. I was so proud of what I had. I sometimes would take out all the money just to look at it. I was afraid all the time that I would come home from school to find that my brother was home on a visit from the boys' home and would magically find my secret hiding place. I had nightmares of it. Some nights I would wake in a cold sweat from chasing him endlessly, only to fall behind and be unable to get my money back. Fear dreams. The kinds that have you waking up in the morning more exhausted than when you went to bed.

My route of travel the next day took me through a neighborhood adjacent to mine. Separated by a couple of miles and a barbed wire fence, this was an actual housing neighborhood. I used to get bags of candy here on Halloween. The people here were the closest to an actual suburban lifestyle that Bend had to offer at the time. Everyone had their garage and boats and basketball hoops. I don't think that I actually had a reason to be there. I just saddled the horse for a ride and found myself going through that place as a spur of the moment thing. That's how I knew what I was doing there had a meaning. For one, you never ride a horse through a paved road neighborhood when there is any other way. Hard pavement is hard on their legs as well as the shoes they wear. If you want to throw a shoe, ride on streets a lot. Plus, a car and a horse are still bitter rivals even after all of these years.

An open garage, a barking dog, a Mach 1 Mustang in midnight blue, these all drew my attention. Without them, I might never have seen the white v-shape hung from the ceiling of the garage. Blue and red stripes went from the nose and spread and widened as they approached the tail. I couldn't deny it. Fate was stepping in and showing me what I had been saving my money for. A hang glider!

I dismounted from old Butte, my horse and tied her to their tree in the front yard. The owner of the house came out and greeted me, wondering why I would be at his house with a horse. "I was just wondering if you could tell me how much the hang glider cost and where I could get one." My heart was in my throat.

"Well, let's see. How much you looking to spend?" he asked with my answer held for ransom.

"I have some money saved up but I have no idea how much I will need." I saw a look cross his face that told me he was considering my answer more than just passively.

"Have you ever flown one before?" asked with a light tone.

"No. I haven't ever even seen one up close before." I told him realizing that he had not answered a single question of mine yet.

"Well come on in and let me show you." I entered his garage looking for meat hooks on the wall or anything that might indicate the need to turn around and run. This guy was a little too interested in helping me. But I didn't see anything that would make me believe that he was a serial killer.

He showed me the glider and all of the harness equipment that I would need to buy. He was helpful and knowledgeable enough about everything. "What makes you think that you want a glider?" he asked.

"I was with a friend..." I told him the story of how it all came about. He laughed out loud and by the time my story was over, he not only had a gut ache from my wild adventures, but he was wanting to try a few of my stunts for himself.

"I'll tell you what. This one is a couple of years old and I don't get out with it as much as I would like. It cost me $1000 just for the wing. The gear cost a lot on top of that. There's a minor tear here and here. You can patch those up easy enough. I would be glad to help with that. What do ya say? $800." His offer was good. I don't know where he thought a guy my age, fifteen, was going to come up with that, but I was willing to see if he would haggle.

"Well, let me tell ya. I was looking for a different color. But, I love America and I would love to fly her colors. The harness and all looks like it could use a cleaning and as you said, it is a couple of years old. The tears in the fabric tell me that I may be in for future repairs pretty soon. These cables will need to be replaced soon as well. They are showing rust here at the connectors. How about $400 cash?" I tried not to let him see me holding my breath.

The haggling went on for a few minutes. I was shooting bull droppings his way with a slingshot and he was trying to speak to me like a kid. Butte was tied loosely out front and I swear she listened to every word. She and I knew that I didn't have a clue what I was talking about. I took the words that he used to reference the parts of the glider and then slinging them back at him as if I had any idea what I was talking about. "Fine, let me get this straight. You want the harness, storage bags for it, and the glider, help with the patchwork, the wing, and the helmet for $500. Is that about it?" He was flustered to the point of sweating.

"Sure, so we have a deal?" I was not cocky, but feigning belief that he was agreeing.

"No. No we don't. My helmet wouldn't fit you. Plus, I like that helmet. How about $575 without the helmet?"

"Naw, $550 though and you got it…and you get to keep the helmet." Now I was cocky. I left there with an agreement to return in an hour with the cash. I was now the owner of a freedom hang glider.

That day, there wasn't enough light left to go out and try my new toy. So the following day I took my glider to the river. There was a point where the river ran between two rock walls. Cliffs where I had seen eagles fly unchallenged for years. I thought that if I was going to try this for the first time, it was going to be some place grand. Butte always liked that trail, and I needed her to get me and the glider to the river. Don't let the lack of structure fool you. A glider has more to it than it looks. I think it was around twelve feet long or so even after it was stowed away.

Looking over the edge of the cliff, a gust would blow your hair back. My adrenaline was working against me, keeping me from rather than rushing to. The falls were rapid and unrelenting below. Hesitation is not my strong suit. I was just crossing my fingers that the flight would be a success. I stood back from the edge. I breathed a few of what could be my last breaths. Then my feet took off running toward the edge. "Okay, we're just going to—wait! Feet, where are you going?" Just a little bit of speed and I could feel the lift affect the glider. My stomach came quickly to my throat. As I leaped off of the cliff, I became a human kite. But I was like Pinocchio, I had no strings.

I would never attempt to assume that my writing is good enough to describe what the feeling of flight feels like. I learned the feeling of turns and rising and falling and the use of air currents. But what I learned that was probably more important is that eagles are much larger up close than they are on a TV screen. Also, they can get really protective if you get too close to their nest. I flew with an eagle escort almost immediately. They came up fast like they were sent by NORAD (North American Radar Air Defense) from the limbs to me at trained jet speed. Direct and efficient, they intercepted my path and soon realized that I was a human. After that, they seemed to understand that I was just there to emulate them and not to be a danger to the nest that they so aptly guarded.

I flew many times that summer and the following as well. I used every cent that that glider had cost me and so much more. I never replaced a part or had a single crash. I took to the skies as if I lived there and my landings, although not always flawless, were easier than I thought that they would be. Eventually, I got so that I needed little hill to go great distances. I read that people now have GPS and two-way radio in their helmets as well as full sleeping bag looking harness. I don't get it. In order to be as free as one can ever feel, people trap themselves in the confines of technology. I don't even like to have a helmet, and in fact, never used one. I was cold up high but would never want to be encased in order to go up.

My buddy never did get to try out the glider. He was a little different when he got back. We never really had the chance to go out and get him in the air. My life would be away from Bend as the next couple of years would be the beginning of adulthood. I would make different friends and do different things. Needless to say, I wasn't able to power my way up to Portland. My glider was pure wind power and the power of will.

SOMEWHERE BETWEEN
A BOY AND A MAN

In the days prior to me going into the army, my mother showed me a side of her that I had never seen. She was the cool mom. I had never suspected a change in that way. She started suggesting that I try things that I had never tried, like going to parties and hanging out with friends and staying out for whole weekends. I don't know that I have ever told her what a great time of my life she set into play by those actions.

I was in a welding and metals class in high school. The auto repair class was located and taught in the same class area, if you can call a giant garage a classroom. There were guys in the auto class that I knew by reputation and by an occasional nod in the hall, but I had never had anything to do with them.

Tony was the tall skinny blond-haired silent type. His passion was a 1977 Chevy Nova. He and his brother had jacked up the back end, installed shackles to raise it up and put a set of bad a—, wide tires on the beast. The front end was stock height with spring tensioners and anti-sway bars. The back had a sturdy set of anti-sways as well. It was canary yellow with black interior and a 350 doing the dirty work for kicks.

Tony's brother was a shorter, dark-haired version of his older sibling. He was also silently cool and pretty much seemed to be always in for the game, along for the ride, so to speak, and game for whatever crazy thing came into play. The boys had lost their parents in a car crash some time before. With my addled brain I cannot remember how long before, but the parents had left trust accounts for the boys that they would receive when they each hit eighteen.

The third member of the posse seemed to be the leader, sharing the reigns with Tony. I will try to remember his name, but again, head injuries have played some real funny jokes on my ability to remember names. (I'm just glad that it wasn't something serious that my brain screwed up, like peeing outside the pot instead of into it.) He was about five feet six or eight inches tall. He was known as Tony was, for having a good fight in him and he, too, was always up for the adventure.

I would have never been with these guys if not for Allan. He was somewhere in between five foot nine inches tall and six feet. (It's hard to pinpoint when I am six foot four.) He was the guy with a beard in the ninth grade. He had dark curly hair that led me to believe he may have been Greek, but I can't be sure. Allan saw me kick the crap out of a jerk who desperately deserved it one time and was kind of drawn to me like a magnet afterward. We started talking and joking around. Once, when one of the jerks who regularly attempted to draw me into a fight was coming into my face and starting something, Allan actually defended me. I was the defender and was actually milliseconds from laying this punk out when Allan came from across the cafeteria, screaming something as he did about what a bitch this guy was, and two hands pushed the guy onto his butt at a full run. When he hit him, the guy flew back about ten feet, no joke. I was stupefied. I am not sure and I can never ask him now, but I think it was Allan's way of proving to me that he had my back.

Allan's mother let him do pretty much whatever he wanted. She was a heavyset woman and she spent a great deal of time at her boy toy's house. Since his father had drowned on a trapping expedition a year before, she let Allen throw parties whenever he liked and get away with other things that I could never have imagined. That was how I became part of this bunch of fun-loving, adrenaline junkies. It was all because Allen asked me to come over and help him patch the porch one time.

Allen and the guys got me drunk for the first time in my life. Honestly, I held the cans, bottles and what have you, but they were my happy enablers. It was the winter of '86. I went over, as I said, to help fix a porch. When I got there, I knew I was in for a wild ride. The hole was caused by two guys trying to carry an engine into the house to fix in the living room, and they had dropped it through the porch. It was still sitting in the hole and we had to remove it. He was impressed with my strength. For helping them, I got to stay for the party. The guys from the shop class, Allan's girlfriend, and another girl that came with Tony were all the party consisted of. We had beer for the most part of the night until some wise a— found a stash of the hard stuff in a cabinet. I had never been drunk before, so I hadn't the slightest idea how much I could handle or of what. So when the bottles got passed, I drank more than a fair amount.

I remember eating the worm out of the Tequila. I remember the nasty taste of Southern Comfort. I remember tilting the bottle of V.O. I don't remember much else. The next thing I knew I was on the kitchen floor and one of the guys was trying to get me up to go to bed. Apparently, I didn't want to be bothered though. I lay there on the floor, grabbed hold of a broom handle, and swung it across the kitchen floor. If I remember right, he was fast enough to evade, but I can't be sure. Fog is thick when years have passed on a rough drunk night.

Earlier in the evening, the girls and I had gotten along really well. I wasn't afraid to admit that I had never drank, and Allan's girl was put in charge of me. In retrospect, I think he was done with her and just hoped I would take her off of his hands, but I was no Casanova, especially in a drunken stupor.

When I woke the next day, around 2:30 in the afternoon, the girls were both there taking care of me. They had been there all night and cared enough to make sure the guys left me alone. The utter sweetness they showed me was one for the books. As I look back, I can never remember being treated so well by people I knew so little. They had rags for my head and had taken great care with me in the night to make sure that I didn't drown in my own vomit. They made me a breakfast of eggs and bacon and just petted me like a child with the flu. Fingers through my hair and petting my arms as a lover might do. It was an amazing time that has stuck with me as the kindest I have ever been treated, and they both belonged to someone else in the house.

The parties could go on at any given time. One night, I got a call to be ready to get cold in twenty minutes. Allan lived a few miles from me, I didn't have any friends closer actually, so twenty minutes was a hard target to believe. It had snowed two feet the night before and was snowing hard that night as well. So I just took him at his word and got ready to go. It was eight o'clock when he called and at eight-twenty on the dot, we heard a screaming, wining sound that almost made me giggle like a schoolgirl, for over a mile away in the silent, frozen winter's night. Allen, his girlfriend, Tony, and his brother all pulled up through the drifts on three snowmobiles. The temperature outside was about five degrees so the snow was powder. The three came in so fast that they nearly cleared the driveway for Dad. The snow just cleared a path as they road in like hell's snow angels.

This was the way it would be for me in my last month in Bend. These guys made it one of the few happy times of my life. They knew how to live, and it seemed to me they were all trying to cram a lifetime into that month.

In that time, I bought my first car as well. A friend of ours had a 1965 Ford Falcon. I had seen the car over time, in the same shop class. I watched the guys put tall Ford tires on this silly little car that they had found in a farmer's field. Then, when they couldn't afford to replace the shocks, they tried to weld square tube steel straight to the axles. It was a riot. The car had no suspension whatsoever. So every corner at every speed squealed the tire. This car with the barely running straight six cylinder engine was one of the best cars at roasting a doughnut. (Doughnuts are when you turn one direction and step on the gas, burning off the tires and leaving a skid mark in a circle like a doughnut.) When the car was offered to me for twenty-five dollars, I couldn't pass it up. I had to consult my mother for ten dollars of the money.

Have you ever had a secret that one parent knows and the other doesn't? Well I did. I didn't have a driver's license, so I couldn't bring the car home. I also couldn't leave it at anybody else's house or why bother having a car so I hid it out in the woods, up the road from our house. All of the properties away from our house, with only two exceptions, were vacant, abandoned, or just undeveloped. There is a canal that runs from east to west about three quarter of a mile, or two properties from our house. Sometime in the past, a red-lava-rock road was drawn in to the canal from the dirt road that went past the front of our house to the last property before the canal. The road ended at the canal in a cul-de-sac like area and everything else up to that area was wild. I hid the car there when it wasn't in use.

My new chariot was definitely badly cared for. It was baby blue. The seats were badly torn and smelled of old foam rubber. When I got the car it had no brakes at all. (I drove it home that way.) I wasn't much of a mechanic but I did manage to bleed the brakes well enough to get the front passenger side brake working. Only! The shocks were in a dumpster in the back of the school or something. I rode on springs alone, as some time before I was able to get my hands on the car, they had removed the steel bars due to police attention. It still had the Ford work truck style, all terrain tires. Ford must have been proud of that engine design. As far as I know, and as far as the guy I bought it from new, the valve cover gaskets had never been on this car. Oil would flow so quickly out of the engine that we just didn't put any in it. When the temperature would rise, I would pull over and let the car cool. As long as the temperature was up, the car would start great, but on the freezing days and nights that I would sneak out to drive, I had to bring rubbing alcohol to substitute for starting fluid. It was a stubborn beast, but somehow durable. I was a new driver and found learning to brake for turns especially difficult. I tended to forget that I couldn't stop on dirt or gravel due to the skinny front tires with only one side working. More than once I would jump from dirt to paved crossroad at over 35 mph having almost missed my turn, which would be a bad thing because there wasn't any more of the road I was on past the main paved road. There was no place to pass my turn for. I would oftentimes finding myself on two tires briefly due to lack of suspension dampening devices and high speeds. (I swear! I had passengers who got their first gray hairs riding with me.)

{I just had a conversation with a teenager that told me that he never wanted to get an old car like that. He wants a good first car. My response to him was, "It's the details that make the story worth telling."

If I had gotten a Porsche with all the bells and whistles, that would be the end of the story. What fun is that? If that was the end of my story, the baby blue, Ford Falcon coup, It would be a great story, but wait, there's more.}

I fully planned on giving the car to Allan's girlfriend when I left for the army. She and I had discussed it and, after some convincing, I got her to accept the gift, "if it lived that long" was the joke. I used to take her home in the Falcon for the brief time that I had it. I enjoyed her company, and it was the closest I had ever been to going on a first date in my own car. My Dad had refused me a driver's license as long as I lived at home when he found out about me skipping school and failing everything but PE. So this was it. When we got to her house, she always invited me in. I was shy and unaccustomed to the attention. Every word felt as if it were a gift. At the time I am sure that I was in the "friend" zone, but I didn't care. I just enjoyed the time I was with her. I was going into the army anyhow. She just treated me sweeter than I had ever known. She was warm and soft and huggable and smelled nice.

As I often tell my kids, the future can change in the blink of an eye. It may be taking the wrong turn, choosing the wrong road or waiting seconds too long or not long enough to do what you're going to do. You could miss the ride that would have taken your life as Buddy Holley, The Big Bopper, and Richie Valens did or you could catch the train and find the connection to your future waiting in the seat next to you. We can't always make the right choices even when we make the right decisions.

One snowy night after leaving Allan's house, I was on my way home. The roads were icy, and I was very unsure still about the highway. I headed home via the back road just hoping that the snow wasn't impassable. On this end of the road were a few homes so the trail was often blazed for the first ¾ mile. With plowed snow and only about six inches on the actual road, I could attempt to go over the steep hill, in which case coming down the other side would have meant slowing to a crawl to traverse extreme holes and 4x4 ruts, or I could go around the hill and not have to worry about the ruts or attempting to climb the slippery hill. With the temperature in the low teens to zero margin, a little snow was still as slick as ice as it was too cold to pack or bond to the surface of the road. I chose the latter. I went around. I must have blinked and missed the future changing because as I went around the hill, my foot stayed firmly planted on the floor. Speed picked up so slowly with this car that I never realized how fast I was going. The road came around slowly until suddenly I was at the merge. The lights were focused too low for me to have seen how fast I was approaching. The corner was there so fast that I couldn't gain traction to steer in time. Being a new driver, I had never heard of plowing, but at that second the meaning of the term would have been crystal clear. I oversteered to the left as I came into the merge from the left. As my car and I swept across the road that was barely wide enough for one and a half lanes, we ricochet off of the snow pile, turning the car to the left. The direction that I thought that I had wanted to go was now more than I wanted. I cranked the wheel to the right as fast as I could, now having my foot lightly planted on the brake. I didn't want to lock up my one braking tire, thereby losing traction with half of my steering. This time there was an abundance of steering, whipping the car to the right so fast that I couldn't catch up with steering. When I did however, I repeated the action to the left and then the right once more. If my journey had been caught on tape, it would have made for a funny video with an abrupt and startling conclusion. This area wasn't exactly void of trees, but they were scarce as this area was a valley with an incline on one side and near cliffs on the other. Much like a wash. So for me to find a tree less than five feet from the right side of the road was really lucky—in a bad way.

I wrapped the front end of the car squarely around the tree. An archer would have had trouble centering an arrow much better than I centered that car. My knees went through the dash, bruising them entirely. Pain coursed through my legs, and I was severely worried that I had done damage that might keep me from the service with only days left before I was to leave.

I was a scared kid. I didn't have a license or insurance. "But wait, the car isn't in my name." I left the car there. In a short time, I would be in Georgia at the infantry training center and I will be so far away that this can never touch me."

"So long as I can walk to get to the bus, that is."

I walked home from the accident scene. It was freezing cold but I didn't feel any chill. I was too worried about getting caught. I never told a soul. My mother never asked what happened to that car, which surprised me. But maybe in my retrospect, I should accept that she and my father never really did know or seem to care about the happenings in my life. As long as I came home alive, the world was in perfect order.

Nobody ever knew except for Allan's girlfriend. She was told because it gave me a reason to see her one last time. Besides that, she wouldn't be getting the car. I was gone from Bend the next morning after I told her about the accident. Bend would just be a haunting memory in the life of a perpetually optimistic boy, far from a place that never felt like home.

IN THE ARMY NOW

When I was sixteen, life in Bend was getting pretty harsh. After my grades fell, my father had me drop out of wrestling. I know that in most cases, his decision was probably correct; but in my case, wrestling had given me the one place where I was accepted. I was very good. I had been to state wrestling championships my last year of junior high and my freshman year in high school. I guess my parents didn't know that though. They had only been to one of my matches ever.

A friend and wrestling partner of mine, Bob, and I were eating M&M's out of a two pound bag. The chocolate contains caffeine as well as sugar, and we wanted the rush for our matches. As I took a swig of soda, which was probably a bad thing, more than a good one for strength, I was called to the floor for my match. I stood and looked up just in time to see my parents walking into the gym. They sat in the front row. I was so proud. Two years of wrestling and they never shown a bit of interest in the fact that I was wrestling. I was a winner, and they had never seen it. I squared off against my opponent as the referee sounded his whistle. With lightning speed, I slammed my opponent to the mat. I then took a leg in one arm and his head in the other and clasped my hand together. As he had no way out and was too late to struggle, I rolled him over in what is called a tight cradle, onto his shoulders, using my weight to hold him there. Pinned.

I won the match very quickly. Yes I was showing off, but isn't the point to win?

I let my opponent go and rose to my feet. I guess sprung to my feet would be more accurate. As I rose triumphantly and the referee was approaching to raise my hand, I looked for the approval of my father. I knew my mother would be clapping and smiling and yelling her voice out, but she wasn't. I couldn't believe my eyes. As I was being cheered by a crowd of people whom I didn't know, my parents were gathering their jackets and walking out. They chose to leave without so much as a word. I wasn't really sure what to make of it and even today, as a father and an adult son, I can't explain what happened that day. I have never asked or talked to them about it. It is one of those subjects that I will take with me to my grave as a failure. Somehow, I was unable to garner the interest of my parents.

My grades being what they were, I was not surprised when my father told me, in no uncertain terms, that I was to quit the wrestling team. I was carrying a .49 grade point average. There was no chance of me graduating at that rate. I would have ended up in school well into my adulthood.

My grades plummeted after the accident in '84. When I was hit by the truck, I was issued a tutor who had not turned in my work to the school. Even though I had done all of the work and passed it with flying colors, I failed for not turning in the work that I had no ability to turn in. The tutor had just not done her job. So I failed the eighth grade and was forced to repeat it. All of my classmates whom I had been with were moving on as I stayed in the same place with many of their younger siblings. Some of the kids I had protected because they were younger were now in my class and I felt belittled, inferior, and like an injustice had been done to me. That coupled with these injustices put upon me by all of the California haters that had tortured me my whole life in Oregon, and the new principal at the school who had seemed to follow me through my school life, Brian Lock (name changed). I was unable to recover the interest in school. I became bored and disinterested. My IQ being highly above average was probably a factor as I felt that I was smarter than most of my instructors. I felt as if they had nothing to teach me. (I know in retrospect that I did not know their subjects better than them.)

I never questioned my father. Baird was a stern man of uncompromising values and beliefs. He was also uncompromising in his commands. You just did not question him. All my life, I would strive to prove to him that Mom and I were worth all of the pain he had endured from my sister and brother. I felt as if he were infallible and whatever he said or wanted was absolute. I looked at him as a hero. I quit wrestling the next morning.

The main wrestling coach was what I now know to be in constant steroid rage. His body was built to the extreme. He was the only man that I have ever seen developed to the extent. His temper was short and his grudges long. After I quit wrestling, I applied for weight lifting as an elective, but the coach was in charge of the weight lifting class. He showed up in my PE class the day I put in my class schedule sheet for the coming semester. He said that he had an announcement to present in front of the classes all waiting for instruction. He then made this very short speech:

> "I never accept failure. Quitters exemplify failure. To make my point this morning, I point out one Bryan Johnson, a state champion in his junior high school and a state champion on my team last year. He quit the team this year and let all of you down. Now he wants to join my weight lifting team, a team of tough, strong, winners. But Mr. Johnson is not a winner. He is a loser. So,

because he is a loser and a quitter, he will not
be joining my winning team."

He then pointed his comments directly at me. "As long as
you're at this school, everyone will know what a loser you are."
He then went on with his class, separating them from ours.

It was that day that took me from a school-aged teen to an
adult. (I thought that I was anyway.) I decided that I would do
whatever it took to get out of that place. I had been the subject of
torment from fellow students, a vice principal turned principal,
teachers, and now the coach whom I had performed so admirably
for. As far as I could tell, there wasn't a thing to lose. Life had
not been kind to me in Oregon. I needed a way out. Even if it
meant—wait—how does a sixteen-year-old kid get out of a town
where he can't seem to get a real job? With no driver's license or
car or money?

I was riding my bike on the far side of town on a cold winter's
day. Snow piles on the edges of the road formed by the plows
were making for a treacherous ride when I spotted the recruiters
office. The army, navy, air force, and marines had offices next to
one another in a small strip mall. I rode up onto the sidewalk and
put down my kickstand, dismounted my bike and walked inside
the nearest office. It was the army. I spoke to the man in uniform
and asked if he had any information about the age requirement
for joining. He gave me a pamphlet and sent me on my way. So, I
walked into the Marine recruiters and asked the same questions.
The marine recruiter gave me a cold response. He wasn't showing
any interest in signing me up. Just then, another recruit came
through the door. "Drop and give me fifty!" barked the recruiter.
The scared-looking, long-haired-freaky person dropped to the
floor and started pumping out four count push-ups. Then from
behind a temporary wall in the back of the office, another recruit
who also had long hair, was banging with his palm on the back

office door. "Sir! I have finished my testing, sir!" he yelled in a just passed puberty yell. "Drop and give me twenty, maggot!" was commanded from inside the little office.

I turned and left that recruiter's office. I didn't like the fact that these guys were being treated the way I had been for the last six years, and they hadn't even signed on the dotted line. Now, if I had given it a little more thought, I may have gone into the air force or the navy offices. I may have found a better gig than I did, but I never went into those offices because of the startling things I had just witnessed.

That night when I got home, I chopped the wood and took it into the house, cleaned the kitchen and vacuumed as I usually would. I just couldn't get past the army allure. It did require that I have a high school diploma or the equivalent. I had heard that the community college offered courses that could be transferred to high school credits. It was my hope that I could get into the courses and get the credits to receive my diploma. I knew my grades in school were terrible and that I would have to work hard. My father had always been clear that in life we are all responsible for what we do. I had always known that I was responsible for my own future as well as my own failures. That's when I discovered the Tamarack Learning Center (TLC). I signed up for classes at both the community college and TLC. I never told my parents until it was way late in the game.

I went into the recruiting station and talked to the recruiters. They had a few choices, but for the most part, they were pushing me toward an infantry unit. The Reagan Buildup of the forces was in full force. He wanted to be as strong a deterrent as possible against the Soviet Union. They offered me a $4000 bonus for signing up and completing basic training. I had never seen that kind of money. I knew that I could get out of Bend and see a wad of cash. My plan was to buy my mother a "Wedge car." She had always called sports cars that. The latest was a Subaru four-wheel-drive car. (I now know they were lemons and hard to maintain.)

I signed up without my parents' knowledge. I did the testing and passed pretty well but the scores couldn't count until I had my diploma. I could take the test over again but the score was already better than it needed to be to get in.

I started classes after school. I would ride my bike to the classes and then ride home, do my chores and build up my courage. I had to tell my parents at some point. They would have to pay for the classes or I couldn't get the grades. So the time would eventually come for me to tell them about my plan.

The time did come. I had been sent a mailing from the recruiter that Dad had opened by mistake. It told of the requirements, test score verification, unit assignment, and date of entry. Dad was pretty surprised. Mom was pissed. She blew a gasket. I tried to calmly explain why and how and when. That stuff wasn't important to her. I was her youngest and essentially her slave. I did everything around there. Dad washed the occasional dish, but all Mom ever did was cook and do laundry, which would have been plenty in most cases; but we had a lot more than that to be done each day. After all, I cleaned the kitchen before they got home in the evening and after we ate dinner every day. I split the wood and brought it in. I vacuumed and mopped and kept my own area clean. I was the TV remote control and the massage therapist. I ground down her callouses and massaged her feet and fixed all of the broken things around the house.

My argument was sound. "Mom, there isn't anything for me here. I am not going to graduate high school unless the place burns down and all of the records are lost. Because of that, Dad won't ever allow me to get my driver's license. I can't find a regular job. I am not happy. There are things at school that happen that you and Dad never even hear about. I just need a way to grow up."

Dad was actually on my side. Of course, he had the misgivings that his house would finally be rid of kids, but nevertheless, he was on my side.

"How are you planning on paying for the schools?"

"I get a bonus of $4000 for joining." I said calmly. "I'll pay you back if you cover me on this." I had never asked Dad for money before. I had gotten a couple of dollars on rare occasion from him for running around town but never had I even asked for anything else. My sister had always gone around him to Mom when she wanted something. I was a man, I figured. I would consult him face to face for anything I ever needed. I didn't plan to need very much. I was shocked that he went along with it so well.

I had never been a rebellious teen. I never wanted to get out just to get out. I did skip school, fake their voices calling the school for attendance, and forge their signatures, however. I had to forge Mom's because Dad was left-handed and had the most beautiful writing you have ever seen (must have been from being raised before the formation of the Dept. of Education and the nationalization of the school system). But I never wanted to hurt them emotionally or to leave just to leave. I never lost respect for them or questioned their judgment either. This time, I felt it was in my best interest to stand for something important to me. This was the first time I had ever argued with my parents, and it really was just arguing with Mom. Dad was mad that I went behind their backs for so long. It had to be quite a shock to find out that their son had already signed the papers and signed up for the two schools and began classes. Now for the biggie.

"I want to quit going to school to focus on classes that matter."

Silence.

"I don't think I am going to be able to do all of this at the same time."

I received a nod from Dad after Moms crying retreat from the kitchen. I had set in motion the necessary pieces to get a diploma, not a GED. I was going to graduate my sophomore year, midyear, nearly in concert with my seventeenth birthday and soon after, I would be a United States soldier.

RETURNING HOME

After the army, I went back to Bend for a time. I went to work for Bend Millworks. I assumed that to work for the mill was about my only option and that I would work for them until I retired. It seemed that I would live a middle class life with a middle class wife like all of the country songs that I loved in my youth.

Getting hired required me to file an application with a hiring service, one of those temporary workplaces. They would do all of the drug testing and background research for the mill. They also got a percentage of my wages for the time I went through their service. If I was with the company for thirty days, my hire would become permanent.

I started on a machine that cut veneer. I fed the machine all of the thin cuts of wood that the machine would then make paper thin. Soon I was moved to a position more suited to my size. I stacked laminated wood beams and would switch off with a guy called "Bear." We took turns as the weight of the beams and the lengths were incredible. Figure that one or two of these are used in the manufacture of your home and no one wants to be the guy lifting them. We each did pallet after pallet of them. Each break time, we would come back to our machine and switch off to the feeder. Bear was the lead on this circuit of machinery. First the boards, (2x4, 2x6,2x8, etc.) would be fed into the machine.

A conveyer would take them to the next station which would be the laminate that would glue them. So the feeder would have to load the pieces in a good stack. Then the veneer, for appearance, would be laid onto the surface. Finally, they would come back out having gone full circle, and we would stack them. The glue was usually still hot. I went through several pairs of gloves in the time I was there.

I worked nights. I became accustomed to my new life pretty quickly. The money wasn't very good but the aspect of permanence sounded great, and I would receive a full pay and benefits package as soon as I got on full time. (I guess my 8–10 hour shifts are not full time.) I had time to get reacquainted with a couple of my old friends, mostly the one who got me the job. I got to get to know my family a little better as an adult. I stayed with my parents out on the property, and it felt good to be home.

Then one day, I showed up for work and received word that I no longer worked there. The agency had gotten into a confrontation with the mill. Whatever happened, I was out of a job. The worst part was that if I had worked that day, I would have been on for the required thirty days and been permanent. It turned out that, that was the reason I was let go before work instead of after, as usual. Someone caught the fact that I was going to get on permanent and had me stopped upon entry. The news hit me hard. But Bear was pissed.

Bear was a 350–400-pound man. He stood a head taller than me, and I was six-four. His mood was calm; but his life had been spent working jobs no other man could do, except me. He had finally found a guy who, with a little time to get those muscles in shape, could keep up with him physically in the challenging work field we were in. To say that our job was physically demanding is an understatement. No sane person puts out that much for work. I was just the man for the job. So, when he found out that I had been let go, he threw a temper tantrum, as the story is told. He had grown men shut down their machines and run from him in fear as he yelled at the boss and threw two-hundred pound beams as if they were tooth picks. Then he went over to the forklift; and as I have been told by eyewitnesses, grabbed the cage, pulled, pushed, pulled, and with a mighty push, rolled a full-size lift onto its side. I have never known these witnesses to be exaggerators, and I heard the story from more than one person. Bear must really have liked the way I worked.

I stayed with my sister for a few days after that all happened. Then one day, I called an old friend, a girl I had known since the fifth grade. She invited me to come to eastern Oregon to see her. I didn't have a car and I wasn't sure if I could find work soon and I felt as if the world was just a little out of kilter for me at the time. I felt lost for the future, so I went to the edge of town and stuck out my thumb. There was no way I could have known that my little excursion to eastern Oregon would lead me into a traveling binge, spanning rail and road, highway and boxcar for the next two and a half years. How could I have foreseen the magic of seeing a stream flow uphill in New Mexico (or was it Texas by then? It's hard to tell one from the other in the boxcar of a train), or the wonder of a Ghostly encounter in Santa Cruz, California. I never expected to pick fruit on a farm in California or Peaches in Georgia or run a combine in Ohio. Visiting the Liberty Bell on less than a dollar a day or delivering a baby in the back of a cab in New York, New York.

My life changed the moment that old mill let me go. In the blink of an eye my future had, once and for all, been cursed to travel and blessed to live. Every error I made would come to pass as something that happens because it does; and every good I did would find a way to sabotage my next step forward. I would learn the ropes of life and work as no other to find that my life would never really settle. I would forever find small respites of hope to one day settle down only to have carpet and rug taken from under my feet. Sometimes literally and other times so figuratively that they would only feel literal. From trucking the United States to traveling through states with wives I was destined to lose or give away, my life had been set into a motion that for all intents and purposes, had no singular purpose.

"I got a steel plate in my head, Clang, clang!"

I was on the road to nowhere. I didn't have a destination, and I figured that I would know it when I got there. I had gotten a ride here from somewhere before. I was dropped by a guy who turned off of the highway and said his place was about ten miles up the dirt road. I wasn't sure if we had passed a town in a long time, and I could see in the dark that there were fields all around. There are overpasses built over the roads for the farm workers to better access fields from one side of the highway to the other, but they do not help a guy who needs a main road and traffic to get to where he is going. The roads on either side end within the fields. The good part is the shelter from the elements that they provide. I slept under one of these overpasses until the sun woke me in the morning. It wasn't a bad place to be. The sun was nice and a breeze blew through the cultivated soil that would one day have crops growing in it. I had full water containers with me and shade could be had under the overpass if needed.

The first day that I sat on that lonely road, was one of hope. I hoped that someone would come my way and pick me up. I threw dirt clods from one side of the road to the other. I told myself stories of wishful lives that I had never lived. I day dreamed for hours before I realized that for hours I had not seen a single car. Then I thought about it for a minute. I had not seen a car since I woke up that morning.

I went to bed that night and achieved a night's sleep full of funny musings about how I had ended up in the twilight zone somehow. I remember that the sky was clear, and I set up my sleeping arrangements to view the stars. I thought that perhaps the next day would be better. I would get a ride from some farmer who needed someone to work his farm. He would have a beautiful daughter, and we would fall in love. My life would be spent raising children in Ohio as a farmer with a bunch of wonderful family all around me. I thought that I heard a car go by in the wee hours of the morning, but I couldn't be sure.

The next day went the same as the first. I was truly in a world apart. The traffic never came. I sat and sat and sat for the entire day from sunup until sundown. Somewhere Gawd was laughing at me, I just knew it.

The third day was much like the first and second. Asking the field to answer why people would build a road where no one would use it; did me no good. The fields and sky were silent on the matter. By the late afternoon, on the third day, I was anxious to wave at airplanes flying over at five miles above the earth. They were the closest to company I had had. I was also starting to feel desperately hungry. I hadn't eaten since the morning before I was dropped off here. I thought to myself how funny it would be to starve to death in the middle of some of the most fertile fields in the world. A place that provides vegetables for much of the United States, and I got trapped here when they were between plantings.

A dog. I saw a dog. Now, where in the world did he come from? He was coming down the road, crossing and searching and sniffing for a very long way. I saw him for far longer than would be reasonable to call him. So, I just watched him come closer until I felt as if calling him would not be foolish. "Here Poochie!" I called to him. He looked up from his sniffing and returned his nose to the ground. A while later, "Here Poochie." He ignored me and continued his mission. It seemed as if hours were passing as he slowly came closer. I got up on top of the overpass for the umpteenth time to try and see if a house or farm or anything was within sight. And for the umpteenth time it was confirmed that there wasn't a blasted thing for miles around.

Finally, I could hear a car over the breeze. It was coming from so far off. I got my back pack on my back. I wrestled with looking nonchalant. I was very excited but didn't want to come across as a loon. I was starving and could barely stand. My water was almost gone, and I was dehydrated to the point of passing out. The car flew passed me.

"What the hell?" I shouted at the wash of air that followed the pickup truck. I turned toward his taillights to reassure myself that he had indeed kept on driving. Just then, the dog was crossing the road. The pickup ran the dog over. It looked almost intentional, but who can say. Whatever the case, he continued driving on as if nothing had happened.

I ran over to the dog that was lying limp in the road after having tumbled endlessly under the fast moving truck. He was dead and gone. The life was stolen from him in the time it took him to stop rolling. I still had no one to talk to.

An hour passed and I was alone once again, hungry, almost out of water, and wondering if I would ever get a ride from here. I have always thought that things happen for a reason. I wandered over to the dog which I had taken off of the side of the road. His hind leg was nearly severed in the accident.

I chose to remove his leg, build a fire, and cook it.

I was almost in tears over the thought of eating man's best friend; but I reasoned that if I were on a snowy mountain with few survivors and time running out for the rest of us, I would definitely eat another person to survive. The problem was that dogs were better people than most people that I have met in my lifetime. As I cooked the hind quarter over a small campfire under the overpass that was quickly becoming my permanent address, I remembered the dogs we had owned in my youth: Gracie and Calamity Jane were Great Danes we had at separate times. Claude the St. Bernard had gotten his name when he stepped on my mother's foot coming out of the kennel at the animal control shelter where she found him. Clancy, another Great Dane I had gotten as a gift that my sister sold before he was a year old. Bo was a German shepherd police dog retired to our home. He was huge for a shepherd. Boy was a German shepherd as well, Dad found him and brought him to live with us. He protected our property in Bend really well against everything to include the neighbor's two dogs. A Rottweiler and a wolf/collie mix. I came home to find him shot to death beneath my parents' bedroom window. He apparently won another fight and the old man next door couldn't break it up. Amber and Sunny were our breeding pair of poodles. Amber was my "dog" so I took her with me everywhere. She was fat and loved to swim. And no list could be complete without the living Muppet, Ben. He was a long-haired Drawthour. He would bounce so high when he wanted in that he would hit the overhang. We got him in 1984 when he and I had the same broken leg and the same pins in our legs. We used to limp together on walks.

Once cooked, I hesitated to take a bite. I had skinned it and added spices that I carried with me in my pack: pepper, garlic salt, and a couple secret spices. But the will wasn't really there. It smelled great though. Finally, I gave in. I almost puked from the thought even though the taste was perfect. I had done a great job cooking it.

Just then, up the road I saw a swerving car from about a mile away. He was on one side and then the other. He crossed as if the lines didn't exist. Smoothly back and forth until he came close enough for me to see his face. I had been letting the fire die and so putting it out the rest of the way was pretty easy. I stood up with my "Leg-o-mongrel" in hand. The car skidded to a stop in front of me. A man with a full beard of white and a scar crossing his entire forehead jumped out of the car as if he knew me. "Well, you want a ride or don't ya'?" The classic song *The Ride* came to mind but for only one verse. "I knew there was something strange about this ride."

I opened the passenger side door and beer cans fell out. I threw my backpack into the can pile that took over his backseat. I shuffled my feet through the beer cans on the floorboard on my side. "So, you look like you've had a couple, you want me to drive?" I asked him with the hope of a yes in mind. "Nope." He said proudly as if announcing that he was about to say something grand.

We drove for about forty-five minutes, swerving the whole way (and counting the cars as we drove. Four (where were they before?), before I saw a town. Granted we were only going about eighty, but I thought how right I was to wait for a ride to come to me. In that time I didn't see anything of interest. The town we did come to consisted of a small gas station and mini mart. We stopped for more beer since I had drank the first of the beers in his last six-pack and he had beaten me to the finish with the other five. He could drink! I went to the bathroom and he got another one and a half cases. I got out the door in time to see him pulling away. I shouted, "Hey, my bag!" He stopped and opened the door on my side and beer cans fell out.

In his scratchy tone he said, "I thought you left without me."

"I couldn't," I told him. You have all the beer. With that he laughed and asked me, "Here…It's a burger…they taste like shit but they ain't dog."

"Have I ever told you about my head?"

"Sir, in all the time I've known you, I don't think you've mentioned it." I said with a sarcastic grin. Because the whole forty-five-minute ride from where he picked me up, he had spoken of an experience in Vietnam.

Then he would yell very loud, "I got a steel plate in my head, Clang! Clang!" And wrap his fist against his head in a knocking motion. HARD! If not for that plate he would have a concussion in his head. He did this every couple of minutes and it was very startling the first twenty times or so. I was six foot four and two hundred plus pounds and it made me worry at first.

We talked, mostly repeating the same subjects, and drove for hours. He was quite a character. I drank two or three beers the whole time I was in his car. He was almost out of beer and had to stop for more. He put away that entire case and a half in a couple of hundred miles.

I left his car with new story and very tired butt cheeks from clenching the material as we weaved through the lanes in the dark of night. To this day, I still think of him and wonder if he ever made it to his destination. The problem is, he didn't really have one. When he dropped me off, he turned around and headed back to where he had come from. I don't know where that was but I think he saved my life that night as he gave me a new found respect for the strength of cloth seats.

GEORGIA CARPENTRY

A friend of mine from my military days invited me to come to Georgia to visit him when we got out. He never gave me an address to come visiting to, he just left me a few bread crumb clues, if you will. I don't think that he ever expected me to show up in the South lands.

I was told that if I wanted to find him, I should find James Venable. The use of the name was supposed to mean something to me, I think. People from the South all knew the name as he was the grand wizard of the Ku Klux Klan. I guess if you are a white boy from a suburb of Atlanta, this would be a pride point to claim personal friendship with the grand wizard.

James Venable was more than the iconic symbol for the whites- only organization. He had been mayor of Stone Mountain village from 1946-1949. He was an attorney with a long career in the field. He was a direct conduit to history. His name was plastered on almost every baseball or softball field in the area, as well. He was a generous man who had donated his family property for the children of the area. He was also the owner of much of the lands that "Stone Mountain" rested on and had donated all of the land to the national park service as well. His holdings had shrunken over the years as he donated them to the betterment of the local society, and the man I knew showed a soft side that would betray his purported past.

I met the man while looking for Bill in Stone Mountain, the city. I only knew a little about the past that my friend had told me. I knew that he had been forced to join the army because of a torrid affair with an underage girl, who so happened to be a judge's daughter. He had been sent away rather than expose the family to the shame of this all becoming public. I also had heard tails from him of the old KKK leader. This led me to the doorstep of Mr. Venable.

I looked up the address in the phone book as soon as I got into town. I didn't have a quarter, so I walked through town asking directions as I did. I found his home very easily and soon was knocking at his door. I stood on the step of the old, dilapidated mansion that was in dire need for a lawn mower, when a large woman came to the door. "Good evening, ma'am. Is Mr. Venable at home?" I asked her, hoping that I was at the right address.

"Do you have a meeting with him?" she asked.

"No ma'am. I have just come from Oregon and I am looking for an old army buddy who claims to be a friend of the gentleman, and I was hoping I could find my friend through him." I said. She retreated through the door and turned back away from the screen. "Jimmy! Can you come here for a minute?" she shouted over her shoulder. "There is a young man here looking for a friend of yours."

I could smell the food on the stove cooking. I had somehow found my way to the backdoor. I assume it was because of the angle of the house to the newer road that confused me. The aroma was almost too much to bear as I stood waiting to meet the friend of my friend. He walked into the kitchen. I was very surprised to see an old man. I didn't know of him or of the things he had done or of his affiliation to the Klan, at this point. I only knew that my braggadocios friend had claimed to know him. "Hey, what can I do for you?" he asked with sincerity as he traded places with his female companion. "My friend, Bill Brown has claimed to know you and to be a friend. He said that if I got into town, I should look you up and find him through you." I tried to explain myself, all the while knowing that he was not someone who would know a twenty-three-year-old man. The two of them discussed if they remembered a name like that and if he could be so and so's kid or a case he may have worked on. The conclusion was clear from the moment they started their banter. Bill was full of it and had probably never met this man in his life.

"I don't think that I can help you," he said with a bit of sorrow.

"Well, I am sorry to have bothered you. Please excuse my interruption."

"We'll have none of that," came the voice from within the room. "Invite the young man in. We can't send him away hungry."

That was the start to a really interesting time in my life. I was in the room with a man who knew several presidents, dozens of governors, and could get a trial dropped with a request over the phone. I had witnessed on several occasions, Mr. Venable talk on the phone and get a man's trial dropped or his sentence reduced to a fraction. A black man named Marcus was the first one that I overheard. His was a murder trial and the short call got it dropped to self-defense. He was released on his own recognizance that night and only had to show up two days later as a technicality. (I met Marcus. He was the most appreciative man on the planet. He came over and mowed the lawn for the old lawyer. That was the fee asked for the services rendered. Marcus would mow his lawn every week that summer and his debt would be paid.)

I ate dinner there every Wednesday and Sunday for several months. As long as I was in the area, I had a standing invitation to come and learn history from one of the men who had written and witnessed the writing of it. We would discuss all of the important people in the Klan who had gone on to power. We spoke of the mistakes and those who made it look bad to be a Klan member. His most ardent complaint was that the Klan was supposed to be an underground army for the good of man. But those men- in-white sheets had ruined the image over the years. He believed that the Klan had a just task to preserve the race but that in doing so, it didn't mean that other races weren't equal or were not capable of coexistence within the community. He thought that Jessie Jackson was a fraud. So he brought out a file to show me that Jessie Jackson had done some very bad things and that he was a Black Panther leader. But we all know that. What he also had was evidence in the slaying of MLK and a possible link that put Sharpton, Jackson and a couple others in a cabal. He said that the message of peaceful revolt was always lost on them and that in his men's research, they found it very likely that these men may have been involved.

I also learned of the modern beginning to the Klan that most people would never know. It happens that Thanksgiving night, 1915, Mr. Venable and his cousin, Col. William Simmons and one other man, a Mr. Green went to the top of Stone Mountain in the middle of the night and had a ceremony where Mr. Simmons became the first grand wizard of the new KKK. Three members of the original Klan swore them in. They restarted, reshaped, and began again the secret society aimed at the protection of the white family and community. Since then, the Klan has had at times, more than two million members. More than the modern NRA or any other organization has had at any one time. Still today, the true followers are in the shadows and not seen. That was the original intention. If you see them on TV, they are not in the true Klan. If you see a march down Main Street, USA, with their hoods and guns, that is not the real deal. I know. I met the only wizard to ever wear the purple uniform with a gold sash. I touched and felt the material for myself, and I learned from the man who was there on that hill top, ninety six years ago.

It was Mr. Venable that told me to go to the VFW (Veterans of Foreign Wars) to find work. I learned very quickly that if he said something, I should follow his instructions. He rarely said to do something that wasn't in your best interest. Even though I was clear from the start that I was not a Klansman or a want to be, we got along very well and I learned so much from him that I only wish that our time as friends had been longer.

I went to the VFW and asked around about my friend Bill. I also asked about work. "Yeah," came a voice from the back. "I got the call. I'll set you up."

I met the man in the back of the room. I cannot remember his name, but he was as old as Venable and not nearly in the shape that the old man was. He took me to his one room apartment and showed me to a roll away cot. I was instructed to stay as long as I liked and that in the morning, two young men would stop by to pick me up. I washed and showered and we shared a meal. TV dinners. In the morning, I was woken by a shake on the arm and told it was time to get up and that my ride would be there soon.

As told, two men in a small car came for me in the morning. They were two young, southern boys about my age, 19. I jumped in the car and asked, "What kind of work we doin?"

"You's going to be a carpenter." We stopped to get some tools and a belt at the hardware store on the way. I was shocked in a couple of ways. One was that these strangers came to pick me up to take me to a job that I had not applied for. The other, that they would buy me a hammer, measure, and belt without question. Yet another, that anyone would be able to drive while getting that stoned, that early in the morning and still make it to work, let alone actually be able to work. I mean these boys were roasting joint after joint after joint. As they passed them around, I was offered, but refused. I don't smoke it and certainly not before a first day at a job I had never done before. But these guys, they were baked.

Jim, the driver, gave me a piece of advice. He said, "The boss don't like to have to train new guys who think they know it all. So, you got ta let him know you don't. You ever swung a hammer 'afore?"

"Nope." I said with confidence that I had somehow made out the words despite his heavy accent.

"Good. Then when he asks what you know, you tells him like it is. Say, I Know Nothin!"

Sure enough, I arrived on the job site with these boys and a contact buzz that you can't imagine.

The boss looked me in the eye and asked me, "So, what do ya know?"

Without hesitation, I told him my entire framing history in one great little phrase that has served me well on many occasions since. I looked him square in the eye and said, "I Know Nothin!"

"Your hired."

I loved that job. I loved the smell of the wood and the swing of the hammer; the sun beating down on my shoulders and the monkeying around up on the sides and the roof. I never got tired of handing up the boards or fetching the boss a couple more hand full of nails. We never used air equipment with that crew, and the standards we used in our framing were the same that he had been raised to use when he was a kid working with his father as a younger man. All of the roofing decking and every two by four were nailed by hand and we were quick. The holler of "Gyp that gable!" could be heard throughout the yard as we set the final gypsum board onto the gables of the houses. One man would yell it and then another. It was a sign that our job at that location was almost over and that the next house would be on tomorrow's list. Or the call of, "Toe nail it!" Another term used that would start a chain reaction of copy cat hollers.

Each day we would go for lunch, me and the guys that I rode with in the mornings. Usually our lunch was from Arby's or some other fast-food joint. I was introduced to sweet tea there and have loved it ever since. I also discovered peach tea from the fountain drink section. On the West Coast, it's all about raspberry tea. I don't care for raspberry. I like peach.

I searched for Bill in the spare time that I had. I wasn't really that desperately trying to find him. I liked the air I breathed and the job that I did. But one day I did find him. I soon moved in with him and his red-haired, judge's daughter. She was a sweetie. I got Bill on at the job. But I have to be honest, I wish I hadn't found him. I may still be in Georgia today. But fate does its bidding.

On a lazy Tuesday, I was up on the roof with the boss. We were fixing in a few of the fancy decking boards when the clouds opened up and dumped on us. He laughed and stood up. "Well, we are just about done here anyways. Come on there, young man. It's lunch time." With that, he took the next step and it was his last. The boards we put in place have bumps on one side. The reason for these bumps is to give footing to the roofers and men putting decking up. Somehow, one of the boards had been put on face down and the rain had made the surface so slick that my boss was off the roof and flailing in midair before he had a chance to realize what had just happened. I was stunned. I climbed down the face of the three-story house so fast that I wasn't really even sure of the route I had taken.

There in the middle of the scrap wood pile, lay my favorite employer of all time. He was face up with a two by four pine stud through his back and out of his chest. His heart separated from his chest and now out on display as if from the script of a horror movie. I was now unemployed.

One of the things that life has kept for me as a constant lesson is that if fate has something in store for you, it is going to happen whether you like it or not. The only thing that I have ever been sure of is that if things are going too well for me, wait for the rub. Something will come along to make sure that I pay for the good feelings of comfort.

One of the guys on the crew had it in mind to start his company. He felt sure enough of his skills to begin another crew. He invited me and accepted Bill as an accompaniment.

We started for him and all went well for the first couple of days. Everything was fine except for Bill's unwillingness to get out of bed. He lost us that job. We were too far from the site for me to get there from the house without a car, and he would refuse to get out of bed until we lost our jobs. His girlfriend had given him her all, and he was done with her as well so we loaded our few things and headed to Florida.

James R. Venable died on a Monday, in January, 1993. He was 92 years old and the obituary reads that he had Alzheimer's, cancer, and pneumonia. Well, I hope to shout. If you live that long, and it takes that much to kill you, you are a tough old bugger.

NEVER FALL ASLEEP IN
THE GULF STREAM

It was Florida, 1989. My friend from the army had gotten us fired from a great job framing houses in Georgia, and we decided to go to Panama City Beach, Florida. I got a job in a pizza place on the beach, serving pies to the most beautiful girls in bikinis. We lived in a motel that cost next to nothing. It wasn't important to have a great place to stay, because we didn't plan to be at the motel very often anyway. One of the girls at work told me that she and a friend needed two male escorts for the night and asked if I had a friend to bring along. I was happy to oblige.

My buddy had a Datsun 260z 2+2, a collector's item car; but this night we would be the guests, so we took the girls' car. Honestly, I had never been on a date with a black girl before and had no idea what to expect. They were both very attractive and friendly and right off the bat, we had a lot of laughs.

The girls drove us a couple of miles from the beach to a small bar where their friends wanted to meet them for drinks and dancing. When we arrived at the bar, we parked down the street at the nearest opening on the side of the road. We all got out and walked to the bar, only to be met at the front door by several angry black men. The girls had failed to tell us that the bar was the local hang out for a gang that they were associated with. Black men of all sizes and shapes were flooding out of this little building like a clown car at a circus. Right away, they went after my buddy, Bill. He was overwhelmed very quickly and was struggling to get away. His shirt was torn from his body in a flash. I was working on talking some sense into the guys approaching me. I told the one who was both closest and seemed to be in charge, "Hold on there big guy. I was invited out by these girls as a friend. We aren't taking your women or invading your turf."

"You sure chose a bad place to take her on a first date," he said as he cocked back to swing.

"Man, I don't wanna hurt you and your boys. Me and my friend are just in the wrong place with the wrong chicks." I told him, keeping my composure better than I should have. He laughed at my hurting him and his boys.

"You gonna take all of us?"

"I don't want to take any of you. I just wanted to dance with a pretty girl." Backing across the street. Just then I heard Bill yell.

"Back off! Back off or I'll shoot." The girl he was with had a .38-caliber revolver in her purse and had gotten it to him.

"Don't make me kill you!" He yelled as he got on one knee instead of heading to the car. Just as he had them backed off enough to get a breath, the cylinder that holds the bullets in the gun, fell to the side. Opening for all the world to see that the gun was broken. The crew, seeing that he was unable to shoot, even if he had the will, immediately reacted. Bill vanished into violence.

"Oh shit. Back away...toward your car." I guess he liked what I had to say as the largest guy in the whole group told me how to live through this night. I walked back, he slung verbal threats toward me as if he were going to kill me. All the while, the other group attacking Bill had closed him off from view with a mountain of bodies.

"Grab your friend." He almost whispered to me as I nearly backed passed Bill. This man who was going to take a swing at me moments ago was getting me out of the trouble that I had no Idea how I got into. I reached over and actually picked Bill up by the skin on his back and yanked him out of the pile of humanity that was on top of him. The girls were holding the car doors open a few feet away. I threw bill into the car and jumped in behind him expecting a speedy get away. But a speedy anything did not happen. The girls were hurriedly in the car, just to roll the windows down and talk with a couple of the guys for a few minutes. They made excuses for bringing us to the hangout and for not calling one of the guys and for.

After that ordeal, the ride back to the pizza joint was awash with "what the" talk. We were dropped at the pizza parlor and went over the whole scene together. Neither of us had any way of knowing what had happened to the other during the confrontation, but let it be known that Bill was none too happy to find out that I neither had to throw a punch nor receive one. I was happy about that, so his anger over it really didn't affect me very much.

As the sun came up, we left his car at the pizza joint where it would be safe for a while. I had the next day off. (Bill had not gotten a job, he isn't a real reliable person when it comes to employment or anything else for that matter.) I wanted to go down to the beach and watch the sun come up. As we walked down the beach and he nursed his ego, we found a couple of flotation devices on the back deck of a hotel—little air mattresses. I wanted to go out and float away the troubles of the night before so we walked out into the water and each took up a position of rest on the mattress we had. I laid in the burgeoning sun and felt its warmth just starting to come over me. Then it was dark. I had slept for a while. I don't know how long. Bill was not near me. The shore was not near me. "Hold on, are there sharks in this water?" As I woke a little more, I was on my belly still. I couldn't hear the gentle slosh of the small waves of the gulf on the shore. I looked past my feet for the beach. Nothing. Just water and sky and clouds. I lifted my gaze to look over my head. In the distance I could barely make out the pier. The land was very far away. I was floating out to sea. "Well now, this isn't good," I told myself. "Perhaps if I close my eyes again and open them...No, that won't work."

"Ok, time to start paddling."

The trouble with cheap air mattresses is that they have a pronounced seam. It digs into your arm pit as you travel from the gulf stream back to the safety of the shore. I was paddling for over two hours, from what one eye witness told me. I was not trying to fight the current as much as trying to go at an angle. I have always been kind of intelligent and so I knew that to make a fuss or let your fear get the better of you, will draw sharks to your location. Besides, I wasn't scared. I don't know why. Maybe it's because I was so happy to be in the ocean among the sun-and-sand-drenched beaches and the bikini clad women. I will never know exactly, I guess. Fear just never set in. I just rowed my arms gently along just enough strength to feel the floaty move through the water. I knew it was to be a long trip and a lot of strokes; I'm just glad I was in great shape.

After an exhaustive two-plus hour, I got to shore. I was a few miles from where we had started. Bill had gone back at one point to get his car and had driven to the site where I first woke up. He had been on the beach trying to get my attention until he lost sight of me and figured he would go out on the pier. He said he and about thirty other people were waving and yelling and watching as I drifted out to sea, completely unaware of my predicament.

(Nobody called for help? I could be living in Cuba today if I hadn't woken up and nobody called the coast guard or the police. I traveled out of the site of several eye witnesses and out into the sharky waters of the Gulf of Mexico, in route to the Atlantic Ocean and nobody called for help. Granted, nobody had cell phones, but Bill drove for a few miles between the start of my nap and the finish and he never stopped at a pay phone. (Just sayin.) We returned to our motel room that night and I rested out of the sun, which had given me a good working over in the salty air. I relaxed on the old, rusty chairs out in front of our room. I just took in what had happened to me and how karma had worked her magic for me stealing the floaty mattress.

The next morning I took a walk out to the pond behind the motel. A man was walking his poodle on a leash. The little dog was so excited and bouncy that it made me glad to be still around after the happenings of the last couple of days. As he walked the little dog around the edge of the water, the little dog stopped for a drink and "Wham!" A large alligator came out from under the surface and ate the little dog in one bite. One mouthful and he was gone. The gator raised his head toward the sky, opened, and closed his jaws enough to drop the puppy dog straight into his stomach; the leash still attached as the little dog's master just froze in horror. He didn't yell or run or drop the leash or pull on it, he just stood there with his mouth open as the leash got shorter between him and the alligator. I ran over, freeing my Buck knife from its case, grasping the blade, and flicking my wrist to extend it; then flipping it into the air to catch the handle, putting the Buck into a useful position while at an all-out sprint. I stepped onto the snout of the animal using the footing to push the man away. As I did, the gator's mouth slammed shut, and I cut the leash before the man became a main course for the reptile. We both stood staring as the alligator returned to the depths. It is about the only time you might say an alligator looks silly is when he has a pink leash sticking out of his mouth. I kept that thought to myself. I was sure that the man with the other end still in his grasp would not appreciate the humor. All that was left of the encounter were bubbles. I picked him up off of the ground and put my arm around the guy and patted his back before leaving him there in shock. I thought to myself, *If Bill had floated out to sea, I would have swam out and gotten him or called for help or stolen a jet ski or something.*

I could see that my time in Florida was coming to an end. Something was trying to tell me to get out while I still could. I never have gotten to live in Florida again, although I have visited Miami once while waiting for and returning from a cruise. I, one day, plan to live in the ocean breezes again. Be it Florida or not. I just have to wait for fate to invite me back.

HOUSTON, WE HAVE
A PROBLEM

Bill had been in a shelter in Atlanta with his new wife and stepson when I found him the second time. I was delivering pizza in a car that I had bought in California. I saved up change in thirty-two-ounce cups from work and everything I bought came from that money. Bill's wife was an ex-bodybuilder and her son, Topher they called him, was about three years old.

Bill was sitting in the shelter doing his usual nothing when I came across them. I had been looking for him and happened to find one of the few people in Atlanta who would admit to knowing him. I convinced him to go job hunting and gave him a ride to an apartment complex for an interview as grounds keeper and maintenance man. He had a few skills that he could use for the position and it came with an apartment.

Bill's wife knew he had a restless…um…heart. She was well aware, when I showed up, that he was soon to leave. She tried all the best moves to keep him around. She went through me figuring that if I wanted to stay, so would he. She set me up with one of her friends—cute, young, dirty-blonde, and Jewish.

I don't know that Jewish makes any difference, but it turned me on. I thought that she was a doll. The only thing that kept me shy was that she was very wild. I didn't know how to take her. So, when she spent the night and I slept on the couch, I had no idea

I was supposed to do anything. The following day when I was asked why I didn't, I made the fatal error of saying "she's not my type." (What was I thinking?) She was so my type.

The next friend was a bit chubby but nice, same church as the other, but not near the body, fun or body. I passed due to bad timing on her. And so Bill's want to travel included me.

We caught a train out of Atlanta; but before we did, I gave his wife my car, snake, and all of my stuff that might help her and Topher. Then I gave Bill a piece of my mind about what a piece of work he was. I was displeased with him as a human being. Too bad it took so long to see how much of an ass he really was. We jumped the first open boxcar we could as the westbound train started to move. Bill's escape from responsibility and my continuing journey to find a home, was finally on its way. Then the train stopped. I don't think it traveled fifty yards after we got on. We sat there all afternoon with the expectation that at any moment our transportation would continue on its journey. Hours passed and no movement.

Finally, around five in the evening the train started to move. First, the sound of the impact, the engine, or unit, colliding to hook. We were out to meet our destiny, but I could barely contain my urge to throw Bill off of the train. As far as I was concerned, he had just committed the ultimate sin. Bill had walked out of the door on a woman that he had promised to love, honor, and cherish. He had done even worse by betraying the trust of a little boy who had grown to call him daddy, a boy who loved him as if he were made from his own flesh. Topher idolized the man, I was now riding a train to nowhere with.

We planned to be headed towards the West. Not toward a destination but rather away from life and the confines of responsibility. I pictured my life as this for the rest of my time on earth. I had come to grips with the fact that I would always be alone. I knew I could only take so much of being around my old friend. He was a self-centered, egotistical man with no worthwhile saving grace to account for his existence. His story, which commonly comes into questions about validity, was that he had been forced to go into the army when a judge found him with his underage daughter. Oddly, the first time I saw him after the I returned home from the military, he was shacked up with her in a nice apartment. The difference between you and me having a nice apartment, and Bill having one, is that he moved into it with her and then caused her to lose her job. He then sold her furnishings and cost her the money for her power. So when I found them there the first time, I came into a situation where I first had to fix her car (he had spent the money for parts on beer and weed), then I got him a job (we worked until the death of the owner). He then refused to get out of bed to drive us to the next job; I got us with another framer. And finally, I had to console her that he was leaving, because that is what he does.

She was a wonderful, beautiful girl—red, long hair. She was petite with firm breast and a cute round little but that made her jeans the envy of most guys in town. She was a head turner for sure. Her big blue eyes, which could cause a wreck on the highway the way they shown against her light, freckled complexion, and that red hair framing her face, should have trapped him but all he saw was the ability to make her cry and long for his return. He had strung her along for so long, returned long enough to ruin her life again, and then left her to try and reclaim the lost pieces. Her father had found out about his return and disowned her for seeing Bill again. The judge had thought that he would send away a boy and have him return a man but what came back was worse than what had left. A games man and a letch. Of course, Bill always had the best of women. He is the guy we good guys have to come in after. Every girl seems to have been with a guy like him, and with his number of conquest in just the time I knew him, they could have all been with him.

I fell asleep as the train wound around in an endless run. The vibration of the tracks helped to ease my sorrow and allowed me to sleep in my bag like a baby in the womb. Sounds of a train are loud and steady, a rhythm of clacks, chings, and rumble. Odd as it may seem, the sound soothes the soul as if we were meant to be riders for life. As one gets used to the noise, it becomes home. You find that you can make out the sounds of birds over it without trying.

We had copied a map of the rail system in America from a book in the library. It was old but relevant. The map showed us how to get from place to place, and which tracks go out of which yard and in what direction they traveled. What it could not show was the direction of track that a particular train might switch tracks and follow.

When I woke up, the sun was about to rise. The foliage around us was swampy and green, many of the same kinds of trees and bushes that we had been watching the day before. I saw a signal for the train posted along the track that announced our soon arrival in Waycross, Georgia. Waycross? Wait, Waycross is south of Atlanta. "Bill get up!" I yelled over the train noise. "The train turned in the middle of the night. We're in Waycross!" Bill woke faster than I had ever seen him wake before.

"What the hell?"

"We can't go into that yard." He went on to explain that in the world of trains, it was legendary that the end of all things took place in Waycross, at least for tramps it did. Bulls were plenty and they hated the tramps as if it were in their DNA. The stories of guys getting beaten half to death and then taken to jail, kept most wiser men from attempting an entry. What Bill hadn't said was how darn big that yard was.

We grabbed our packs, looked out the door to make sure that we weren't approaching any signs, bridges, rails or what have you. We were forced to jump before the train even slowed. Somewhere in the morning dusk, I missed seeing the sign. I stepped out the door of the train for my first time ever leaving a boxcar in motion. I no sooner relaxed my knees, put my arms across my chest holding my backpack straps, and went airborne when I came to an abrupt stop. The sound of aluminum impacted my eardrums in concert with my body crashing into a sign that stood silent vigil warning of pedestrian traffic ahead. The posts, cemented in the ground, gave great resistance to being uprooted. I won the battle, however. As the sign gave to a lean, the angle catapulted me many feet into the air. I contemplated releasing the straps that I, as of the instant, had a death grip on but wiser heads prevailed. At that speed and flight pattern, my inner child grabbed a parachute and bailed out of my ear. This ride was one I would have to take alone. Much like a slider in baseball, my spin was slight. My knees stayed slightly bent, legs together, feet and heals together as well. *I hope I don't shit myself.* I thought as I contemplated the idea that I might not survive impact. Bill found it quite amusing somehow as he flipped and tumbled through soft grass and wound up in a bush, never having missed a moment of my disaster.

When a disaster takes place in my life, clarity rules and wisdom always seems to prevail. It matters not whether I am facing a gunman or flying through the window of a truck. If water is rising and the flames of hell are licking your left butt cheek, I am the one you want to be with. Even without experience in a circumstance, I can always come through. I have walked through hell to go see friends and tamed the demons for personal pets, all because I kept my head. This may have been early on in my hell-walking days, but I chose to keep my sanity in presence of chaos.

Resisting the urge to scream like a schoolgirl with a frog down her new dress, I clenched my teeth. It was then that I realized that my inner child had landed safely on the ground. In order to hallucinate this, I had to be upside down. Uh, oh! I had rotated into an earth watching orbit and was now forced to watch the ground come rushing to me.

The rail was coming to a road crossing is why a sign was located where it was. From our vantage on the train, we were unable to see it. The road was below the level of the tracks and our view was probably blocked by a big sign that read, "Pedestrian Crossing!" The gravel widened out along the roadside. This meant that my smooth Cape Canaveral landing should have been redirected to anywhere but Waycross, Georgia. Where our landing was supposed to take us was down a fauna covered embankment. The rail is built up on a steep incline of dirt and rocks. (Need I mention sharp rocks?) We were supposed to land as if parachuting from a plane. Instead, I had gained altitude, distance, and momentum. I was coming upon where the lower ground had been built up to the road. Sort of like the corner of your room when you are a kid but made of dirt. Impact always speeds things back up to real time. Just beneath the rise, about two feet or so, I hit with an amazing amount of force. So much that I bounced me up in the air, and I spun like a corkscrew, about five feet in the air. I leveled out onto my back as I hit the ground. A twelve-inch-diameter stone as a pillow, I lay mere feet from a blue car waiting for the train to cross. The driver looked down as I released my left hand from the death grip on the strap that I had been wishing for a time was a parachute. I waved and smiled. He slowly shook his head and looked forward again. I guess he sees flying hobos all the time.

RAINBOW GATHERING 1989

I had found an old friend and was close to the point of realization that he would never be anything but a no good moocher. As we traveled around the country, keeping our home base in Colorado Springs, we would work for a couple of days and then move on with a few dollars in our pockets. We traded food stamps for cash or worked for a couple of days and somehow a couple of dollars could last a week. We jumped trains using the map we copied from the library to places unknown. Sure, sometimes there was some sort of destination in mind, but it really didn't matter. The whole point was to get away. Away from what? I didn't know. Responsibility is always worth escaping from. I didn't have any to escape from, though. Bill would have a warrant in Georgia now. He had jumped bail that I had posted for him right before we left Atlanta, $1200 I had earned by delivering pizza in Atlanta. I saved all of my change each night in milk carton shaped soda cups. Thirty-two-ounce cups hold a lot of change. I had to go to the bank and have the change sorted to become bills before I got Bill out. The teller was not happy. She was downright huffy.

Somewhere along the way, Bill and I heard tale of a gathering of the tribes. Okay, Indians still get together for powwows. No, the gathering they spoke of was a bunch of hippies from the sixties and the people who wish they were hippies from the sixties getting together with homeless, transient (us), free spirits, and the occasional person that wants to hang out with 35,000 screaming naked hippies in the woods. My own term:

1. They rarely scream. More commonly they chant or om, sometimes sing but always need love.

2. Not all of them are naked. A whole bunch of them are, thank Gawd, but not all.

3. The gathering is not always located in the woods. It changes every year. The national forestry keeps record of where they are to be and all you have to do is ask or look it up.

We heard that to eat there was free. You get to camp without interruption, swim in the river or whatever water source is available, see people who are in the same place in life as yourself (some permanently) and get lost for a prolonged period and it took place in July but you could come whenever you wanted in June to help set up as well as staying through August to help clean up and replant any damaged areas. We were in.

We found out that the location was in Nevada on a map. No freaking way! How does a hobo get to that location? All of the signs seemed to steer us toward a desert region that wasn't real hospitable. We had to leave the trains and hitchhike our butts into the camping area. At the time that we discovered where it was going to be held, we were in Colorado Springs, Colorado.

June 5 was the day we decided to leave. (I have no idea what importance that plays in my memory or why I remembered the date.) We both had money coming to us that would come in the end of the month. We figured that we could figure that out then. The temptation to go was just too strong. We left town and started hiking. Bill had carried a can of boot oil around with us for several months. In a rainstorm in some unknown location along the way, we stopped to set up camp. I attempted to get a broken pallet to burn from under a pile of leaves and trash, when I was attacked by a burning sensation throughout my entire arm. A mound of fire ants had engulfed the lower half of the pallet. In the melee to get them off of my arm, Bill had somehow ruptured the can, leaving it unable to be sealed. We scavenged as much as we could for our boots and tossed the rest of the can. In doing so (using so much on our boots), I inadvertently caused the leather that mine were made from, to be unable to breath. In a homeless situation, oftentimes one does not have the opportunity to take off one's shoes for days on end. In our journey to the gathering, my feet became very ill. Yes, sick feet.

Once we arrived, we saw desert for miles around. The wind was terrible and there were no tents or water sources to be seen. The people we traveled in with were as worried as we were. Just as we parked and had started discussing leaving, a man came to the window and said, "Welcome home brothers and sisters."

I turned and looked around the dilapidated cutlass supreme and said in a voice that showed far too much enthusiasm, "Okay, I have got to see this. Who's game?"

Everybody climbed hesitantly out of the car. Bill and I grabbed our gear and walked with the "Brother" to the edge of the established trail. "Are we camping here?" I pleaded for a "no" answer.

I waited for the answer as he turned to me, looked at me, and said, "Yes, we've got a couple of spaces available over there." He pointed away from where we were standing. "If you get set up quickly, the drum circle will be starting in about an hour." My hesitation to believe must have been evident. Our new "Brother" couldn't hold back his smile. He laughed and started a veiled attempt to stifle a giggle.

"Walk forward to the end of the parking lot," through his now outright laugh. "I think that you'll be happy with you accommodations."

I looked back at my fellow travelers, turned, and started to walk. All we could see from where we stood was a whole lot of flat land and a few scattered sage brush plants.

As we walked forward, we passed buses of all years and colors. They had curtains and carpets in front of their doorsteps. Many had dream catchers hanging in the windows or beads. There was a bicycle collector that had so many bikes that the bus was nearly hidden. I met a psychic lady in front of her bus that had her professional name emblazoned on the side in four-foot letters of deep purples and crimson. She was the first topless person I saw. She was well older than my mother and was a vast disappointment. I hoped for better quality down the road. Our walk went passed the home of the alcoholic. He had an RV with a tent connected to the side and a roped off drinking section. He informed us as we passed that his was the only place in the entire gathering where a person might find a drink. Alcohol was not allowed anywhere else. We continued. As we walked toward the end of the lot, the trail started downward. "Five miles to go." Came a voice from a sister in a rainbow dress. "Welcome home!" she shouted to us as we waved and smiled.

The walk was long and took us past several camps: bead makers, that's right, makers, vegans, drum makers, dressmakers, first aid station, and many camps that we weren't sure about. As we walked through the deepening valley we rounded a bend. At this point, the valley walls separated into a river valley of green grass and a shallow, fast-moving river. We stopped for a moment as we looked forward at a wall of shale that had a mysterious natural discoloration that resembled Jerry Garcia from the Grateful Dead. (I thought that it looked like Sasquatch, but I guess that's up to interpretation.) The best portion of the grassiest area was occupied by the "Mushroom Tea Kitchen." We chose to visit briefly and were informed that the tea would start brewing around dark on the twentieth. Their supply being limited, private parties were to be had through that time with friends from the preparation party. Since we were there to help build, we were in that friend group.

We considered staying, however the direct shot from the valley entrance led me to believe that the wind could come down that stretch pretty quickly, so we moved on. Unable to cross into private lands, per agreement with the owner through the gathering coordinators, we walked further up river until we found the camp that spoke our language, "Taco Mike's!"

Taco Mike's kitchen was located almost at the end of the road, so to speak. He had intentionally kept it far from the other kitchens due to his kitchen's proclivity towards meat. No other kitchen served meat. We were the carnivores of the group. The kitchen was located back in the tree line with a backdrop of steep shale cliffs that worked as an exceptional wind barrier. It was built of lodge pole pine that the kitchen had taken from location to location, year to year. Each side fitted to the other with notched poles and twine. The inner area was for "cooks and staff only" Somehow, we became "staff" by virtue of being there so early on and helping to build the area and gather firewood each day. This became very important later. We were privy to where the food stuffs were kept, a well-guarded secret for many reasons. One, people do not always tend to be honest, no matter where they find themselves nor how nice they are. The second reason is that most of the people were vegetarians. If they could, they would steal, ceremonially bless and bury our sustenance for the harm we were doing to Mother Earth. We had the advantage, however. We were capable of violence if necessary, even if it wasn't allowed at the gathering; also, we were all the most physically intimidating of anybody in the valley. For intimidation, a big hairy hobo trumps a whiskerless vegan, any day.

When we got our tent set up, I had to take my boots off. My feet had been in them for several days without being removed. The burning was unbearable as we rolled out our bags within the tent, so I removed them to find my feet unrecognizable.

The skin peeling and blistered my toes produced a green color that disgusted me. I feared a hospital visit in my future until I was approached by Taco Mike's wife (I am so sorry that I can't remember your name). She sweetly told me of a warm spring that was on the other side of the river and said that we had passed it just a short distance past where we had entered.

The springs had an odor of minerals and sulfur. The water bubbled up from deep within the earth where nature warmed it to a very pleasant temperature, and then delivered it to us just feet from the cool waters of the river. Someone had taken the time to make a hot-tub-shaped rock surrounding for the waters to pool into, and then a smartly positioned exit area for the waters to continue their journey to the river. Seating was accomplished using stones gathered out of the river. The stones natural wear form centuries in the river bed had turned them smooth to the touch and amazingly well-cupped for ones bottom. I was told by others on the way that the healing powers were amazing. It made me wonder what kind of healing each of these people needed for them to be such an authority on how well the springs would heal my feet.

I could hardly walk without limping. The only problem is how does one limp on both feet? I approached the warm springs with common sense. Many times in life, doctors ask us if we are allergic to sulfur drugs. I surmised that the sulfur from the earth, directly combined with other minerals and stewed together in a warm liquid for a long time, should have medicinal values. I soaked my feet, as well as the rest of me, in the warm waters for a long period of time, even longer because a group of pretty girls with no clothes on came to soak with me.

They were young and tan. I thought that they could possibly be sisters. With flowers in their hair, one wore braids and seemed to be the center of the group. One had long, dark brown almost to her bottom, and the third had her lighter brown hair playfully squared off in the middle of her back. Her hair glittered infused with blonde strands. In any surrounding other than this, they would stand out with their clothes on. I was thinking as they walked up…Well I can't tell you that, but I also thought how easily they could appear in a Vidal Sassoon commercial together. I was nineteen and they couldn't be older than seventeen to eighteen. It never came up in conversation. If there are molds for teen bodies somewhere, these three came out of the "holy cow" mold, all thin and shapely with medium breast, tan and sunned without tan lines. I was sure somehow that I was dreaming. This just doesn't happen to a guy like me. I would never have even thought of approaching girls of this caliber in high school.

I thought that they were there just to soak, and I was not about to let the three of them see my icky feet. Just as I thought my pruning had completed, and that I had to get out before I became the next meal for Taco Mike's kitchen, our conversation took a turn to the better. One of the girls told me that she was the daughter of one of the older ladies who told me about the springs healing abilities. She had grabbed her two beautiful, naked friends to come cheer me up and see if they could do anything to help. She asked to see my feet and I told them, honestly, "I was trying not to let you see them. I think I'm completely boiled now." I came out from the water and sat on the rocks surrounding the pool. She took my one foot in her hands and another of the girls took my other foot in hers. "Woe!" I exclaimed as I started to fall backwards off of the edge of the pool. The first two attempted to pull down on my feet which each had accidentally lifted at the same time. One lost grip and then the other, sending my feet right up in the air. The third girl came forward and grabbed my hand. I outweighed her by several pounds. She came forward as I fell back. She came out of the water as if climbing stairs as I fell off the edge, landing on top of me. Her body on mine as if we had planned this to happen, she gave me a peck on the lips and said with a giggle, "Thank-you for the moment." She then backed off of me and took my hands, helping me back to the edge where the other two were so tickled about what they had caused that they could hardly contain themselves. Once we all gained our composures, we talked and laughed while they held my feet firmly sandwiched in their hands. They were focusing their energy towards fixing my damaged feet. The third stayed sitting with me with her hand on my back to help in case I should fall again. She too was focusing her energy on me. I was just trying to deny my natural urge to get excited. Soon, I forgot about those worries and just enjoyed the company of the beautiful ladies who cared enough to take care of me. When I asked why they didn't just tell me in the first place, why they had come to the pool, the girls said, "We had to see if you were deserving."

My feet healed miraculously. I walked barefoot for weeks and forgot about my boots all together. A nice sister gave me a pair of slippers to use if I needed, most of the time I remained barefooted, however. The loose skin was missing in a couple of days. The color started to return soon after. I made a trip to "Babylon" (the name they call everywhere that is not in the gathering) in the end of June. While I was in Colorado Springs, I saw a doctor who told me that if she had seen my feet a few days earlier, she might have had to remove my toes and part of one foot, but the reaction she was getting from touch, led her to believe they would recover, which they did in short time.

When I returned from Colorado, I brought back money, tobacco, and candy bars for trading. Bill and I hid the candy in our tent and resolved to trade it for what we may need in the future. The gathering was a few weeks off. People were starting to want for chocolate; but by the time the trading got underway in the full population, and everyone realized that they had forgotten their "wifey be good bars," we would be able to make out like bandits. It had to be a planned and coordinated attack on the sweet tooth to work out correctly, which is to say, to our devastating advantage.

I had traveled to Colorado alone. I was in the throes of rainbow idiocy when I walked out after a discussion that left me wondering about Bill's commitment to me as a friend. I essentially lost the coin toss by default. Bill just refused to go and that leaves only me, with my recovering feet, to go all the way to Colorado to get money and food stamps that would be waiting for us. I left without my pack or extra clothes or even a sleeping bag. I was angry, that helped me to leave so unprepared, but the biggest reason and the reason Bill should have had my back, sucked it up and gone, was that my feet couldn't bear the weight yet because in addition to being injured, I was *barefoot*!

People on top had spoken of freezing nights and dustings of snow when we came for supplies. I wished I had thought about that while I was in route today. The first night I was dropped at a road where little traffic traveled. Little traffic traveled through here anyway because we were on Shoshone tribal land that was mostly leased for preservation, to ranchers for grazing. A small building was off of the side of the road about a hundred yards. I walked up to it as the sun went down and the temperatures dropped. I found a newspaper in the trash and a plastic bag that I pulled up over my legs as far as I could. The snow and wind were such a sharp contrast to the nights we were spending just a couple of miles away. I guess Sasquatch was watching over his valley.

The next morning, I got up with a goodly amount of frost and frozen water on me. I was shaking and cold and cursing myself. I don't remember how I got out of there. I do remember a ride I got down the road a way. I was still cold at that time, if memory serves. The man took me home to dinner with his wife and family. His son and daughter were excited by my stories of travel and adventure. They had endless questions about how a man survives without a home, something they would never have to worry about.

Before I left, the father asked me to stay. He offered for me to come live with them. His son had never been able to speak to strangers but with me he hadn't even hesitated. A total stranger from out of nowhere without a pair of shoes and too dumb to bring what little he had in life, and I was the one he felt a bond with. "He has autism," his dad had told me. "I will let you live with us and all you have to do is be his friend. I'll give you an allotment each week and get you whatever you need to feel comfortable. Please, he really likes you. It's never happened before." I was in a bind, with no reason to turn down the offer. I would have been the "Beverly hills down and out" before the movie came out, but I had my goals.

After I got to Colorado, I had to go to Texas for money as well. We had made a route long before we discovered our "rainbow" dream. I just never thought that I would be doing the foot work for both of us.

I arrived back in Colorado Springs at the right time. My slippers were destroyed, and I had only worn them while on the sharp rocks of the railroad. I entered our home base shelter, checked in, and looked down. In a bin of shoes, there was one pair to fit me, a pair of lightly used, all-leather moccasins that matched my hat perfectly. (I was still wearing my hat.) It only seemed fitting that I should wear what the rainbow gawds had given me.

I wore those moccasins for a long period after the month that I was at the gathering after I returned.

Bill and I had become part of the supply claiming crew. We would hike to the "top" and claim our share of the supply run and carry it back to camp. The time I was there, I never missed a supply run. I was dedicated toward earning our share. Bill was too, I suppose. But we were spending more and more time apart.

I came back to the tent one afternoon to find a wrapper sticking out from under the sleeping bag. I opened our secret stash area to find it empty of chocolate and full of empty wrappers. There were two of the mini bars from the "we can eat" stash that we were supposed to share. Bill walked up as soon as I discovered the missing trading goods with a girl he had been spending the day with. "What the hell, Bill? Where are the candy bars?" I was very angry, to say the least. I had walked, frozen and gone way, way out of my way to get those. "What?" He laughed with his words in a way that usually got me to forgive him for his selfishness. "She needed one." "Get your stuff out of the tent," I told him in a calm voice that Bill had seen me use only when speaking softly to someone as I sent them to the hospital. Bill's face dropped. His girl for the moment started to tease me about how it was just chocolate, when Bill told her, "If you care about our safety, just stand there and look pretty while I get my stuff."

Bill walked off knowing that his life was nearly ended. I know it was just chocolate, but for me it was a journey of thousands of miles without shoes or even the minor comforts that I could normally carry on my back. Any other person would have gone to the hospital and lost their feet, but I was not normal or ordinary. I persevered where others would fail, or worse yet, not be willing to try. Bill and I would never have a relationship again. He had forced my hand. I must have grown out of him at that moment. From that point on, I saw a stranger in him whenever we crossed paths, which is silly because I was used to him being in strangers, women that is.

Supplies were purchased with money donated by the attendees of the gathering. Some had stamps and others would go along and put things on credit cards. Things that we could get for free, like day-old cabbage or lettuce or tomatoes, we would get from the dumpster if we could. Sympathetic stores would save it for us, and they even sorted out the bad stuff. Some fruits were included as well. I remember a load of fresh bananas coming in one day, a truck load, all donated and fresh. Another way they made the needs of the many work so well was that the buying power of that many, even if not a lot, allowed flower, coffee, and sugar to be ordered by the pallet. That saved a lot of money. The people who had nothing to give were usually willing to help out in whatever ways their skills allowed them to. Very few did nothing, but since money donations were anonymous, no one would know or care if you sat around doing nothing.

I made jokes often in my days of hippie heaven. One was for a hat. I said, "All of the hobos have hats, I want a hat." No sooner did I start telling people that I wanted a hat from the rainbow fairies, then I found a leather hat with a full brim that dipped down to protect the eyes—red/brown leather and made forever. I loved that thing.

I frequented the hot springs daily. I saw the girls frequently. They were warm to me as I got to know each better. Two of them sang and played guitar regularly at places that I would visit. I always received hugs and kisses from them to the admiration of all the other men. A few times, I found myself spending entire evenings in there company; I remained a friend to them and nothing further came of it.(That's right, left in the friend zone.) A rumor flew that I was with all of them. The girls turned out to be the ones who started it. I am a pretty big guy and it helped to keep the guys at bay.

Taco Mike got arrested before the start of the actual gathering. His wife stayed in town to arrange his defense with the lawyers from the gathering. The charge was "resin on hemostats." The Nevada State Patrol arrested him for dirt, basically. So we had to take over the kitchen. As all of the other camps were planning to divvy up his stuff and our supplies, and our own campers were leaving to other camps, I was one the first to come forward. I said to the small group that actually did the cooking, "We are not giving up this kitchen. I am not going to spend the next month without meat. We did half of the cooking when Mike was here, we will now do all of the cooking. No problem."

The camp ran very smoothly. I made breakfast and helped with lunch, and we shared the dinner duties. It's never hard to pick a volunteer out of the crowd of hungry people to go for water. We had to keep all of the trippin hippies fed, there was no other choice. Besides, my mother taught me a great lesson. She cooked very well while I was growing up, but the best part of helping Mom in the kitchen was all of the taste testing. I would carry the burden of passing my mother's secret on to the next generation, me.

My life among the hippies was a study in culture. I grew up with a man who was practical but not closed minded. He loved a naked body and had a great and dirty sense of humor. My mother was a "bunny" at Playboy's "Bunny Club" night club in the sixties or early seventies and two of her sisters were go-go dancers in the cages like you see on movies. Both were very open about, well, everything to me. But the hippie culture is one that must be experienced. I have always been a fiscal conservative. Keep your hands out of my pockets and everyone for themselves seems to make a lot of sense to me. On the other hand, for people choosing to live this way and enjoy life this way, it is just one more way Americans can feel freer than any other place on earth. Besides, if you come up with a system in which you can live off of the land, feed yourself off of what you scavenge, so to speak, and everybody is happy with no casualties, not only does that sound like freedom but also like a very efficient kind of capitalism. Think about the generation of Davy Crockett. Now think about what I said…Yep, pretty close only, without the long muzzle loader.

I learned a new art while I was there that I still play with. Early in the morning, if you listened clearly, you could hear the hum and chain of my nun-chucks. I worked them whenever I had the extra energy from a long night out or from having partaken of the spirits offered by the others. I have always been fast. In the army I would work them for the guys and put on a show. Sometimes, I would invite some big-talking-new guy who hadn't seen me work them before to work them as fast as he could and I would snatch them out of his hand. Here, however, I had to work them on the other side of the river. I didn't want anybody being bothered that I was a master of an implement of doom, or anything. As I worked them, I would invent new moves or things to do. I have developed different styles over the years, each completely different than the other.

One day, I had an audience. A couple of guys on the other side were watching me intently as I danced and kicked and flipped with my chucks. I did a few staff moves and incorporated the two together in a strange "kung foo theater" presentation of "Jazzy does the Rainbow."

Later, a man with a red beard and a funny hat came to me and asked if we could talk. His name was Mark. I recognized him from my audience and was happy to hear what he had to say. "I have something for you to try." He pulled from his bag, a couple of strings with wadded rags tied to the end. I watched as he took these things and proceeded to do what was very similar to a fire dance from the islands with it. "If you want, I will teach you to do these to add to your skills." I was interested. I wanted to do what he had shown me. Also, there was a promise of a surprise later if I did well. So I practiced. He would guide me through a move, and I would do it over and over until it was great. Then, he would give me another piece. Not long and I was doing amazing things with them.

After a few days, Mark came to me with a new toy. This is where I came up with his nickname "the toy maker." He handed me a bag. It was black velvet and had a drawstring. In it was a set similar to the ones I had been working, only real. The new set was a nylon string with a fishing swivel attached. This was put through a foam ball like one might find on a paddle ball set. Attached to the end of the swivel, wrapped in rubber bands, I found two rolled up streamers. They were eight foot streamers in red, white, and blue. "Here, practice these for the fourth," he said handing them to me. "I have another surprise for then too, but let's wait." "Practice patience. You move so fast and that is good and that is amazing, but you can't do that with eight feet of tail. Learn to dance like you do with you weapons."

I practiced and practiced, a few hours a day for the last couple of days of June. I got so that I could dance and I could walk and move. I could do whatever I wanted to. When Mark came by after being gone a couple of days from our camp area, he was impressed. I showed him my moves, and I showed him my dance. Then, I showed him my speed.

I stepped into the clearing and dawned the bag. Showtime! It started out with me holding the entire set in my hands, hidden from view. I flipped my right wrist and out came a ball on a string; and like a whip, the streamer unfurled for the small crowd that had started to gather. "Ahhh," they said as if I were onstage. I took a slow start with one lonely dragon flying the world to find its mate. Every voice got quiet as I told my story in a tone that was loud enough to be heard, provided you were quiet enough to listen. I went around the circular clearing searching and flying. "But a dragon's love affair is tricky. A dragon only mates with the strongest, most beautiful mate the world has to offer." With that I flicked my left wrist and out came the second of the set, the same way as the first. Each time I let loose a ball, I insured that the end would "snap" only inches from Mark's ear. (Snapping rip-stock nylon is no easy task. I had to work on it.) Which worked out great because near him was a girl who let out a shrill scream each time I did it. I went on, "A dragon is staunchly protective of its territory. The problem is, a dragon's territory is the entire earth. Haven't you ever wondered why so few dragons exist?" All of this said while having a battle rage with the two "dragons." I leaped through the crowd and worked the toys over people's heads. Everyone was very excited. "As the battle raged, the beasts nearly engulfed the planet in flames," with this, I started to gain speed. The sound from the toys used at normal speed, sounds like a flag in the wind. When you add the excitement of a watchful crowd to a muscle-bound weapons master, the sound becomes that of a twin propeller plane. High-pitched snaps crackled through the air. Eyes got wide as I bared down and went into a concentrated state. From the center, it felt as if I were part of the string and the ball and the streamer. Soon what sounded like a pair of Harley Davidsons on a drag strip, tamed back down and "the dragons had exhausted there anger." The dragons got together in the end, "For the good of the species," I explained to the eager audience. Mark was pleased. "I knew I had the guy for the job," he said.

On the morning of the fourth, he gave me a set of glow sticks set up on strong string. He had thought this out well, before he came. I worked stories all day and glow sticks all night. I was a hit with my show. (He called the things "Scoobies.")

I worked the kitchen and collected the wood and got the groceries. I was pretty happy in my role. I made the coffee all night, most nights. When the pot was done brewing I would holler out "Mud's up!" in a voice that boomed across the camp. Once, we had a complaint that someone was trying to sleep, but he was quickly suppressed and made fun of for being too close and too early to be in bed.

I was serving dinner, asking random people if they had brought the garbage disposal to make my job easier, and watching the crowd one night, when I looked up to see a pair of breast that I didn't recognize. I glanced casually through the corner of my eye, as I had gotten good at doing, when a pair of beautiful eyes stole my glance. I could not help myself. I was lost. There stood a five foot nothing, brown-haired beauty. She had long, dark hair, six- pack abs, and my heart. "Hey gurly, what's your name?" I asked trying not to give myself away. She was standing with two others in a long line for food. "Lori." She was shy and more clothed than the other two she was with. We talked a minute and she came up again after she ate to talk some more. "I will be done here in about forty-five minutes. Do you want to walk around and see the sites with me?" I asked with my heart pounding and expecting her to sweetly decline. In a tone near to a whisper, "Sure."

Honestly, I don't remember much more than that we were inseparable after that. I can't say as that we parted for more than a few minutes at a time for the next seven, wonderful days. She would leave for a while to check her camp while I did my duties, but most of the time she sat and waited. For hours, she would sit. I had things for her to do as well, but my memory fades as to exactly what we did because in my memory, it was me. I felt so at ease with her and so in heaven that everything we did felt as one. I looked at her and felt so at home, a feeling I have never felt since.

Lori and I spent those days in wonder. But time has a way of stealing our dreams. Mine left on July 8, 1989. We spent the morning together. Both trying not to give away the way we really felt, I was glad it was her that shed the tears, because if she hadn't I would have. She left me there and had to accompany her friends back to Santa Cruz, California. Before she went, she wrote her phone number and address on a small slip of paper. She signed it with a heart and we kissed our goodbye a dozen times. "You poor guy, you never did get your garbage disposal." She consoled as she laughed and cried at the same time.

I wanted to walk her out, but she insisted that to do so would be too hard for her. We held on as long as we could. Then she was gone. People had seen us together so much that they often asked after her and if I would be going to see her.

The days after were a mixed sense of loss and excitement for me. I wanted to go see her, but my days were full and my services needed for the clean-up effort. I wandered around in a daze. I did what had to be done, had some fun in the process, but my soul was in Santa Cruz.

Leaving the "Gathering of the Tribes" was sad. Every day was well-ordered and my duties were of my own choosing. I had found rainbow magic in so many ways. As with life however, all change comes. I had to leave. I couldn't live there in that spot forever. Soon, no one would be left. In the waning days, I was one of about fifteen left. It was time.

Walking out, everyone said their goodbyes and exclaimed "Come home next year." I was most shocked when I arrived at the top and saw a couple of guys who I barely remembered. They were on an expedition for food in Babylon when they came across a gift for me. Both were grinning like a couple of Cheshire cats when they lured me back to their truck, and there sat a garbage disposal. They even had a battery they had planned to haul all the way to my camp. Boy, were they disappointed that I was leaving. I guess they weren't ready for it to be over either.

I got a ride to a small town with a railroad. I caught a slow mover leaving a driver change stop and headed west towards my parents. I sat in the door rolling a smoke and dreaming that I was headed to there instead of away when a sudden gust of wind took my hat. Rainbow magic stays with the rainbow, I figure.

A few rules and fun facts for a gathering:

Welcome home means just that.

1. Babylon is anywhere not within the boundaries of the gathering.

2. Nudity is a great way to let down your defenses but it can get cold.

3. No one says you have to take off your clothes and an equal amount of people choose not to.

4. Vegans and vegetarians often would sneak and eat at our camp. They are not always honest to the people they work so hard to impress.

5. Any substance offered in the borders of the gathering are free or bartered; no money allowed, except to give for food and supplies.

6. Take chocolate, save it for the second half of your stay when everybody else is dying for some, and barter to your heart's content. (They are human, after all.)

7. Never, ever, ever throw cigarette butts, cellophane, or plastic into a fire. They have a sixth sense for that and get very nasty.

8. No Styrofoam should ever be brought into the gathering unless that's the only thing you like to talk about. Ever! They hate it. Remember that the hippies lost the sixties when you come home. Not everyone can live like that. It is just a dream and as such, must be enjoyed and then left.

INVISIBLE SANTA CRUZ MONSTER

After the Rainbow Gathering of 1989, I went home for a visit to my parents in Bend, Oregon. My mother was happy to see me but had made plans to go to San Francisco a week or two after I arrived. She gave me a small, battery-powered word processor to write my memoirs. I wrote on it, but it wasn't a memoir as much as a collection of stories. I originally called it "Please don't read this." I would describe it as "sixty-seven page to page and half stories dealing with anything from why I hate cats to ten things to do while falling off a building." The stories were funny and thought provoking. I would tell people, "I think people reading it will come away thinking more and saying things like 'Hmm. That's all I ask.'"

I caught a ride with my mother down to San Francisco. I then stuck my thumb in the air and caught a ride to Santa Cruz. My goal there was to find the girl whom I had lost my heart to at the Rainbow Gathering. I had spent the best seven days of my life in the company of an angel, and I wanted to see if my angel would still have wings in the coal fires of hell that was everyday life. (Okay, my outlook wasn't that grim but it sounded great as I wrote it just now.) The light of day, so to speak, could shed light on a person that you never knew. It could be good or it could be bad. There was only one way to find out, and I was on a quest. I knew that this girl could settle me into a wonderful place without trying very hard.

I had her address when I left the gathering but had lost it along the way. I did, however, remember the name of the street that she lived on. I was going to go up the street and hope to be seen by her; and if that didn't work, I would walk the street and knock on every door until she or someone she knew answered.

The day that I got into town, I went straight to the mall. The mall was (and I do mean was) a nice place to sit and walk and visit with other street people like myself. I could spend long hours writing or not. I could go to the coffee shop and smoke with a nice cup of coffee or buy a muffin and share it with someone else who had nothing as long as I didn't get caught sharing because feeding the poor in Santa Cruz is against the law. Many days I would just go down to the beach and see the people and families enjoying their days as I had done as a child. Most nights there were shows at the elevated, cement stage on the beach. Late at night one could go under the stage with other people and joke or play music or just sit.

Every evening, food could be had from the Buddhist temple just off of the strip. The peace and tranquility of the temple was warming to my soul. No matter who you were prior to entering the gates, you were a Buddhist once you entered. Every night was a soup or curry something or other. Bread was always available and was almost a main course in its self. I learned chants and to meditate while I watched others come and go just for a bite to eat. The monks were kind, no matter why you were there and they, more than anyone, knew that every life is a story to be lived. No two people are the same and even the monastery residents themselves were once something completely different from who they were now. I learned a great reverence for them and the lives they chose to lead. I can only wish to one day find the inner peace to be as loving an individual as they were as a whole to people they didn't even know.

The second night that I was in town, I had to find a place to rest. I had stayed awake with excitement the first night, but that was not going to be possible the second. I was exhausted. I hiked out of town with two other people, a boy and girl. We were all teens with backpacks, but I was the only traveler. These two lived on the streets out of refusal to go home and follow the rules. I needed a separate camp site from them. They were a couple, and I felt that what they really wanted was to be together for a little one on one. As we turned off of the road onto the rocky shores of the river, they walked a bit ahead, showing me where they intended to stay and pointing out that up the river a little was a small clearing that others had used for parties in the past and that I would be welcome to use it. I thanked them and wandered up the water's edge until I found where I was going.

The trail cut from the edge, no more than twenty yards into the tree and berry bush line. Then the trail ended as a sharp right turn forced you into a cleared area. The area was about twelve feet across in all directions, almost a perfect circle. In the center was an old couch that I wondered out loud to myself, "Who the hell carried that thing all the way down here?"

I set up camp which took all of ten seconds. I untied, rolled out and unzipped my sleeping bag, pulled my pistol to the top of my pack for easy access and was out cold before the light had fallen into the ocean.

In the full moon light, something tussled the bushes loud enough to wake me from exhausted slumber. I could hear it from the other side of the couch but far off in the distance. It took me a few seconds to get my bearings enough to remember that if the river was to my back then the woods to my front had no trail. The couch gave me perfect cover to peer off into the distance. The cloudless night with a full moon bright, (sorry, had to rhyme that) let me see clearly. The bushes were moving off in the distance of about thirty to fifty yards, a long distance. The disruption got worse as if something were escaping a trap. It reminded me of a fish's final attempt to escape the hook as it gets pulled from the water. *A raccoon?* I thought. "No, too much commotion." "A bear? Possible. They are common here." Just as I thought that I had figured out what it could be, it started moving through the bushes in my direction. First, slowly enough that I wasn't sure I was seeing what I thought I was seeing, then fast, damn fast! I reached back and grabbed for the .44 magnum pistol in the top of my pack. My eyes averted for an instant, it closed the gap in the time it took me to grab my readily available pistol. I took quick aim, cocking the hammer on the fly and prepared to fire. Whatever it was, it tore bushes up and spread them wide. *Berry bushes!* Thorns and thickets and all. It came toward me with no sound that didn't belong to the screaming of torn branches and vines, but it was loud, none the less. My aim sure, I knew where and when it would emerge from the bushes. I would have a split second more time as it had to get me through or over this couch. Not a lot of protection, but at this point I would take any split second that I could get. As it came to the edge, I felt it leap from the bushes, but I saw nothing. It was a clear sky and the moon was full and directly or nearly, above my head. It leaped directly over me and hit the bushes on the other side. I kept my aim perfectly in sync with where it should have been the entire time, even if the entire time was the blink of an eye, and I still saw nothing. No shadow. No form. Nothing. But I felt it clear me like Evel Knievel over...wait, he never really cleared anything. He would have landed on me, but you get the picture. It hit the bushes on the other side and tore through them to the water's edge. Once there, I didn't hear a thing. No rustling of rocks on the shore. No splash, for sure; nothing at all. I stayed awake for several minutes before deciding that the thing was not coming back. I didn't even realize that the hammer was still cocked on my pistol until I went to set it down on my chest. I slept with it on my chest for the rest of the night. The next morning, I woke with the sun as it shown through the trees. It would be a warm day, I could tell by the early heat and the steam off of the bushes. I jumped out of bed with the thought. The bushes held the answer. Whatever happened last night would be told in the morning light.

I walked the trail left by the invisible beast. The berry bushes were torn off as if by a car racing through. The broken and spread branches were evident that for at least this incident, I wasn't as crazy as I had given myself credit for. The trail led back for at least fifty yards. At the beginning of the charge, there was plenty of evidence of some ruckus that seemed to come from nowhere at all. The undergrowth was dense and undisturbed. It was as if it came from the ground or fell from the sky at this point, caught a tortured fight, and darted toward the water. After examining it for myself, I walked out to the bank of the river and found that as the beastly thing went to the edge of the bushes, the trail ran cold. Not a rock lay turned, but the bushes looked as if blasted out of the tree line; the same as I had found in the clearing. Whatever had done this had left the couch opposite my side, with a smattering of thorny vines. That thing was moving.

The young couple was still in their camp when I came to them. I had them return to my camp after explaining my story to them with all of the detail that I could come up with. They both seemed to be bright, and I really wanted their opinion on what it could be and if they had ever heard or seen anything like it before. So, we returned to my site and sure enough they had never seen a thing like it. Both confirmed with me that all of the broken limbs had fresh, wet wounds. The trail showed no sign of foot prints and the spot of origin showed no sign of entry from any other direction. The couch did have branches from the vines and the limbs on trees were broken as well.

I no longer remember the street, but there were three of them in Santa Cruz County. I chose the closest first. I did as I had planned and walked up the street. No one came running out of their house with arms swung wide for that long awaited hug. No one noticed me in the least. So, I walked door to door and asked each person if they knew of the girl I longed to be reunited with. This first street was only a block long. The fact that I did not find her was more expected than not. Plus, I think it was the wrong ending, as in it was a street not an avenue or some such thing; but I was determined to do my best to hit every street with that name. Since I didn't have the small slip of paper that she had written her address on, I couldn't be too careful or I might miss her for lack of memory.

The next day, I went to the next street on my list. This one a bit longer but still not the street that I needed. I followed the same routine that had gotten me nowhere the day before. I got the same result. I went back to the mall for the day and enjoyed the peace and the smell of the ocean breeze on the wind. The Platters were playing on the beach that night. I was never a big fan, but hey, it's a free show. I watched and dreamed that I would see Lori on that beach. I imagined that we would see one another and find true happiness; so that all of my travels may be over, and we would have our lives here in the sun of California on my favorite beach from childhood. I strolled along checking the crowd, certain to see her any time now, but I did not.

I sat under the pier after the show. I had one more road with the same name. This one was six miles long, and I would need bus fare to get there. I wasn't sure if I would find her but I had to give it one last shot. I sat under the pier singing, "Under the board walk... Down by the s—e—a On a blanket with my sweet baby, is where I'll be."

The morning came, and I was off to find true love. I packed up all of my stuff into my pack, hoisted it onto my back, and went into town. The mall was nice, and I got into a conversation with a couple that had just come in from out of town and wanted to know why I was homeless. They bought me breakfast, and we walked and talked our way down to the beach. They bought me lunch; and we walked as I told them stories of my travels, and we discovered that we had met at the gathering briefly. When they heard my story, they both thought that they remembered seeing her with me. The thought of a romantic reunification teased there curiosity and they gave me bus fare. Wishing me well and for love to last the ages, we parted ways. I caught the bus up to where I was headed at about three-thirty in the afternoon.

The driver of the bus was a romantic as well, I guess. I told him my story on the trip out of town to the intersection where the road began. As I exited the bus, the driver told me, "It's clear you're broke, be back here when I come by at 6:30, and I'll give you a ride back on my last turn." Thanking him, I left the bus and looked down the daunting task. I could see that the houses on this stretch were farther apart and the driveways longer than the suburban houses that I had been trying. This was closer to a country road than the others. We were approximately four miles from town. I didn't have time for the "walk by" that I had done with the first couple of streets. I just started knocking on doors. I walked from door to door and several of the homes had no answer. I considered missing the bus just to go back to the homes where the people could be at work or whatever. In making my plan for the six-mile walk, I kept a piece of paper and a pen out to write the addresses down that weren't home. I looked along the road as I walked from door to door for a place to spend the night. I had water and canned food with me that I could easily last a night or two.

Ultimately, I decided to catch the bus. The Buddhist temple had showers, and the road I was on was dusty and the sun was hot. I felt that it would be best if I just went back into town and got cleaned up, and I would come back out tomorrow and try the missed houses again at a later time. I knew the bus would run out this way until 6:30 pm. The driver had said that his last run came by here at 6:30, and that he would give me a free ride back to town; so I figured that I would come out clean at 6:30 tomorrow night and stay in the tree line if I didn't find her and catch the bus the next morning. That way I would be clean when I found her, if I found her.

I got back to the intersection with about ten minutes to spare. I sat down in the dusty center where the roads merge. It is where the bus dropped me off and was not marked by a bus stop. As I got comfortable, the sound of an accelerating car coming up the road caught my attention. I could hear the telltale sound of exhaust that only one type of car makes. There is a distinct sound when a car accelerates. Some cars are beefed up and have an engine sound that roars. Other cars have kits that make them sound good. This car was so specific because the car was fast from the factory. What we call "chipped" these days is only one of the many lucky features that you can get when the actual factory gets involved. They call it the "police interceptor." Only law enforcement can have a four-door sedan that can catch a Porsche, Corvette, Jaguar, (don't fool yourself, 12 cylinders, that's all we need to say) and some even have had to catch Ferraris and Lamborghinis. The *Police Interceptor* is one of the finest shows of American automobile superiority ever. Only the best suspensions and transmissions have been allowed in a police car. Even their electrical systems are superior. All cars should be built like this in America. We should send cars like that to the auto shows around the world and refuse to sell them abroad. I watched as the sound came around the corner, followed by the sight that confirmed what I had already deduced. "I wonder where he's going in such a hurry," I said to myself. Just as he came around the corner, he applied the brakes hard. As the car slowed near me, the officer locked up the breaks and slid to a stop in front of me. The officer was out of the car, gun drawn but not aimed at me, almost before the car stopped. He yelled. "Let me see your hands," as he kept the barrel of his gun pointed toward the ground in standard police training fashion. His face was serious and his eyes were covered by dark, pilot sunglasses. I cleared my hands from their previous position on my lap and held them up, kind of nonchalant. "Stay where you are or I'll have to shoot," he instructed me in what he must have thought was an intimidating voice.

My mother was in law enforcement my whole life. I was trained my whole life to be friendly with law enforcement especially if they have a gun out of the holster and are saying that they might feel the need to shoot you. Since this guy obviously felt the need to tell me, point blank that he may need to shoot me, nice was on the top of my list as to how to treat him. Honestly, what else would I do?

The officer told me to roll onto my stomach on the ground and put my hands above my head, separated on the ground. I did. He then put a knee in my back as he took my hands behind my back and cuffed me. A quick pat down and he sat me back up. The officer asked for identification. I gave my identification to him, or at least directed him to it. He asked me my name. I told him my name. He asked my social security number. I told it to him. He then says, "I don't think that this is you. Please stand up." He helped me to my feet and walked me to the car. He then asked me, "If you are who you say, why do you have this identification for Mr. Brown?"

I had completely forgotten I had my friend's identification in my stuff. I carried it with me when I had gone to Colorado Springs for some money and food stamps that were there waiting for us while we were at the gathering. A disagreement had caused me to separate our partnership before I got a chance to give it back. I was supposed to give it back, of course. I had never gotten the proper opportunity to return it to him. I explained this to the officer to no avail. My only consolation was that I had hidden my gun before all of this. I had suspected that I could be stopped and questioned and it would not look good for a person under twenty-one to be carrying a pistol, hidden in his backpack, in California especially a .44 Magnum!

I was taken to the police department and placed into a small holding cell. They chained me to the bench in a room that was eight by eight with a window for the officers to keep an eye on this dangerous criminal. After a short time, the officers took off the hand cuffs. I was allowed the freedom to wander my cell and see all of the fine things available in an eight by eight space—a toilet, sink and hard bench. After the enormous time it took me to investigate my new surroundings, I sat uncomfortably on the hard bench. I reached for the knife scabbard on my side, strapped to my belt. My Buck knife usually took up the space, but I had put my harmonica into it for some reason. (I don't remember why exactly. I have been trying to remember but it escapes me.) I played low and sad. Like hell! I played a fun and exciting tune. Then a blues tune. The officers passing by heard the harmonica and laughed. Everybody just let me go on and sing my little songs for about thirty minutes. Then the shift commander instructed them to take away my instrument. I was bummed, then booked and put into general population. I was given a cell in the middle of the room and an orange jumpsuit. Orange is usually for felons. No crime I could think of that they could charge me with would be a felony. There were cells for the long term guys but overpopulation of the jails had caused them to put bunk beds in the middle of the cell. I think there were about eight sets of beds for a total of sixteen extra beds. The front of the cell was probably about fifty feet across? The entire jail cell area was in a triangle shape (sort of) with the front being the widest part. Believe it or not, the entire front of the cell was glass!

They weren't going to throw away the key on me, of this I was sure. How? Because every half an hour I was removed from the cell and questioned. "Did you break into this house?"

"No." Returned to the cell.

Removed from the cell. "Where'd you get the typewriter?"

"My mother." They actually called her. Returned, removed.

"Where were you on this day?"

"Why are you in this county?"

"How did you get here?"

"Where is the girl if you came to find her?" For that I had an answer.

"You know guys, you could help me with that." Returned and so on.

For three days they did this. I couldn't figure out why they didn't just ask all of the questions at once. They tried to pin every crime in the county on me. Finally, I asked them, "Haven't you guys ever solved a single crime? Who are all the guys in the cell with me, renters?"

During my stay in the county jail, I made a great friend. He was in for killing a couple of people. I can't say what he said about whether he did it or not, but he is probably still in prison. We chatted all day. As long as I was in the cell, between my question and answer periods, we played cards and joked around. I kept a couple of jerks from beating him to death with a chair because he wouldn't give up his breakfast one morning. These guys were pretty hard core until they were nursing a few bruised and nearly broken bones. (I didn't want to draw attention to myself with the guards by breaking these guys to bad. It might disrupt their search through the cold case files trying to find other things that I didn't do.)

That first night, everybody was sleeping. Some snored, some cried, some just slept. The sound is usually the first thing that everybody reports. The rumble sounds like a train rolling through the room. I would say that I am an expert on the sound of trains. I can confirm, a train sounds very similar to the sound of a strong quake. "Earthquake!" came the screams of terror. "Shut up and go back to sleep," I yelled. "You morons live in California, how can you be afraid of earthquakes?"

"I don't want to die in jail!" guys were screaming.

The pre-tremors were strong and each one felt like a full scale quake. They came each night as we lay down to sleep. We were awakened by them so often that I finally slept through the last few.

On day three, I was taken out of the cell with several other men for our arraignment. I had handcuffs, leg shackles, and a chain around my waist that went down between my legs and connected in the back like a sumo wrestler's G-string. Both the handcuffs and the shackles were connected by a chain to the G-string. Then, just in case I decided to fight the guards and fight my way out of a well-guarded hallway, through a well occupied jailhouse, and out the front door, I was chained to everybody else in the group by a long chain. My friend, the murderer was handcuffed, period. They walked us to the courtroom and unchained us, one by one. I was led to my seat by two guards, one on each arm. Everybody else walked single file to their seats without escort to include the murderer! We were all instructed to stay standing, me with my guards, until our names were called. The judge entered. The audience sat. The bailiff called each name in alphabetical order until I was the only person standing. My guards had left me there alone while all of the names were being read. "Sir, why are you still standing?" The judge asked me with discontent, as if it hadn't ever happened that the names were finished and someone would still be standing. "My name has not been called, your honor." I said with glee in my voice knowing fully well that this was a time for lighthearted humor. "Give the bailiff your name, son." The judge signaled the bailiff to come to me and get my information.

After all of the men in my group had been arraigned, with the exception of the murderer who was being arraigned, the bailiff returned to the courtroom with a look of astonishment on his face. He handed a form to the judge and the judge stopped the proceedings by holding up his hand to the lawyers. He leaned in close to the bailiff and spoke angrily but in a whisper. A short back and forth between them and the bailiff returned to his position beside the door. The judge reread the form in his hands and a lawyer made the mistake of saying, "Your honor..." with a quick show of authority, the judge held his hand, palm out as if to signal a car to stop, firmly toward the attorney.

"Mr. Johnson, will you please stand?" he ordered. His words sounded, well, respectful. With the sounds of chains preceding my movements, I stood. "I will." I quipped.

"Sir, are you the one here for looking suspicious?" there was humor in his voice. "Damn straight, your honor," I said with a pride that would belie my circumstance. "Well," he thought for a moment, "how do you plea?"

"Guilty as hell, your honor!" thinking that the worst that could happen was a laugh from the courtroom, I figured that someone walking door to door with an eighty-pound backpack, dirty clothes, and a disappointed appearance would look a bit suspicious. The courtroom did indeed laugh at my answer, as did the judge. After all, when you hear people that you know are guilty plead their innocence all day long, and you have to hear the inhuman ways people treat one another, and the criminal cases he does and the boring drawl of lawyer after lawyer (which is nothing like you see on TV), to have a guy stand before you in chains and shackles just because someone determined that he might do something wrong even know he was guilty of nothing more than knocking on the wrong door (several doors actually), then to plead guilty for a crime that isn't really a crime at all, with manner of pride and dignity, who wouldn't laugh?

"Okay, well sir, in Santa Cruz county, looking suspicious is a crime, a misdemeanor. I sentence you to time served. 'Clack'," he wrapped the gavel hard on the desk. "By the way son, who was your arresting officer?" I pointed from my waist, as I was still chained. "That man over there, your honor." I pointed to the prosecution area where the officer who had arrested me sat with his face in his hands. He looked up at the judge and lightly waved. He had also arrested my friend the murderer who stood beside me now with just his handcuffs on. My friend was able to lift his hands above his waste as he pointed and smiled a big toothy grin at the officer who was responsible for both of us being in the same courtroom, side by side.

"Oh, you don't say? Officer enter name here, our officer of the month." The judge's voice dripped with sarcastic sweetness as he tortured the officer a little more. "Maybe you should take a bow, son," he said now focused in my direction. "Just seat yourself there and I'm sure you will able to leave soon enough, but with all that iron. It's a little distracting to have your multiple escorts take you out right now." He had seen the silly display of force when I was brought in.

When fate speaks, I listen. I had been unable to find my girl. I got locked away for three days for nothing. The quakes were pretty strong. I felt that it was time to leave. In case no one has noticed, when fate speaks, I listen. So when I spent the night under the bridge in San Francisco that night and woke up, I was headed home. I didn't have a plan. My plan had been to live in Santa Cruz. I was going to try and live with the girl of my dreams in the place of my most favorite memories. I stuck my thumb in the air because that's what I did. It was just habit and nature. The fact that the first car to pick me up that day was a police car was fate's irony. He drove me at one hundred miles per hour over the double-decker bridge to the other side of the water. A couple of miles later, he dropped me off and even gave me a couple of dollars for a cup of coffee and a snack.

My aunt was at the *World Series* when the big one hit San Francisco. They stopped the game. The first site I got of the disaster was on the television in Mt. Shasta where a ride had let me off at a small restaurant. I went in for coffee and the lady asked me if I had heard the news as she signaled toward the TV. First, I saw the exact place that I had slept under bridge. It was on the ground with people trapped between the layers in their cars. Next, it flashed to Santa Cruz, where the epicenter was. The mall and the temple were destroyed completely. Stores I had been in hours before, gone. The jail had sunk eight feet in the ground, and the officers and prisoners alike, were all prisoners together. I sat mesmerized, pleading silently to the universe that my girl was alright.

BAR FIGHT:
THREE NIGHTS OF HELL

I was hitchhiking through the Southern United States near the border of Mexico in 1989. It was over a hundred degrees outside. The sun beat down and scorched the earth, so you can imagine what it was doing to me. I stopped in a little bar, on a dirty street, in a part of town that looked like a ghost town. The only way that I knew the place was open, was because there were several cars outside. I was out of water. The only reason I walked through the door of that bar was to get a drink of cold water. Even if my water jug had been full, the water would have been hot to the point of nearly undrinkable.

As I walked through the door, I became nearly blind in the darkness. I removed my pack and carried it by the frame as I attempted to find my way through the room. There were several men drinking and carousing in booths along the wall on the left side of the room while several more were turned that direction on chairs taken from the tables in the center. The bar was on the right and a few scattered tables in the center. A bartender sat on a stool at the near end of the bar. He signaled me to put my gear near him in the corner, where the bar ends. As I propped it up against the wall, I attempted to order icewater. Instead, I opened my mouth and the equivalent of dust came out. No sound other than breath through a nearly closed air passage.

I would love to say I sauntered up to the bar like John Wayne, I didn't manage this, however, so I dragged my overheated, sorry soul up to the bar. I tried again to ask for water. At this time, the bartender got up off of his stool, scooped up some ice in a glass, and filled it with water. He set it down in front of me and turned. He then reached for a pitcher, which he filled and placed in front of me. I downed the water, fighting the ice but thankful for it. I then filled it again and again. Just as I finished the third glass, the bartender said, "Your gonna make yourself sick. Slow it down and hydrate slowly." Just then, I got that tingling in my throat that told me I may be sick.

As the feeling was passing, I realized that from the moment I entered, a growing number of the guys behind me were making remarks and taunting me. Now, one of them was behind me. "You didn't hear me say to get out?" I could smell the beer he had been drinking. "You got a hearing problem?" I could feel him in my space and his breath on my neck. His line of questioning was familiar to that of a drill sergeant. My mind raced delusional back to basic training.

"I'm just here for water." I managed to get out.

"F——— water!" he made it abundantly clear that he didn't like water.

The spittle on my neck led me to believe that he may be still in the water closet. I assume that he had to hide his habit from his friends at the booth.

"I apologize, sir. I wasn't aware that water was so hated here. Bartender, get me a shot of what this guy has been drinking, drunken bum spit!" I quipped with a wink at the bartender who was waving his hand back and forth with his palm out and mouthing the words "don't" over and over. With that, the drunk punched me in back of the head.

My life has been lived under the shadow of hatred. I have put up with crap from people my whole life, from my brother to the kids at school. I came through it with the strength to ignore comments from all angles. Tough guys are only tough in their own eyes, as far as I'm concerned, because I fear no man. I have fought enough to know my own abilities, and they are great. My inner child has a black belt in humility, a master's in humanity, a doctorate in psychology, the patience of Mother Teresa, and the temper of a red-headed prostitute on crack. I only have certain lines that should not be crossed. First, never touch my friends or, Gawd forbid, my family. Second, never gang up on a single person. Everybody should stand a chance to defend themselves. And third/fourth combined in this instance, never touch me with malice, especially from behind.

Grabbing the lip of the bar with my right hand, I spun to the left on the swivel bar stool. With the back of my left fist, I impacted the side of his head with the force of a sledge hammer. As the impact waved throughout his body, his feet left the ground toward the direction of the blast. His head had no choice but to lead my fist as my follow through brought me full circle back to facing the bar.

His flight in a semi-circle ended with his right side of his head impacting as his feet nearly achieved full vertical. My follow through ended with my right hand picking up my glass as it re-arrived at the bar.

The bar erupted behind me as the entire room rose to their feet in shock. I turned my head to look behind me and saw a frozen group, better than half were uniformed police officers that I had been unable to see when I entered the dark bar from the bright sunlight. As they fought to be the first to get their hands on me as if racing for a doughnut, the bartender looked at my "oh no" expression and said, "I am real sorry, Mack."

I swallowed my mouthful of water and turned to take the heat. My mother was a sheriff's deputy and a city cop as well, in my early years, so I knew how unnaturally protective these guys were about their own. In my estimation, the least I would expect was jail time. An upgrade from that would be a beat down, next and most likely both. Or, well, there is an awful lot of desert out here. Whatever the case, I knew that to fight back against this many pissed off deputies was a pointless way to get in even deeper, so as the sticks came out and the gloves went on, like they all thought that they might leave fingerprints on me or something, I would have to take it like a scared school girl… er…I mean man.

First the beating was unorganized and chaotic until one of the guys, tired from hitting me, started to lead the show. As they came on with so many people swinging, I had ducked the first blows and went low to avoid facial reconstruction. My arms held in a boxing guard but tightly to my chest, I let them hit my arms instead of my ribs, kidneys, and stomach. For the first moments, I thought, *This ain't so bad.* I then feigned a fall and went down where I suspected that one or two might kick me in the ribs a few times and even a shot to the face for good measure. Not a problem. I have ribs of steal and if I turn my face in the right instant, the blow to my head instead would hurt far less. After they get their fill of violence, they may stop and leave me there or throw me out, either way I will survive with little or no damage. Not so lucky. This guy had already taken his name tag off. He had a brain and wanted to prove it to his friends at my expense. While he started to organize the troops for a long-term stay for me in a "discrete location, another guy gave me a shot to the jewels. Two guys were trying to wake their buddy whom I had laid out in the first place, yet another went to bring his patrol car around. The remaining jerks leaned against the bar, huffing, and puffing with exhaustion from the fine work they did on me. Each would take a shot kicking at my ribs and then return to the bar.

I wasn't any worse for wear at this point but I stayed down and cursed in my head at the guy who kicked me in the crotch. I wanted to laugh because of all of this manpower, not one could muster a good beating. I wasn't about to say that though. While I lay there, just pretending to be hurt, somebody let this no name idiot convince them to cuff me, to pick me up, put me into the trunk of the police cruiser, in hundred plus degree weather, and drive me to the "old jail."

I didn't know where the old jail was but I was pretty certain that I did not want to go there. As I lay in the trunk, I was looking for a latch or something to let myself out. I didn't find one. I wasn't in there long enough to look real hard, as we arrived at the old jail very quickly. They drove me into sally port, where prisoners are removed from the car and brought into the building. One of the guys unlocked the trunk and reached in to get me when he noticed that my face didn't look very beaten up. He then took out a pair of handcuffs, put his hand through them like brass knuckles and hit me square between the eyes. It didn't break my nose, but a gush of blood did come down and the skin split, giving him the result he seemed to long for.

They hauled me into the nearly deserted building. The power was on though it looked like just barely. Many of the deputies were there from the bar, and it was quickly decided to put me in the solitary cell. One of them looked for the keys while another turned the power on to the control panel. Things were not looking well for this young traveler.

My cell was in a wing of the jail with no windows. I passed many cells with bars on the way to where they intended to keep me. If I was ever in a worse situation, I couldn't think of it. Once we got to where they wanted me, I was stripped naked and hosed down. The guys enjoyed having me at their mercy to joke and punch. Several of the guys started trying to step on my toes, as if it were a big game. I avoided them as much as I could without letting on how not badly beaten I was. No name kept his hand on his gun. He acted as if he expected me to do a first-blood move and start killing everyone and running away. I suppose I could have done something, but I was a little scared and 19 years old.

The first night, they threw me in the cell after a round of "Have you ever heard of a rubber hose?" They beat me with a hose like you would find in your yard. I'm not sure, I lost count after fifty, but I estimate that all together the three guys using the hose hit me one hundred times. I didn't make a sound and that made them angry. So I was placed in the cell and chained to a ring in the floor with a standard pair of handcuffs, which severely restricted my movement. I couldn't stand or stretch. I had one hand free and the other stuck in place. The one who found the hose on the floor above us to use in my new game, found a serving tray in the kitchen. He pissed in it and slid it through the slot, "Drink up," he sounded over jubilant. "It's all you get tonight."

I still felt resistant to any serious injury. My toes were sore and my back, arms, legs, and torso bruised, but other than the blood on my face, which they kept reopening, I was doing alright. I sat naked on the cement floor in the dark and heard them shut down the power. The humming of the electrical circuits stopped as did the air vent. The lock was mechanical so I wasn't lucky enough for a release from a magnetic lock. I sat there taking in what had happened and wondering what I had done in a past life that karma would choose this for me. I got the chance to think about my surroundings and what I had seen coming in. The building was very old. The paint was peeling from the walls and every metal surface had thick layers of lead-based paint with several layers showing in places. I swear I saw dirt floors in some of the cell areas. It could have been a mistake. I was pretty dehydrated so I could be wrong. It did appear that way.

In the dark, alone I fell asleep. I woke to the sound of the lock clunking open. I saw the beams of three flashlights that burned through my eyes and ruined the night vision, and three guys in plain clothes came rushing in. I attempted to jump to my feet out of habit but the wrist restraint kept me from rising more than to my knees. One had a miniature bat that one usually uses to end the life of fish or thump truck tires with. He repeatedly hit me in the head in rapid succession.

"Hurt one of our own, will you." One voice sounded very angry. I didn't recognize it from the bar.

"F—— him up," said another as he stepped on my toes with his boot heal.

"What's with the toes? You guys got a foot fetish or what?" the first words I had spoken since the bartender.

I was sure they were the wrong words when the little bat bounced off of my chin in an attempt to knock out my teeth, I think. Someone attempted to kick me in the groin, but his aim was off in the dark, lucky for me. Then two of them held me while the other kept hitting me with that darned little bat. The thing must have been made of oak, because it hurt. I received a few punches in the gut from each guy in succession before they left me in the dark once more. I outweighed each of them and, although I didn't fight back, I was able to overpower them enough to cover up some of the attempts to injure me.

When they were done, I was strongly considering that this could be the end. Any time one of them could enter the cell and put a bullet through my head. I had seen all of their faces and new that they were all cops. But they were enjoying this too much to end it that quickly. I couldn't tell the difference between night and day. No windows and no meal times meant no way to even set my mental clock. I was so near sun stroke when I entered the bar that I didn't ever find out what time it was. I had walked for so long in the hot sun and summer days were so long that I had no baseline from which to guess. The cell was hot and the cement walls kept the heat so well that I wasn't even able to venture a guess from that. The guys were sure not to mention anything to comfort me while they were there.

The visits were frequent and time slipped by. I slowly got more cuts on my face and more bruises until I looked as if I had fallen off of a ten story building. In between each, I would sleep or pass out depending on the mood and quality of pummeling I had taken. I was never sure which to do, so I let my inner child flip a coin. Each man seemed to have a favorite spot or area to injure. One had a serious thing with hitting me in the ankles with his night stick. I was pleasantly surprised each time that he was not with the group. My hair was caked with blood, and I had stopped sweating. I wasn't sure if the dizziness was from severe dehydration or the endless blows to my head. I became familiar with the little baseball bat. He wasn't my most frequent visitor, but he did do the most damage to my head. The rubber hose found its way back a few times as well.

I hadn't eaten in over a day when all of this went down. At times I would think of how hungry I was. Shortly, it came to mind that it was a good thing that I was starving. If they wanted me to stay alive for longer, I would rob them of the opportunity to beat me one day when they came in and found me dead. More importantly to me was that I didn't have to go to the bathroom. The toilet was in the cell, yet had no water in it. Even if it had been functional, I had no way to reach it. My hand was cuffed to the floor. I did have a plan if it came to that, however. I would reach it by lying across the floor and reaching my arm to its full length. I would be able to get there feet first, if only just. But that wasn't ever necessary.

At the time, I didn't know what day or time it was when two men came to the cell. I was almost unable to lift my head by this time. "Hold still," the voice behind the light said. He reached for my handcuffed wrist. A click and zip later and I was free from the floor. He collected the other cuff, and the two of them helped me try and walk from the cage. I stunk so bad that I offended myself. My eyes were swollen nearly shut. My ankles were bruised and swollen and pain shot through me each time I took a step. The world was in a perpetual spin that would have caused me to vomit if there was anything to send out. I was ready to pass out before I could walk the distance to be put out of my misery.

We stopped at the shower room where the hose was hooked up. As I was sprayed down, I snuck gulps of water and pretended to enjoy the high pressure shower even though every drop felt as little fists on my beaten flesh, washing my pits, and pretending to wash with an invisible bar of soap. I started to scrub my hair when I caught my nails in a gash on the top of my head. The ripping feeling was excruciating and started the bleeding again. "Sorry guys, but I may bleed to death before you get to shoot me." I gurgled through the water as I washed my butt. I hadn't made an audible noise since the gaff about the foot fetish.

"We're not going to have to kill you if you cooperate." I think it was the one holding the hose who spoke.

"You good?" The other asked. I thought that a rhetorical question because he couldn't be serious. I could almost make out shapes. The flashlights were bright but not directed at me with full intensity. My energy was increasing, and I figured that I could last a bit longer if I had to now. I must have drunk two quarts of water mixed with my own blood, sweat and stink. I had been looking for a chance to escape and now might be the time. There were only two of them, and I was sure that I could overpower them. By my estimation, I had been here almost two days. Surely, I could muster the power to escape two guys who were preoccupied with killing me. They would be trying to keep their minds on the task at hand. Where to bury my remains, where to shoot me, in the back of the head or the front? Who got to have the honors? the fingerprint issue? whether to use a blue tarp or green? Wait, I was getting caught up in the details that they were to get caught up in to distract them long enough for me to escape.

The water stopped and the blood wasn't flowing from my head as bad as I had expected. My heart was starting to beat a little lighter now that I was formulating a plan. The water helped immensely. One handed me my pants. The other held my shirt. I dressed and pondered the burning question of escape. I was grabbed by the arm and sat on a bench once my clothes were on. My socks and boots were there on the bench, as dirty as when I had last seen them. "Remind me to get a new dry cleaner," I said as I made what I hoped looked like a disgusted face at the three-day-worn-smelly socks.

They led me through the area where we had come in. I remembered windows but the place was dark. I knew it had to be night time. *Great*, I thought. "It's only been a few hours and I thought that it had been two days." I chastised myself for my weakness. "Next time I get kidnapped and beaten I must show more strength and resolve." "And more humor. Those guys seriously need to hear more funny jokes in their lives." Then it occurred to me. No handcuffs. They had forgotten to handcuff me.

As we neared the sally port I was starting to see my chance as they led me to the car, maybe. The gate would be closed before I was secured and only opened once I was locked in, so that won't work. If they put me in the back seat, I have a method for that but it includes a possible crash depending on my success and speed. I wasn't sure yet, but it would come to me. I wasn't going to die peacefully. I would try to escape or take one of them with me. Fight or flight, normally fight, but I could accept flight in this, the most peculiar of circumstance.

"What they did was wrong." one of my executioners told me.

"Dicks. They give us all a bad name." the other said.

"You need to leave and don't look back. There's nothing you can do here but get killed." said the first.

"We'll give you a ride to the county limits. Don't look back and don't tell anybody or they'll come find you. You almost killed Don." said the second. I thought about what they were saying. Don must be the one who hit me in the back of the head.

"You broke his neck." said the second, speaking out of turn for my story.

"Hop in." The first officer opened a patrol car door.

"Any chance you might just let me walk?" I waited for the violence to start, but instead, the other man pushed the button to open the gate. As it opened, I was still waiting for someone to take an arm or aim a gun or…nothing.

"You're a free man. You can do whatever you like, but you can't take long. We don't know how long till someone comes to check on you."

I climbed into the car and asked, "Can I get a ride back to the bar to get my stuff first?" "Sure thing." The door closed and I wondered if I had made a bad choice. But the car pulled out, stopped for the other officer and drove away from my personal prison a place where the most important person was me. I had been housed in a facility built for fifteen-hundred, all alone. Now I was to be free. Or so I hoped.

The bar came into view and the driver circled the block. The two of them were talking low voiced among themselves. "Do you see 'em?"

"Naw. You called him, right? Wait! There he is."

"I see him. Alright back there, make this fast." He spoke to me a soft, firm tone like he was trying not to be heard outside of the car. I could tell that these guys were worried.

I was let out on the sidewalk and the car then backed up, swinging tail end first, into the alley out of view. I headed for the front door that the bartender was holding open. I could scantly make out the details of his face or of the officer with me through the slits that were left of my eyes. The bartender took me by the arm as I passed him and left the door to my rescuer who stood at the door with his hand on his gun. I was guided to the back of the bar behind the counter where he led me to a storage and office area. My bag was there untouched and unmolested.

"That makes one of us." I said.

"What?" the bartender asked me. He must have thought I had gotten one too many head injuries.

"Nothing. Just noting how well cared for my bag was."

"I just left it back here for ya. Hey, you need a few snacks for the road?" he sounded as if he was about to cry.

"I was the sheriff here for years. We wouldn't have ever done that to a guy." He packed my bag full of chips and cookies and pretzels. In the side pouch he put a couple bottles of water and handed one to me that I couldn't open. I hadn't even noticed the pain in my hands. My left was chaffed and torn to shreds. My wrist looked as though it had barely survived a shredder. My right was smashed from boot heels and various wrist locks applied (unsuccessfully and without skill) by my captors. So the bartender turned, took it from me, and opened it, returned it to me and returned to what he was doing without stopping. I drank hungrily from the bottle, almost dropping it. He then picked up my bag and helped me with the straps. I handed him the empty bottle which he placed on the counter. "Thank-you for everything." I said, truly thankful.

"I thought that they were taking you to the city limits to scare you out of town, not keep you for three days doing Gawd knows what." His disgrace over their actions was clear. "Three days?" I was shocked.

"And the night they took you." He realized from my response that I really had no idea how long it had been. He tucked a $20 bill in my pocket and guided me out the door. The car pulled around and collected me and the other officer, and we left the downtown area.

We drove for several miles without a word. Both the driver and passenger watched as we left, to see that no cars showed up behind us. I was trusting in them to not pull over and snuff me. I was none too sure about what to expect as we finally did pull to the side of the road.

The passenger got out and opened the door. I climbed out as he looked around as if we were in a war zone instead of an endlessly flat desert. I reached for my pack and drug it across the back seat to me. I stood it up because I couldn't grip the straps, turned, and put my arms through. I stood up and stepped away from the car. With this, the door was slammed and the officer started to enter the car. As he did, the driver handed him something. He then reached for his wallet and pulled out a twenty to add to what the driver had handed him. The officer signaled to me to come closer. I did. He then shoved the money into my pocket, pulled his leg in, and slammed the door. The car made a quick U-turn and sped off toward where we had come from.

I watched them drive off as far as I could. The sun was just coming up when they left my sight. I reached into my pocket with my tortured fingers. I felt for the bills but couldn't make out their shape with my tattered, crushed digits. I pulled from my pocket the bills from my rescuers and then re-entered the pocket for the twenty that had been placed there in the bar. I smoothed them together. The sun shone through between my elbow and my waist onto the currency a smile welled on my face as it hit me, "I got sixty dollars!"

NEW YORK: BABIES ARE ADORABLE...AFTER THEY'RE CLEANED OFF

A young man, a thumb, and a plan, I was going to the scene of all of those Charles Bronson films. I wanted to meet the angels who protected the innocent and the hookers on the street corners. Hollywood had filled my mind with a myriad of ridiculous falsehoods. I was trusting in my better judgment not to meet a budding "son of Sam."

NEW YORK CITY!

I had no idea about the five boroughs or the Staten Island vs. the city. I just wanted to see the icon. But I asked a guy for a ride in a diner and he had no idea that I didn't know my way around. I said I was going to New York City, and he was going there as well so he took me to the city. He dropped me off on the sidewalk on the side of a skyscraper. I had seen those before and was not yet impressed. But I thanked him for the ride and got out of the car. I started to look around and then up and up and up. Okay, now I was impressed. These were much taller than words can express. I felt small and more than a little dizzy. I started to walk down the street, don't ask me which one, when a cab screeched to a halt alongside the sidewalk.

The driver hopped out and stormed around the car. He opened the backdoor on the passenger's side and started, in broken English to yell at the woman inside. His accent was thick middle-eastern and he was very angry. "You get out now. Go do that with your own!" his tone spat out the command. I thought that someone must have been shooting up heroin in the backseat or something. I waited to see the low-life chick come out in a dazed shame. "You get out, I say!" I heard moaning from within the cab, a woman in anguish. My thoughts were of the drugs she had done. What they were doing to her. Experience told me to let the situation play out until I saw her.

She was on her back in the backseat of the car with her legs up as if in stirrups. She was breathing in and out like a well-timed watch. Her lamas classes were paying off. The driver grabbed her by the arm, and I grabbed him by the scruff of the neck. I slooped off my pack that I had slung over my right shoulder and let it fall lightly to the ground while I contemplated letting him do the same with my left. I pulled my left arm out straight and he released her as I put him out further from me. When I let go, he was beside the trunk of the taxi, and I was where he had been a minute before. From this point, I could see her water had broken all over the backseat and the floorboard. I turned my attention to him briefly saying, "Watch my pack you prick. Hey, right that down. I might right a country song."

I had never seen a baby born before this point and all of the experience that I would have after this point would do me no good now. It had fallen on me to help this poor woman whom the cabdriver was going to throw out onto the street in her most vulnerable of times. First I told her, "I'm no doctor nor do I play one on TV, but today, we can just pretend that I am, okay?" she nodded her agreement as she entered another contraction. They could not have been more than a minute or less apart. I knew that meant that I was about to witness more than I wanted to. I asked her, "Is there anything that I can do for you," as I rolled up my jacket, reached around behind her, and laid it under her head. "Check the dilation." Her voice was strained but calm and peaceful, considering what she must have been feeling.

"I'm sorry, I don't speak Latin (a joke about being a doctor), I failed that part of med school. What is it that you want me to do?" she smiled and looked upward as if embarrassment was setting in. Meanwhile, I was readying myself to look up a strangers dress.

"Well (explanation), and that will let us know if the baby is coming yet." She had said a lot in a couple of sentences. I know I blushed but I tried to hide it.

"Okay, then in that case…" I turned and told the driver and the small crowd that had grown behind me. "This is a time for privacy guys. Ladies," I signaled them to me. "Block us so I can deliver this kid for her, okay?" the women moved in and put the men in their place. They took over like a pride of lioness guarding one of their own. So, with their backs to me, I started the check.

I had been with very few women in my life as of this point. I was an expert on the book learned part of a woman's anatomy from a young age. The reality of what I was going into was very different. She did instruct me, and I followed her instructions to the letter. But what I found wasn't a cervix, it was a furry little babies head. "I don't think you have long to wait. This one is on its way." I smiled from ear to ear with the realization that I was delivering a child. The relief of the child's cooperation was far too great to enumerate here, but let it be said that I was more spectator than actual doctor.

While we were busy, the driver was ranting to the people in the crowd as they tried to shut him up. He was not only angry that she was messing up his cab; but he was going on and on about how indecent she was, and how he couldn't make money that way and who was going to clean it up. "Not me, that is who. Not Me!"

The scene where we were was better. I was asking her gentle questions about herself to try and soothe her in between contractions. "Are you married?" I saw the ring and knew the answer.

"Yes. He's meeting me at the hospital."

"Boy will you have a surprise for him."

"Yeah!" she almost yelled as the contraction came on. Soon, though, I saw the top of the head appear. From that point, it was just conversation about pushing. In no time I was able to hold the top of his slimy little head. One more push and he was out in the world for all to see. I reached a finger into his mouth and swept out some of the slime. He hacked up more and coughed. He started to wind up for a good scream.

"It's a Boy!" I said it out loud for the now sizable crowd to hear. The baby cried to announce his arrival. The people all around us cheered as I covered his mother back up.

I set the newborn baby in his mother's arms. He tried to look around but babies can't see very well. A man stepped forward, patted me on the back, and gave his clean T-shirt to the baby for something to help keep him warm. The weather wasn't bad, but it wasn't a womb. "Alright, let's get you two to the hospital." I looked at the two of them together. Her eyes wet with happy tears and the new baby just looking up at his mommy. "Thank-you," she said without taking her gaze from his innocence. I helped to scoot her further into the seat and closed the door. "Cabbie!" I used my commanding voice. He came forward, disgruntled, and more than a little disgraced. He was not impressed that his cab was the scene of something beautiful. "We are going to the hospital. Get in." I pointed to the driver's seat and then climbed in the passenger side.

The trip was silent as the mother and her child cuddled in the back, and I stayed with a firm look in the front. I didn't want this self-absorbed jerk to speak to me. We arrived at the hospital, and I sent him inside to get the nurse. "I am not..." he attempted to speak. I put up my hand and pushed my palm toward him. His silence was followed by a snort. He then went into the ER and soon came back out with a nurse and a couple of others driving a gurney. They gently took her up and into the bed then drove her into the doors.

The driver stood too close to me with his eyes trained on me.

"What?" I questioned. Daring him to ask.

"My money." They were the first calm words he had spoken all morning.

"I suggest that you go ask the ladies husband. He should be in a fine mood when I tell him that you wanted to throw his bride out in the street as she was giving birth to his only son. I hear he plays ball for the Jets." A small fib to cause worry to a man who desperately deserves it. The cabdriver stepped back a step. He looked to see my expression which was jovial and sure. He then walked around the car mumbling under his breath in whatever language he called his own. I snickered to myself and went for my bag in the passenger side before he could leave me without it. I then rolled a cigarette and smoked it slowly, content with my days work.

"I wonder if I could get her obstetricians cut." I pondered. I finished my smoke and went into the emergency room and straight to the men's room to change my shirt.

The families were in the waiting room in the nursery when I got to the second floor. Between his and hers, this was a huge family and this child was going to get lots of love. My plan was to sneak through unnoticed, say good-bye and good luck to the baby through a window in the viewing gallery like you see on TV and be on my way. What actually happened was that as the elevator doors opened, the nurse from downstairs noticed me and said, "That's got to be your guy right there."

Soon, I was surrounded by people I didn't know. Each was happy to thank me. I was hugged and patted and almost tackled. My cheeks were kissed many times, and I wished that I had been more clean and presentable. I had in my hand a rolled up shirt. "Is this from the baby? Let me take care of that for you." The woman was the new grandmother on the mother's side. She spoke with a thick Greek accent and looked the part as I had seen in movies all of my life. "Go, she waits to say thank-you. She waits down there." She pointed and pushed me a little. Each of the family ushered me toward the hall. "Third door." The father's father pointed out.

I walked toward the door wanting to leave. I had done my part and just wanted to leave the child in the more-than-capable hands of his family. Embarrassed by attention, I knew deep down that this was how it should be, but my stomach flipped around; and I was nervous about meeting the father and seeing the woman whom I had seen in ways that even he hadn't. I wasn't sure, now that it was all over, if I should see that much of someone I had never met before. I don't know. I was young and shy and inexperienced in the ways of people.

I peered into the doorway. Mom and Dad were embracing. I didn't see junior anywhere. I assumed that he was in getting baby stuff checked out in another room. "I wonder if I can at least get attending physician, honorable mention." This crossed my mind. I pulled my head back just in time to get spotted. "Come in," she called in a weak voice. "This is my husband." I quickly let out, "I sure hope so."

Her husband was no football player, but he was a really nice guy. He was in tears with happiness. I got one big hug from him and about a dozen thank-yous. We chatted about how good it was to have someone when his wife needed them most and on and on until the nurse brought in the baby boy with a clean bill of health. I held him for the first time all cleaned up and not slippery. He just slept through everything. Then it was time to go. "Wait, we wanted to ask you something." She looked at her husband as she called to me. He nodded his approval.

"We want you to be his godfather." I didn't know exactly what that entailed.

"What would I need to do?"

"There is a ceremony and we get your information so we can keep in touch. You have rights in the child's life; and if anything happens to us, you agree to take care of him. Will you do it?" Her explanation sounded like the responsibility that I had been avoiding for a while.

"Sounds like a privilege for someone close to you guys." I was flattered and really wanted to say yes.

"Who is closer to my wife than the man who steps forward in her most intimate moment and delivers our child and her from an insane cabbie?" His words had truth and sounded as if they had come from my own mouth. I was destined to say yes, and I had a feeling that to not accept would have been a grave insult.

After a few more hugs and a few more tears and some moderate plan making without actual plans, I left the room glowing with pride. I looked for the grandmother whom I was having held my clothes.

"She went to wash your shirts. She insisted," her son informed me.

"How long till she gets back?" I asked with a little hesitation.

"Not long. You are staying there tonight. You will get a hot meal and a warm bed. It's the least we can do. Her words," he said it as if I had become a part of the family. Little did I know, in being the godfather, I was.

I stayed with them for four weeks as the church ceremony was planned, and it was so beautiful. I got to be with the baby every day and had such a wonderful time with everybody. I went to work with several of the family members and was asked a few times to stay and take a job. I never took or asked for pay. I was just seeing what each did and how my godchild was going to be raised, or so I would tell them. I have a lifelong open invitation to return and have received many updates on this, my first of seven godchildren. Thank goodness, no one from the family was lost on 9/11. My godchild is in his twenties now.

FIRST TIME GUARDIAN

After hitchhiking around the country and attending the "Rainbow Gathering" in Nevada among other travels, I came to visit some of the friends that I had made in the army. The family of one of my friends had treated me like family for my entire enlistment, so I went to their house to visit.

The family had several children aging from my friend who was two years younger than me to the baby who was about two. Two of the boys went to the same school right up the block from their home. They were both very adventurous types who loved playing with explosives that they had made from fireworks. Commonly, they would go to the lake near their home and dig trenches for hours, just to play war with friends. They were the two kids that every other kid looked to for inspiration and mischief.

One afternoon, the boys came home with a bad story to tell. There was a drug dealer visiting their school and selling to the grade school kids. He caught one of them and the other stood by to help, but what could a kid do against an adult? The dealer knew the family either by reputation or by association and told the boys that if they told anybody what was going on, he would kill their entire family, starting with the dog.

I was pretty upset to hear the story unfold. I didn't know how, but I had to do something. My father and I watched all of the hero movies growing up; John Wayne, Clint Eastwood, Charles Bronson, etc. I knew that if they were in a situation like this that they would do something to handle the problem. So I put my mind to work as we all ate dinner and discussed the events that unfolded.

That night, I took a stroll by the house where the drugs were coming from. As usual, there were many people coming in and out of the place. I stood in the shadows watching them. Some were there and gone, and some would not leave. There was a constant vigil at the front window by one tweaker or the other. All high on their dope, all thinking they were being watched. This night, they were right.

I left my shadow perch and walked down the street. Without a car, I found myself walking a lot. I walked up the street turning down the road to the main drag. I walked the street from one end to the other and back. Thinking. Thinking about my option. Thinking about the consequences. Wondering how I would go about doing what I needed to do, getting rid of the drug dealer. On my walk, I returned to where I had my backpack stashed at the end of town. I grabbed a road flare and tucked it into my inside pocket. Though I wasn't sure what I would use it for, I knew it had enough uses that I would find something to do with it. Besides, I had carried it for a long time and had found it hard to keep. I strapped on my .44 magnum pistol that I had picked up in my travels as well.

I came by the pistol in an odd sequence of trading ventures. First, I traded a cigarette for a dollar, and then I traded the dollar for rolling tobacco. Then I traded the newly opened tobacco for a pair of boots. I traded the boots for twenty dollars in food stamps. I traded the food stamps for fifteen dollars in cash. I traded the cash for another bag of tobacco and a knife that I didn't need. I traded the knife for another pair of shoes. I traded the shoes and the tobacco for a .22 caliber semiautomatic pistol. All in about an hour. The next day, I was leaving town when a guy pulled the

.44 on me out behind a warehouse that bordered the railroad tracks. I saw that the cylinders were empty so I pulled out the .22. "You're not loaded," I told him. "Hand it over."

"What?" he asked as I closed the gap between us with my palm outstretched for the gun. "I'm loaded and your little holes are empty. Hand it over," I said grasping the end of the big gun. He let go of the pistol and took a step back. I reached behind my back to my pack and rooted through a side pocket. I found the single .44 mag bullet that I kept for good luck. I opened the cylinder on the larger gun and placed the bullet in the chamber, closed the cylinder, cocked the hammer, and let it forward four times and spun it as my heroes of the old western movie would. I stopped it in my hand and cocked the hammer one more time. "Now, what you got in your pockets?"

"You gotta be kidding me!" he exclaimed in a voice two octaves higher than he had used while he thought that he had the advantage.

"Nope, I am not kidding. You took the risk and lost. Never go to Vegas," I said with too much self-satisfaction. "Now empty your pockets." I got another twenty-five dollars and a pack and half of smokes.

A few hours passed as I waited for the time to be right to return to the drug house. When I went back, the house was quiet, no one entering or leaving. The front window was blacked out so I couldn't tell if there was a light on or not. I slowly and cautiously walked closer. No movement. I stepped up my pace and climbed the steps to the front door. I listened. No one made a sound. I walked down the steps and went around the back. I checked the windows as I walked around. They were all covered. I had no way of knowing what I was going to find in the house. I walked to the back and up to the back door. To my surprise, it was not fully closed. Apparently, somebody was too high to be cautious. So I entered the back of the house into the laundry room. I spied around the corner into the kitchen, and there was nobody in the room. The lights were on in the kitchen but not in the adjoining living room. People were asleep on the couches and on the floor. I walked past the sleeping people and to the front door area where there were stairs leading to the second floor. I climbed the stairs. I opened each door in the upstairs hall. First was the bath. I stopped and used the toilet. Flushing the toilet sounded like a jet airplane going through the dead silence of the house. I felt as if every step was going to give me away.

I opened the next door and found a disgusting, smelly mess. The room had no occupant. The bed was without sheets and the mirror was on the bed with dusted leavings of lines already snorted. I was procrastinating. I must move on. The last door had to be the one I was looking for. There were no other choices. I gripped the knob. As it turned in my fist, I half expected to find an armed man on the other side like in all the movies. Life has taught me since, that people are people and their habits are very similar, but then, I was new to people stalking. I kept turning the knob. I heard the metal mechanisms clicking and grinding against one another. The sounds vibrated in my hand and through my body. I was certain that the entire house could hear it as well. Suddenly, the latch came free and the door pulled itself open. It felt as if someone were pulling it from the other side but it was just badly fitting in its frame. The occupants in the room slept while I entered.

As I stepped through the door, I gave some thought as to what I was going to say. I approached the bed, my eyes completely accustomed to the light. I saw the girl in the bed, naked, and only partly covered. She was pretty. I couldn't help but to think of the terrible things that would happen to her body if she was using. He was there before me. I stood over him trying to figure out what to say or do to make certain that the family would be safe from his anger. I knew it had to make an impression. It had to make him feel so insecure that he would run for good.

I pulled my gun from the holster and opened the cylinder. I removed one of the only six rounds that I had for it. I closed the cylinders and shifted the gun into my left hand. I held the bullet in my right. I bent over and shoved the bullet up his nostril. "Mmmphph!" He tried to scream but I muffled his mouth with my hand and pushed my full two-hundred pounds down on his face. With my left hand, I held the barrel of the gun to his head with enough force to leave a mark.

Just then, the girl, awakened from her sleep by the sudden jostle of the bed and his attempt to yell out, leaped from the bed in all her nude glory, screamed a blood-curdling scream that would have made a horror movie sound track. Startled, I looked at her calmly and said, "Are you sure you want to do that?" with that thought in mind, she stopped, and closed her lips. She slowly covered her mouth with her hands and watched as I told him what I had come to say. I said it so low that one could barely here it. I whispered in his ear from in front of his face, if you know what I mean. They were both silent as they tried so hard to hear the message. "This is a message from the (insert name here), the next bullet will be moving much faster and will have your name on it. I really think that you should leave town." With that said, I let loose of his face, and confident that I saw no gun, just a bat near the door, holstered my weapon. I looked on the floor and saw a pile of clothes so I took the flare from my pocket. As I backed towards the door, I struck the road flare and it ignited, defeating the darkness and replacing it with eye gouging red light. I held one eye closed as I had learned in the military and said, "You might want to get out. Your house is on fire," as I tossed the flare into the clothes, turned, and walked out of the room, down the stairs and into the living room. I then kicked one of the sleeping people on the floor in the ribs, "Wake these people up and get out, this house is on fire."

Walking outside, I didn't turn to see my efforts rewarded until I reached the shadows. I wanted a mystique to follow me.

When I did turn, I saw all of the people rushing out of the house, some nearly naked and all still groggy from sleep after days of partying. The guy with the bullet in his sinus was holding his nose and crying like a baby. His girl ran down the road with a sheet wrapped around her, and I dare say nothing else. The house was fully ablaze. No amount of water would save it.

I went to the family's house. It was three in the morning or later. The second son answered the door and let me in. He greeted me by name and asked if I was hungry. I looked him in the eye and said, "I have handled the problem." With that I walked over to the window and pulled at the blanket that they had as a curtain. In the distance one could see the blaze above the other homes. The whole of the sky was lit up like the coming of Christ.

The next day the paper read that a drug lab had exploded and that authorities were investigating the homeowner. Around town, my reputation was set into motion. Before I got up that morning, the local tough guys were talking about how not to get on my bad side. I heard the story from people who didn't know who I was as if the Archangel Michael had come to earth and set it ablaze with his fiery sword of truth. Oddly, it was all pretty accurate, with the exception that nobody ever mentioned that I had used the bathroom.

HOW NOT TO ENTER
A DOORWAY

They say that in less than a minute, your life can change (whoever "they" are). Touch someone I care for, and I'll show you how. I had heard from a friend who had heard from a friend that an ex-girlfriend of mine was being treated badly. I looked her up and found out that the rumors were understated. Her situation was very similar to the tales I had lived with my own mother growing up. Many of the stalking and kidnapping tales were resounding of deja vu. My stomach turned as I welled with anger that I had been a stranger to for so long.

One thing that a man must remember is that when you allow anger to enter your thought process, no amount of planning can save you from disaster. Either you go too far or jump too soon. A simple act of rescue could turn into life without parole or failure. Planning and research must remain free from pollution. Anger is pollution, the worst deteriorating acid of a clear mind. I had not been actually angry for a long time. I had been in a life where anger was never in the cards. I did what I wanted and lived as free as one can be. I set up a tent or slept on a couch or just left for another place as the wind blew. I had disappeared from the area so many times that the legend of my deeds seemed an urban legend, not that I am sure if that term had been coined yet.

I hugged her gently to avoid paining her bruised body and left with the intent of finding this guy and having him beg to apologize to her. As I came into his complex, it escaped my normally complete research that he would be warned of my arrival before I even finished getting her side of the story. Her neighbor called him on the phone to tell him that she was setting something up. I was walking into a trap. Lucky for me, he didn't take people at their words as much as he should have. I was told later by someone in the room when it went down, that he thought that they were exaggerating. He also assumed that the guy he was warned would come get him if he touched her again, was just a figment of her imagination. He never put the stories together.

His apartment was on the second floor (Aren't they all?), so my arrival would be hard to hide in broad daylight. (Rule to follow: Darkness is a hero's best friend.) I strode up the steps (thanks to a mother who worked nights during my childhood, my 220-pound frame moves relatively silent up stair and across areas) and walked the balcony. As I came to his window, I saw him and a friend in the living room. He with a very short, sawed-off shotgun. I proceeded to the door.

The blast from the gun coincided with an earth-shattering crash that swung the door open, off of the hinges and onto the second man in the room who was sitting on the couch. It felt as if someone had climbed the balcony and grabbed my leg, yanked it out from under me, and then let go, leaving my foot against the rails, my pant leg shredded and me feeling insulted. I fell forward, sort of, landing with my left leg straight out behind me but catching my weight on my right toes and hands both on the ground in a weird sort of runners position. From there I shot at him like a leopard. I was on him before he had realized that he had just shot me. My right hand grabbed the gun from his right, but he didn't immediately come free from the gun. With a twist of my wrist and ducking under his now taught arm, I pulled upward, raising him off of the ground by the one arm that was now behind him. As his weight was now in motion, I pulled him to my right as he flipped a somersault in the air, and he finally released the gun. I chambered another round, and before the casing hit the floor, aimed it at the person emerging from under the door. At the same time, my flying friend landed on the table where I had directed him, collapsing it under his weight. I recognized the guy from the couch and so I raised the aim of the shotgun off of him. "Wise men know when to leave." The words sounded profound in my mind.

"Um! Um!" That's about all he could mumble on the short trip to the door. The butt of the gun made an angry crack when it came in contact with the bastard on the broken table's forehead. His squeal almost made me laugh. Schoolgirls were known to have a braver scream. A second more and his eyes twitched closed, unconscious. After racking the slide a couple of times I was sure the gun was empty before tossing it to the floor. I then raised my foot straight out in front of me while standing beside his twitching body. I drew it backward, imbedding my heal into his groin. Coming in contact, I could feel the soft tissue through the leather of my size 14 work boot. If he were truly unconscious, I had discovered a way to wake him up. He sat straight up. His eyes were wide and his breath left his body. He turned his head to the right and squinted as tears streamed down. His face went green and before his breath returned, vomit spewed from his mouth. His hands were clasped on his genitals so that's where I broke them. I came down on my knee hard, delivering a blow from my right hand with the full momentum of my body behind it. I then grabbed hold of his limp digits, twisted, lifted as I stood and flipped him onto his belly. His breath was just about to return to him and as he gasped that first squeaking breath, through narrowed passages, I buried his face in his own vomit and resisted the urge to break the elbow of the arm I still held. "You know who sent me. You know why. You won't ever be a problem again, or I will make sure of it." I didn't ask, I told him. Then I left.

This was a refrained gesture. I kept my mind clear after the initial blast, by telling myself that I had made a disastrous error, and now it was time to compensate. I cooled my temper and just focused on the task at hand. When all was said and done, the entire event took less than a minute. If I had not adjusted to the circumstance, he may still be tied up in my basement.

I spent the better part of the day removing blue jeans from my skin. If he hadn't cut the barrel of that 20 gauge off so short, I would need a wooden leg. Fortunately, he didn't load with 00 buckshot or slugs.

FIVE AGAINST ONE:
YOU GUYS NEED MORE BACKUP

This story is of a day in particular that really was spooky neat. It happened when a girlfriend and I were living in a gravel pit in a part of Tacoma, Washington.

It started out as a normal day. My girlfriend and I were homeless together; because I already was homeless, and she was relying on others to support her, who were not her family. I knew these people, though not well, and had come to their home looking for a child molester whom I had knowledge of having done a bad thing. I knocked on the door and the door opened. I walked through the house and cleared the joint. In going through, I had not taken notice of who had answered the door, just that it had not been who I was looking for. So I went into the living room to find that it was this four-foot-eleven girl in oversized sweat pant and shirt that nearly swallowed her. I looked at her and said, "You are adorable. Can I take you home and keep you?" Long story short, I ended up having used that great line on the worst person I could have. I didn't have a home to take her to. I was living beside some railroad track and working full time stocking drywall for seven dollars and fifty cents an hour. But I still ended up keeping her because later I came to take her out on a date, and I had broken my ankle so they wouldn't allow me to leave. I mean I could have left, but she was cute and these were friends. How could I have ever known her temper or that she would end up my first wife?

See, now the story has gotten longer. Where to start? I came into town from the road. I wanted to see old friends that I had made in the army, who were not in the military themselves. After visiting one of them one night, I was just walking down the street when a car pulled over and asked if I remembered her. I did. I wasn't interested. She offered me a place to stay for the night and I was feeling generous, thinking that she wanted to sleep with me. She wasn't very attractive and wasn't very smart. She was overweight and had a laugh that would set you back a row. But, she was very nice and had had a crush on me for a couple of years.

We showed up at her aunt's house where she was staying, and I was shown great hospitality. I was grateful and they asked me to stay when they heard about my travels. At dinner that night, her uncle asked what I did for money, and I told him that I worked where ever I went and would move on when the job was over or I had made enough. So, he offered me a job. He was kinda big in the company that he worked for and could easily get me on-site unseen as they were looking for a guy, and I fit the bill for what they wanted. It could even lead to steady employ. Well, I had never delivered drywall before. I didn't have a clue, but I figured it couldn't be any more difficult than what I had already done for work. I took the job.

Boy was I wrong. Drywall is heavy. Darn heavy. And the edges are beveled. You have to carry two sheets connected together. They are eight-feet long and four-feet high. One guy grabs the front with his near hand on the bottom and his far hand on the top to stabilize the flat sheets. The back guy dose the same only he may want to put his inside hand around the back and grab on. The rule is, never set this stiff down hard or it will shatter the edges. It's made of chalk, so you never set it down one end first or the corner will break. (Notice that I said will and not could.) Never drop it or it will shatter. Never walk it up the stairs because it takes too long, and there are too many sheets to deliver. Now, while this condensed chalk sheet is trying to topple at any slight wind or balance issue, we would come in through a door, window, or place we removed the wall for the delivery and stack, by hand, however many sheets they need on each floor. To get upstairs, under almost every case scenario, there was a header above the steps. Since these things don't bend, every time the guy in front took his end up, the guy in back had to stoop down and get lower and lower until his end was at the bottom step. By the time his end got there, his knuckles would be either dragging on the ground or near enough that they would scrape just for the fun of it. He would then ascend the steps with his hand almost touching each step until he had cleared the header. As one gets better at the job, they watch the header and lift the end until they are back to a full standing position. While we are holding the couple of hundred pound "bundle," the beveled edges eat into the under knuckles of our hands. (Mine bled the entire first two weeks and my hands have always been like leather.) All of this is done at a full frickin run!

Basically, you can't get a more stair-climbing, hand scraping, knuckle busting, weightlifting, back wrenching, dust breathing, carpentry undoing/redoing, energy consuming work if you tried. I've dug ditches all day in the rain and snow, for a long period and never come close to that kind of miserable work. I've shoveled rotten corn out of a giant silo that exploded on the waterfront and would gladly have done that every day, as opposed to drywall hauling. Granted, it could have just been the company that I worked for, or it could be that for a brief stint in my life; I took a break from being a tough guy to be a sissy, but I doubt it.

After a couple of weeks working the job and living under their roof, I was downstairs when the couple's son announced that his mom and dad wanted to have me stay longer. I told him quietly that I had other plans as to where to live but to thank them very much and I was very grateful. He asked me why I wouldn't just stay where there was food and shelter. He asked a couple of times and wouldn't let me shake him so I said to him quietly, "I'm not used to sharing my every move with other people." He was confused, and I would have let it go, but he insisted that I tell him. "Your Mom is kinda nosy," I told him. "She gossips every day and is constantly listening, and it isn't something I am ready to deal with in my life." Just then, we heard screaming upstairs. We were in the basement, and she had been listening through the laundry shoot. She cussed me up and down and yelled at her husband to get me out. Blah, blah. So I went upstairs and looked at her husband. "Please give me a ride to where we work, and I'll be out tonight. As for you, you're screaming about how you are not nosy, but how did you know I said it? I was whispering. You were listening down the laundry shoot again, weren't you?"

I found a place near the railroad tracks and set up a tarp. I slept there at night and worked all day. Once in a while, I would rent a room at the motel for a day or two. On payday, I would go to this little restaurant near my work. For about five dollars I could get a burger that, just the meat weighed one and a half pounds. With the bun and stuff to deck it out, it was three pounds.

On the weekend, I would usually go to my old stomping grounds that were about an hour's drive from where I was staying. On the bus, it took more like three hours. For my birthday that year, I got myself a new tattoo. I had one, so I thought that it would look better if I got one for the other arm. I had a wizard put on. He has flowing brown hair and a blue hat and cape. When you put it together with my bulldog tattoo on the other arm, it weighs out pretty good.

I really had no intention of staying in Washington and certainly knew better than to camp out here in the winter. I was in the snow all night, barely covered by the tarp that I had made a tent out of. My work left little energy to do anything with. I was feeling pretty low. In retrospect, I should have gotten my last check and headed back toward the sun. I really don't know what kept me there.

I took a bus into town where my friends were, finding a few of them together in a restaurant having coffee and soda. I was greeted as usual, with hugs and slaps on the back. The mood was heavy that night and soon I found out why.

They had hesitated to tell me at first, but someone we knew was hurt. She had trusted a man for too long. He was a street fighter whom we will call Beast. (I want this to remain a little sketchy for personal reasons.) A street fighter has people bet on him as he takes on any challenger, and then he gets a cut of the winnings if he wins. If he loses, his broken bones and cuts and scrapes are all he takes away with him.

Beast had beaten her black and blue. But the worst part was that she was eight months along with his child. Everyone knew that I would hunt him down if I found out, so when they told me, they had his whereabouts and schedule all sorted out for me. That was all that was said about what was going to happen, or if I would be the one. My reputation for being the right hand of karma was known far and wide.

After a long while spent with friends, a long time girlfriend gave me a ride over to where he was. She was my unofficial timekeeper. The first time she was with me when I went after someone, she was so astonished by how fast I took him down and how much damage I had caused, that she forever more started a stopwatch to keep an unwritten account of how long it took me to take a tough guy down to a bawling child. This time would be no different.

She accompanied me to the door on the second floor. I signaled her to stand aside and facing her, I jerked my body sideways, leaning heavy into the door. A move I have never seen done on any movie splintered the doorframe and sprung it wide. Beast was standing there stunned, but my partner sprang back and grabbed for her gun. "What?" I asked with surprise. "I saw…a gun," she said with hesitation, one hand on the watch and the other on her side. With that, I turned and stepped into the startled, 300-pound man. I grabbed his collar bones with both hands and threw him across the room. He screamed like a little girl as I side kicked him in the solar plexus, landing him on his own couch. He would not interrupt my lessons with screaming. (A punch, kick, or any jarring to the solar plexus can leave any man, any size, gasping for air.) Jumping in full body, I wrapped an arm around his neck like an old friend, only tight enough to cut off his air that he was panickly gasping for, and started to speak softly into his ear. As I did, I would punctuate every sentence with a punch to the face.

With a conversation that went something like that, I got up off of him. He rose to his hands and knees and regained his voice, although the blood was pouring from his eyes and cheeks. I have to hand it to him, a threat at this stage was pretty gutsy. "I'll get the Crips and we'll come kill you, mother——!" With that I used my 14 ½ EEE boot as a bar of soap to wash his foul mouth. I kicked that steel-toe clean into his mouth. "Shhhhh! You'll wake the neighbors," as I left the door, "47 seconds."

I had never met this guy before. I didn't have any interest in his life or lack thereof. But I did know that a girl I was friends with needed help. The people I trusted in life at the time had given me evidence to substantiate the story, and I did what I did. I don't, nor did I ever feel bad about it. He did try to press charges, but he didn't know who to press them against. He tried to take out a hit on me, but nobody had a clue who I was or how to find me, and if they had tried to find me through my friends. Well, let's just say we watch out for one another. But, because we got wind of the hit, I sent a friend over to where he was hiding out to persuade him to drop the matter.

My large friend showed up outside of another of our friend's house. Beast had no idea that he was in the middle of my people who, each in their own right, owed me some sort of life debt. I had either fed them, protected them, taught them, or quite likely helped them against someone like him. I had a network of people whom I had never asked a thing in return. Each of the countless persons would go to hell if I asked them to, probably because I never had. I just did what no one else would or could, and then I would leave.

Beast came out to meet a man his size, and then some accompanied by a smaller built man with long hair that resembled a rock star. The conversation consisted of hushed tones containing "you might want to..." and "it would be wise for you to..." ending in "if we come back, and we will come back..."

The following day we were talking over the encounter. My large and usually violent to a fault friend was the first to tell me, "Man, what you did to him. I felt so sorry for him, I didn't want to hit him." Beast had a spider web of stitches from each eye. His nose was broken and jaw was wired and his teeth all gone. His eyes were permanently red filled with blood. My smaller friend remains much more dangerous than the larger. He isn't wise, but he makes an effort to think out situations. He acts only when provoked and is quick to fill his hand with whatever he happens to be wearing, be it a gun or a knife. Whereas the larger reacts out of aggression and pure meanness. When they used to get along, they were a pretty good team.

I worked the following week and returned the next weekend. This time I was in the company of the larger friend when he became intoxicated beyond belief. I took it upon myself to drive him home. I don't drink very often. It made sense for me to take him home—that and the fact that it gave me the opportunity to stop at a couple of locations on the way. He had a seventy something Monte Carlo, the perfect wrecking machine.

First, I stopped at the home of a girlfriend of mine who was shacking up with a guy I knew to be trouble. I knocked on the door (it was a friend, after all), which was opened by another of my friends. He didn't quite have his brain working but it worked enough to remember to everybody we knew how I snatched the naked man out of his bed and beat the apartment up with him, then gently put him back in bed with her. She was sound asleep when I whispered the warning that had him heading to Montana the next day.

My second stop was not so friendly. A couple of guys had jumped a soldier and hurt him pretty badly. I went by one of their houses. I was in luck. Not only them, but a couple of their buddies were there. I came into the drive and had to prop my friend up. He had put his head on my shoulder for the last couple of miles. His breath was ninety proofs and he looked to be enjoying the ride too much. I pushed him away from me and against the door. He moaned, hick-upped, and grumbled and I stepped out of the car.

The front steps were clear and a party was going on inside. I took the front stairs, one step across the porch, lifted, and stomped through the door. It wasn't locked so it went down with an impression. The old hinges were no match for my legs formed of years of hard work. The pine door went flat forward and smashed into whoever was behind it. I stomped heavily on him as I crossed the down door into the room and stepped on the side of his head that was showing. The first to try and stand was a gang member wannabe. I guessed his weight to be about 175 as he flew out of the living room window. The guests that were in attendance scrambled as I went to beating on punks. (I almost hit a very pretty young lady with the first gangsta while he was in flight. A thought went through my head to stop her and ask for a date.) The next guy tried to hit me with a bat but I caught it, took it from him with a yank and swept his feet from under him with a blow to his knees. I then flipped the bat in the air and put the handle through his teeth like a spear. I walked a couple of steps into the room and did a few maneuvers on the two caught in the corner that broke bones with a loud cracking sound that you feel through your own bones. They screamed and cried unabashedly. The tough kicked right out of them. One begged me not to touch him any more as the other cried watching his arm bend in places that it shouldn't. The last of the ones I was looking for tried his best to get me from behind, but I caught him out of the corner of my eye, spun, and put my foot under his chin as he jumped to hit me in the back of my head with a bottle. I caught him coming down with enough force to flip him backward in the air. He landed on the back side of his head with a thud. I then stomped my heel into his testicles, pulled my foot back, and buried it from the bottom of his rib cage, up, snapping a couple of ribs, and being rewarded with a breathless scream that made no noise.

My buddy was just starting to dry heave when I got back in the car. I reversed out of the drive and headed down the road, a normal speed, not like in the movies. The only thing I had to worry about was my friends puking. I entered the highway and got up to speed. It was about three thirty in the morning, and not much other traffic was on the freeway. I reached over and leaned my 360 pound friend out the door, holding onto his shirt and belt as he spewed forth. A nights worth of alcohol and food spattered its way down the road. It is amazing how liquid tumbles when it hits the asphalt at sixty miles per hour.

We got to the friend's house where I was taking this passed out gelatin man. I got out of the car, went to his side, and threw him over my shoulder. I walked to the foot of the stairs of the three-story apartments and looked up. "You really need to diet," I told the limp behemoth on my shoulder. I climbed the stairs to the second floor when I heard a familiar voice; "Where you taking him?" "To your place," I retorted in a "duh" tone of voice. "I live down here." I turned around wondering how I could have missed that and thinking how glad I was that I hadn't made a mistake like that earlier. I came down to the last step and turned in mid step. My ankle cracked loudly as I went to the ground on my broken drum stick. *After tonight, I guess I deserved that,* I thought. I protected my out cold friend all the way down, which is silly because he wouldn't have felt a thing. I could have explained away any bruises by saying he had been raped. Hell, it wouldn't have been the first time he was taken advantage of in his sleep. But I just cinched my boot tighter, tried to see if I could stand to walk on it, which I could. Then I plucked him back off of the ground, onto my shoulder and took him in to the couch. That night I went to a young ladies house whom I knew would welcome me into her home and slept off the pain. It had been a good night and I slept the slumber of babes.

In retrospect, forget about the gravel pit. That's a story for another time. It has to do with people, dogs, and cats all choosing the same night to mate; clairvoyance; 5 people in a car jumping out to attack me with hockey sticks and golf clubs, but losing their nerve when I came at them; flying hubcaps and a dog of mine. Just a casual day in the life, you know.

THE INFINITY GHOST

My first apartment with my eventual first wife was a dump. It was a studio apartment with a front door to the kitchen, and then everything else room. No walls between. No separator. The bathroom was to the right as you enter the front door. In the bathroom, the wall partition was made of block glass that barely concealed your identity from the party on the other side. The rent was one hundred seventy five dollars a month, so I wasn't expecting of any great creature comforts.

The first night, we walked in the front door, my buddy Kenney's girlfriend, plopped down on the living room floor, laid back, and was instantly covered with fleas. She screamed and brushed at herself as the rest of us refused to enter the house any further. Kenny and I looked at one another and in two-part harmony said, "Flea Bombs!"

After bombing the apartment with four flea bombs in a 400sq ft. apartment, we vacuumed real fast and moved in. I had a backpack, so did my girlfriend. Moving in was complete. Kenny and his girlfriend had disappeared. I went to the bathroom and found them, doing the deed on the counter—him standing, her sitting. The neighbor washing their hands in the sink on the other side of the glass wall, I went to the bathroom and teased Kenny about his timing, position, technique, and equipment. I gave her compliments on being a great girlfriend for being so open to doing it so soon after we entered the front door and gave her a thumbs up. I then said, "Hey neighbor!" He responded, "Hey man, welcome to the neighborhood," in a tone only slightly muffled by the glass.

The very first night we discovered that our walls were as thick as a quarter-inch-piece of plywood when the neighbors started their nightly ritual of intercourse. The lights were out for only a few minutes, and we were warming up to make love in our new apartment for the first time. After living on the streets for almost two years, it felt good to know I would be settled down for at least a little while. She had not been along for the entire time, but had been for a couple of months since I got into her life and was pretty excited to be in a place herself. This was her first apartment of her own ever. So when the occupants of the next apartment started slapping skin, moaning, banging down the walls, and carrying on, we could not help but laugh. They really put on a good show.

The apartment was partitioned out of a house that had once been a large home in what was now the worst part of the entire state of Washington. Hill Top, it was referred to, was in the middle of, not just gang territory, but the part of gang territory that was most disputed by the Crips, in blue, and the Bloods, in red. You had to beware of what you wore so that you didn't end up on the wrong side of drive by shooting. The fact that we were white didn't help our cause. It was primarily a reputation for being the wrong guy to mess with that kept she and I safe. The agreement was that I would be nice if they were. Shootings happened frequently on the streets around us but our place was located in a back alley away from most of the action.

Our time here was pretty much without outside incident. She was a bit nuts and I was a bit wild, but the outside influences of either gang never affected us. I would sometimes venture out in the streets to get away from our arguments and walk through the drug dealing world that would one day be Martin Luther King blvd. In Tacoma. We all know what that monicker means.

On Christmas eve. We were woken to the sound of a thunderous noise. I thought that someone was coming through the front door. I jumped from my bed only to find that my girlfriend had a solid grip on my testicles. She was wide eyed and frightened and her grip was unrelenting. I looked at her with serious intent, "I'm going to need those," I said with a grimace of pain involved. I went to investigate and found that our bathroom roof had collapsed under the weight of snow. The snow was less than six inches deep, this was just a testament to how shoddy a place this really was. The manager put a tarp over the hole for a few weeks but he never cleaned up the mess. We had to do that.

One night while we were sleeping, I woke to see a figure standing at the foot of the bed. I was on the left side of the bed, (A group of blankets and sleeping bags in the rectangle shape of a bed was really what we had.) and she on the right. The figure was at her feet and seemed to be wearing a sweater. In the center was a figure eight turned sideways and it slightly rotated as I watched. As he came around the bedding, He seemed to watch me. He came to my side and leaned in toward me as if to tell me a secret but there was no sound. His legs were not seen, but he moved as if walking. The chest area that made me see him as having a sweater on was transparent only to the point that is was like looking through summer heat waves off of the pavement, only in multiple directions at once. I don't know why I knew it to be male or how I could lay there without questioning my sanity, but to this day, I know it to be as real as you or I.

My girlfriend and I have compared notes on him so many times over the years. I was on the streets for a long time and so any movement towards my bed brings me awake very fast and I am usually very clear of mind. That night, we both tell Identical stories. We were both asleep and then we were not. Our clear heads were instant as if the thing wanted us to be coherent for the meeting. Neither of us has ever had reason to make up a story like this and after a very tumultuous marriage and divorce, the best things we agree on are that we hate one another and that we saw what we saw that night.

The sideways, moving figure eight on his chest/ stomach area has caused me to call him the infinity ghost. There is just something about a ghost that lets you know you are still alive. (And if you're not careful, that your bowels still work.)

ANTELOPE OREGON: SNOW HELL

At the time my first son was born in January of 1992, my mother worked for the Laborers international union of the North Americas (LIUNA) as a secretary. She had retired from the Des Chutes county Sheriff 's office where she had been a dispatcher and deputy since we had moved to Bend in 1980. She decided that if she got me a book in the union that I would move home. The union offered what seemed to be greater pay and benefits than most positions I had had in the past and mom thought that I would do well. So I moved my little family back to Oregon to try and form some semblance of a normal life.

The move was not without incident. Before we could move, we would need a car big enough to haul us and our stuff, so my first wife and I bought a 1969 Cadillac, Coup deVille. On the way to my aunts house for a last visit and with my cousin and her baby inside, we headed for Sant Rosa from Clear lake. The front end fell promptly out of the old beast on a winding Santa Rosa California road. I drove the car like that all the way into town. The front wheel on the driver's side was free to move back and fourth as it pleased. The several miles we drove to get to where we could stop were pretty exciting. A funny thing happened as we made that drive. A brand new Mercedes passed us on a blind corner. He stayed a couple of car lengths ahead of us until he sideswiped a guard rail, bounced off and then continued to drive at a high rate of speed until we could no longer see it.

My uncle and I went through the want adds to find another car. I found a 1971, Datsun 710 wagon. It was on the side of a building with about 2 years worth of dust and a busted radiator. Believe it or not, I got the guy to repair it for us for free on the spot. $350 and we drove it back to my aunts and uncles house. As for the Cadi, we left it at the local super market and I put my tell tale note on the windshield, "Take me home and keep me. Free to a good home. Keys are on the dash. Front end bracket broken. Have a nice day."

We drove to Oregon in that old Datsun. All the way to my mother's house in Bend. It was great on gas but lacked any real show of power. We weren't at my mother's very long, perhaps an hour when we were told that we would be staying at my sister's house in Antelope*. I fixed a couple of shelves in that time and a few other odds and ends, which seemed to be my normal routine when I visited. I would walk in the door and mom would put me to work on all of the odd fix-its that dad either hadn't done or didn't know how to. So we got back into the car and proceeded to drive the miles and miles to Antelope.

Once there we were shown to the outside shed where we were to stay. My old waterbed was in the middle for us to sleep in so that we would be nice and warm considering the only heat would be a space heater on the floor. There was also a dresser and enough space for us to set down our bags. That was about all that there was to that. We were in the last days of summer so the winter seemed our last concern at the time.

The following day, we decided to go into Bend and see my folks for the visit that we thought we should have had instead of what we perceived as the brush off. On the way out of antelope there is a fifteen-mile road called Lower Antelope Road. Then, you turn west on highway ninety-seven and drive thirty-seven miles into Madras, just off of the Warm Springs Indian reservation.

South bound from there another twenty miles is Redmond and thirty more to Bend. We got just on the southern outskirts of Madras when the car just couldn't give any more. A rattle and a bang told me we had thrown a rod. The oil trail behind and a cloud of embarrassing smoke coming from under the hood said it had pierced the block. We had blown what little money we had on the two cars and gas from Cali. It was going to be a while before this old beast saw the road again.

We parked the car on an old farming road and walked up to the house to tell them not to tow it. We would come back as soon as possible for it. After that the only thing was to get back to my sister's house, so we stuck out our thumbs and hitched a ride.

The following morning I woke to the uncomfortable feeling of flu-like symptoms and backache. I had somehow chosen this time to come down with shingles, a second coming of chicken pox. Symptoms of this included scarring back lesions that felt as if the long tentacles of an octopus were burrowing into my spine, wrapping around my nervous system, and ripping them from my body. I was weak and in pain and every muscle in my body ached and teased as if they would fail at any moment. So I went into town to look for work. After all, nothing would stop me from feeding my new boy, Bryan.

I got two jobs that day. Unfortunately, I heard the first offer and accepted it right away. Instead of working in the warm environment of Denny's as a server, I ended up at the Plumb Fierce gas stop on the three-way intersection of hwy97 and hwy20. It had an old carwash in the back and an old service bay void of any semblance of tool or rack. I don't know how long it had been that way but it was about as empty as it could be. We washed your windows, checked your oil, and filled your tank as it is illegal to fill your own gas in Oregon. I got the occasional tip and the vacuum system sometimes kicked down a buck or two from someone's misplaced change between the car seat cushions. Every night, I would clean out the vacuums and wish for change.

I hitched a ride every afternoon. Hope would carry me into town but to get a ride home most nights was but a fleeting dream. Every night I would close. Paperwork was done, figures tallied, doors locked, and eventually about eleven-thirty I would run out to the corner of 97 and 26 and 20 to try for my ride home. Most nights however, I would come back to the station around 1:00 a.m. to curl up under the back counter in the unheated bay where for some reason they kept two antiquated furniture blankets, the kind for moving furniture with a truck or moving van. At first it wasn't so bad. The weather wasn't to terribly cold so the cement floor wasn't a bad place to rest. And every morning I would get up when the manager opened the doors. I would then try to get a ride into town or just hang out at the convenience store/ bait shop next door.

Next door to us was a pretty convenient place for sure. They had hot food behind glass, hot coffee, and cocoa. So if I had found enough change or had gotten a tip the day before, I could get a small something. But I usually passed on it because I saved every cent for the wife and baby I had at home.

Formula was eight dollars a can and diapers were seven dollars a bag, and we could barely afford them. Plus, I had met a man who said he could find a motor and fix the car so I was paying him half of my wages in order to get the car fixed and back on the road. Two engines were ruined before he finally got it almost right enough to drive but that wouldn't be for months. So, I was stuck in this circle for quite some time.

One day I spent the day with my baby in my arms and playing with my niece and nephew until I had to leave for work. We played in the sprinklers and waded in the kiddie pool all day. It was eighty degrees out and life was pretty sweet for a moment. I was broke and happy with life before me. I was sure that any day now I would get that fateful call from the union and my child would be headed for a life of ease with a father he could be proud of. After all, what else does a father ask then to be seen in the eyes of his son with respect and glory and, at this age, awe?

I grew up in Bend my whole life from the time I was 10 until the ripe old age of 17 when I joined the army. In that time, we got one channel on television for most of the time. It was Channel 21. It carried ABC, NBC, and CBS programming. Eventually we did get Channel 9, PBS but come on, really? Is that really counted as a channel? The only time it has good things to watch is when the pledge drive would force them to. So as I was saying, 21 had a weather forecasting guru named Jack Mercer. He made an art out of never looking out a window, or so it would seem. We could be in the middle of a blizzard and he would call for cooler weather with a slight chance of showers. No Joke! He once called for a warming trend that would bring us out of the freezing weather in the teens where we had hung for the last two weeks. The next morning was one of the coldest on record and it hung close to that for a month. If you wanted to know the weather your guess was better than his. So with that said failing to check the weather was no failure at all.

That day was like all of the others before. I worked as hard for all of those weary travelers as I had for all of the ones before them. Around six, it started to cool enough to make me want my jacket. I didn't have any customers from 9:00 p.m. on, so I was inside waiting to close. At 11:30 p.m., I was already on the corner when a car stopped with an older lady at the wheel. She offered me a ride to Antelope. She believed she had to go through there to go to where she needed to be. I was pretty excited. Two out of three days I was not getting home at all, and this night was shaping up to be pretty cold. As we drove I discovered that this woman had seen Antelope on the map but that the closest she could actually get me was to lower Antelope Road, which was fifteen miles from the house. But, you know what? That was okay. Someone would come along, and if not, it's not really that far to walk. So I gladly continued on with the nice lady driving with a smile on her face feeling as though she were doing the greatest thing for me. Her happiness was contagious.

By the time I got out of the car, small snowflakes had been hitting the windshield for a solid ten minutes. The road had waves of little snakes made of snow floating across as we drove. I was becoming more concerned and was half tempted to turn around after she left and try to head for the safety of town. The only thing that had kept me from that was the knowing that during our drive, only a single semi tractor-trailer had passed in the other direction. I knew my chances were slim to none of getting a ride back to town.

Antelope was the biggest story of 1984. The little town of twenty-five people was taken over by Rashneeshpuram. A sect leader named Bagwan Shree Rashneesh had bought a ranch and started busing in people from all over the United States. Mostly, they were homeless vagrants whom he could sway towards his will and get the skills from them that they had forgotten they knew: builders, plumbers, electricians, engineers. They almost completely succeeded in building a self-sufficient town of their own just outside of Antelope. Meanwhile, they would drive around in their jeeps and pick-up trucks decked out in the colors of the morning sun, threatening to shoot anybody who stood in their way. It all fell apart when the Bagwan had a falling out with his number one wife, Ma Anon Sheila and the feds invaded. Ma Anon Sheila was never caught. She is said to have taken all the Bagwan's gold and escaped to Switzerland. I believe she married an investment banker there. The crazy old Bagwan was never really the head, it would seem. He was just a nutty old pawn. He just came in from wherever it was he was from, and they kept giving him Rolls Royce. He just thought Americans were really nice. He died in 1990 of heart failure. He has world renown as a sex guru.

A town of twenty-five was no doubt a long shot to get a ride in the middle of the night. This night, it was pretty much assured that I would be walking, and I had better get to it. I walked briskly at first. My arms were bare from the elbow down; I hadn't even thought to bring a coat on an eighty-degree day. My eyes were getting stung with ice crystals falling from the sky and whipped by an ever increasing wind. My thin slacks, common attire for a summer-service-station employee were no match for the cold chiseling away at my legs. A bag stubbornly clasped in my hand was a treasure, a gift to the mother of my child. I had nothing else to ward off the cold. My quarter pack of cigarettes? My Zippo lighter? My empty wallet? None of these would wrap me up and warm me from the cold on my long walk home. I had to keep walking. As the snow piled up on the road, my feet were starting to chill in my boots. The only thing I had that even halfway seemed suitable for the weather—work boots. I had worn boots for the last few years. No matter what job I got, I could wear boots. The same couldn't be said for tennis shoes. So at least I had boots. But a lot of good warm feet will do if I freeze from the top down. Have you ever heard the ER doctor say, "His brain is dead as well as his heart and all of his extremities. His penis may have frozen off at the half-mile mark, the sheriff is still looking, but we have some excellent news for you. His feet. We've saved his feet and he is going to be just fine."

What would I do? I realized with the snow at the two to three inch mark at the first mile marker, something was not going my way. By the time I got to where I suspected the second mile marker was usually found, I figured about six inches of snow. By that time I was well into the road between the high cliffs and the wind was unbearable. So I just kept going. The snowfall was nearly white out conditions, and I couldn't pinpoint when my arms and thighs had lost feeling, they just had. I started to formulate a plan. I would get through the draw and build a fire. It would be warm and sustain me and I would make it. Then I would build an igloo. Yeah, and I would move my family in, and we would live there forever! Wait. Something isn't right with that thought. For one, there wouldn't be any electricity to plug in the water bed. Second, I don't want some harp seal hunting polar bear to eat Lil' Bryan. His mother, maybe...so I had better not move them in right away. I must be losing it. Everybody knows it's too hot in the summer for an igloo. Besides that this snow is too dry, dry snow. Any kid growing up in the winter wonderland of Bend would know, if the snow is dry, it's well below freezing. Usually colder than twenty Fahrenheit . Well, I better just start with the fire. Gawd it was cold.

I don't exactly know what time it was or how far I had gotten. The only sure thing is that hypothermia had been in the mix from the moment I left for work that day. My eighty-degree day was a world behind me now, and if I didn't figure out something fast, I was going to die.

The plants were all covered with snow. What a change from the sage brush fires we had been fighting all summer. Antelope is an all-volunteer-fire department. Each farmer and rancher knows that the ranch he defends today may help to save his farm tomorrow. An old engine bought at auction from the sale of Rashneeshpuram had gotten the town a beautiful, fully functioning truck with powerful hoses and the ability to take the fight to the fire in a hurry. So long as someone was there to drive it, that is. When the alarm would go out, every person in town had a call buddy, and I was on the list. If I was at the service station in Madras, I would close up and go in to Antelope with whoever was on their way home from work. It was one of the few times I could get a sure fire ride, no pun intended. Antelope was desert. Sage brush and thin tall strands of sparsely placed wild grass make for rapid burn. Add the occasional juniper tree and you get a fast moving, unobstructed fire with precariously placed bombs. The juniper tree is filled with sap. And when it gets hot, pow! Don't be anywhere near it.

There were no juniper trees here but the sage brush was going to do just fine. I stomped down the spot I wanted, just to the side of the road. Oddly thoughtful of the fire hazard contained in the sage, I tried not to build the fire to big. (In retrospect, I should have lit the darned bush on fire.) I gathered enough for a while and sat huddled with my back to the wind trying to protect my little fire.

It wasn't very big, my fire. At the time I knew I would think myself a sad and pathetic beast for making such a small and ridiculous fire. I knew it was crazy to ask that little fire to heat me against such overwhelming odds. In truth, I thought that I was dead. I had no doubt that I was going to die and I didn't want the last thing I did on this planet to cost some poor family their home. I pictured the families in their beds sleeping through the night after they secured their livestock and being totally unaware of the fire encroaching on their home while they slept. I didn't want that to be the way I was remembered. As I sat there I wondered how long it would be until the snow melted, and I would be found. I wondered if coyotes would eat me after I was gone and no one would ever know I had died there in this blizzard. I hoped that my son was being held tightly in that heated water bed as the wind whipped outside. I started to close my eyes. I had been there for a long time. I could not find a place on my body that had feeling and my legs seemed not to work. My eyes were strained to see through a white out when I could see, and now I could no longer see anything but fuzz. My eyes were frozen.

I remember falling over. I remember not being able to counter the pull of gravity. I just curled as closely to my fire as possible. I know I was in that position for a long time. I remember the sound. The sound of a four-stroke-motor cycle or was it an old- arctic-cat snowmobile. I dreamed it was an old biplane. The engine unsure as if it were going down. A distant sound. Far from, but getting closer. Hey! That's a car!

Before I knew what hit me I was trying to get what used to be my feet. "Oh sure!" I said. "The boots were going to save the last parts of me for science before." How feeble I felt. I thrashed around like a fish. I could not feel my arms. It was like they had been broken off and fed to the fire. I didn't remember doing that. I believed they were still there. My eyes had been closed for a while I guess, because when I opened them I could see a little bit through the ice on my eye lashes. Sure enough, when I looked around me, I was still in one piece. That's all it took. With that I got to my feet, as they were formerly known and looked into the draw. I saw lights. I heard noise. I saw powdery snow flying to get out of the way of some lunatic driver. I waved frantically. I ran over and stomped out my fire, made six or eight attempts to grab the bag I had be holding onto so tightly and I waved my arms over my head wildly and the car approached, approached, and passed me without slowing down.

"You have got to be kidding me!" I wish I could have gotten my mouth to say. I watched tail lights as they left me far behind. I was not sure I had seen what I had seen. "Is this my afterlife?" I thought. "A twilight zone episode?"

I turned back toward my ex-fire. My trusty Zippo would light another. Of that I had no doubt, but about feeling it to do so. I couldn't feel anything. I wasn't even sure if I was a ghost or real, because that guy surely did not see me. Wait, am I going to haunt this spot for eternity? Boy did I get screwed? I don't like this plan at all. But wait. I heard the same engine coming back. I heard it for a long time before I could see it. I almost thought it was an audio-hallucination. Sure enough, that same "whurrrp whurp whurp whuuuurrrrp," sound. I gained my place on what I perceived in a foot and a half of snow was the side of the road. I started flailing my arms wildly way before he could see me. I watched as he flew past me a second time, a second time. I must be a ghost. As he disappeared around the bend in the valley my heart...oh my Gawd. He must have made a wrong turn off of the highway. But you know what? I didn't care. He should have stopped and given me a ride to the nearest place he could. That guy would let me freeze so that he doesn't have to take me with him. Fine, when I have my igloo warming party, he is definitely not on the guest list. He can just..."whurrrp whurp whurp whuuuurrrrp," you can't be serious. He's going to come back just because he risks not being invited to my party? Well, unless he apologizes then he still isn't invited. Here we go again. Waiving the arms? Check! Wishing and hoping? Check! Staring where I believe his eyes are through the headlights? Check!

Just then the car stopped. A long way before he was even close. I stopped waiving so frantically. After all, if he thinks I'm speaking sign language I wouldn't want him confusing this motion for waiving him off. The car inched forward from about 200 yards. I waved a bit more until I figured he knew for sure I was waiving at him. When the car was about forty yards, the driver stopped. So I walked about three steps forward. He backed up about ten feet. *What is wrong with this picture?* I thought. I am out here in short sleeves and this guy won't let me into his car? Just then the driver's door opened. "What's in the bag?" he yelled over the wind and snow and sputter of his AMC hornet's years-past maintenance due engine strain. I looked down at the bag I was holding. As long as I could remember no one had ever questioned me about a paper lunch bag. Of this I was pretty certain, he could not have foreseen me having this bag the first two passes. "Girl Scout Cookies!" I yelled back in his direction.

During the painfully long pause that took place before his next request, I remembered how excited I was to see a camper full of family discard unopened boxes of girl scout cookies. My wife was a big fan and so I grabbed three boxes of them after the people left. I hadn't been able to give her a gift in a long time and these were sure to please. "Show me," he said.

So I turned the bag upside down and out fell three boxes of cookies. I had guarded them with my life, and now they fell to the snow which had tried to take me up on that offer. "Alright," he said as he got back into the car. He waited for me to walk up and try the knob. He made me wait while he finished making up his mind. Finally, he let me in.

The car had no heater fan but as long as we kept moving the air kept flowing. I told him how I came to be in that situation he drove me to my sister's driveway. It was a little over a quarter of a mile from the road to my bed. I shook for eight hours and was awakened in the morning still unsure of being home. When the time came I hitched a ride back to Madras the next day with a friend from town in a jeep with no doors, a soft top, no heater, and a hole where there should be a shifter boot.

ARLINGTON OREGON: NOW THAT'S SICK

While living in Antelope, we moved into a small mobile home in the peaceful Antelope RV Park. There were large trees shading the grassed area and a picnic table. We stayed in a small single wide with a couch that folded out into a bed. Bryan was such a cute little infant. He was just getting to use a jumper and walker. We lived there as the spring and summer came in. I was still working at the gas station and waiting for the union to "kick in." My wife was going to the little store next door for food and minor groceries which they allowed her to run a tab for. The store was also a diner and a single pump gas station. We had gotten to know the neighbor and his wife who had picked me up in the snow that night not so long ago. People in the community brought us fresh milk in big gallon jars which was still warm and so very creamy. If I had been able I would have loved to live there longer. On occasion I would help load hay for transport or some other task to help out and become a member of the community.

I had made a few good friends in town. One was a younger man who had built his jeep himself. It had a Chevrolet 350cu engine, no doors, and a soft top with no sides. Every time he went into town he offered to take me. Sometimes, he would make excuses to go into town and wait for me to get off work to come home usually once a week or so. He had picked me up the day after my near death in the snow and had been the first person to hear my recounting of that night's tale.

My wife's ability to charge food had been taking up every cent I could earn. She was charging meals at the diner. She had no concept of how much she was spending. I really couldn't get it across to her but I was able to talk to the store owner who was also our rental owner. She limited what could be charged but my wife was able to convince her to make "exceptions" at times and it was killing our money. I was shocked sometimes when I would expect to have a couple extra dollars and would go to pay the bill only to find it was more than I had earned. It was especially hard considering how little I was able to eat on those nights when I didn't get a ride home from Madras. A single chicken leg or Jo Jo potatoes from the hot food counter if I was lucky.

I called my boss one night before starting work. I had talked to the manager about borrowing fifteen dollars for diapers and formula. We each had a drawer for cash and change, and I was hoping they might let me make it up in a few days on payday. He said no. I explained to him my situation and what I had gone through on a weekly basis and how even thumbing rides I had never missed a day or been one minute late. I tried to explain the ordeal with my car and how half of every check was going towards getting it fixed. He was unmoved. I had worked there for several months, yet he didn't trust me. I took the fifteen dollars out of my drawer anyway. I needed diapers for my child, and he had to have formula. I didn't want to steal the money, I just needed to borrow it. I finished the day and purchased what I needed at the supermarket that night before getting lucky and running into the owner of that funky homemade jeep at the market. Score! A ride home to boot.

The next day was very normal. I worked the pumps and cleaned the windows and checked the oils. Everything was fine. The sky had not fallen and the world had not ended. (We're going to call the guy with the Jeep Jim from now on, because I can't remember a name from 19 years ago.) So Jim came by the station that night. I hurried and closed on time as he was waiting. During this time, we discussed the fact that he and his parents were concerned that I wasn't able to get home so often. They had all chipped in for the gas and oil to get me home on the few nights that they could. Jim said that they didn't really ever come to town and that other than tractor supplies he had been coming into town visiting other friends each time, just to make an excuse to pick me up. The night before, he had seen me walk into the market from the gas station where he had feared he had missed me. In an effort not to let me know he was there to pick me up he had pretended to be shopping for snacks and "accidentally" run into me. I couldn't believe what a great bunch of people I had fallen in with. No one had ever shown me such kindness. He was driving round trip of over one hundred miles, a couple of times a week just to give me a ride. He said his mother feared for my safety.

When I got to work the next day the sky had fallen. The police and the owner were waiting for me in the office. It seems that in my haste the night before, I had left without locking the bay door. The cold weather caused the springs to raise the door just enough to bring attention from the roving patrol. They called the owner to come down at 3:00 a.m. to lock the doors. When he got there he reviewed all of the drawers to check for theft. My drawer was still eleven dollars shy. I explained how I had been paying it back with the money from tips and change from the canister vacuums. All of my explanation fell on deaf ears. I was going to jail unless I had eleven dollars in my pocket. Furthermore, all of the change from the vacuums was to be repaid as well. He counted that as further evidence of theft. Oh, and just to prove what a dick he could be, he said that if he could prove I had actually received tips, those would be owed him as well because his company had initiated an unwritten no tip policy. The charges were now twenty dollars.

Lo and behold, just as I was being cuffed for the ride to the jail house, who should pull in but my mother. She had driven down to see my sister and was just in time to see my shame. Lucky for me she had a checkbook. As she wrote the check, the owner of the company actually suggested that he might not take it. It was the officer that took him aside and explained the stupidity of what he was doing. The officer had heard my entire tale of woe and shown no sympathy but now he was on my side. What a change? I watched as this unfolded. I was taken from the car and the officer looked over to my mother and asked, "So Cyndi. You got your key on you or should I get these?" referring to the handcuffs. I went with my mother back to Antelope. She drove while I talked, and I told her the whole story. How my wife had been using the little store like a free shopping card and how I had almost died in the blizzard and all about the peace we had found in the little town. I told her about the townspeople who had been so kind when I needed them most. I told her of my humiliation in having to steal the money she had repaid. She told me that she would have done the same thing.

When I got home to my little oasis in the desert, I had to tell my wife that I didn't have a job. I was going to be unable to pay the rent or the bill she had accrued in the store. Even my last check was being withheld to cover "damages." I left with nothing and as the owner of the Plum Fierce station had said, would get nothing. I was at a very low point. I had done everything humanly possible to be the best employee imaginable only to be cast aside and forgotten. And if he thought he was stolen from then I felt as if he had raped me. No dignity can be scavenged from an encounter like we had.

The union called that afternoon. I was using the store as a message phone and man who ran it came running across the grass. "They called!" he said in an excited tone. "The one you've been waiting for."

I returned the call and found out that the job I had was to be installing concrete run off protection for a power station in Bend. I would have to move in with my parents for a short time while my wife and child stayed in Antelope, but that would work. It was a fifteen dollars an hour job. I didn't know how anyone could afford to pay that much, but I was willing to take a fool's money. The gas station job was minimum wage. I was so excited that I did all the calculations in my head for every hour I worked, a practice that I would continue throughout my career. I was always within a few cents.

There was a reason for the wages. We were told, me and one other guy who lasted less than a day. (Shovels didn't agree with him.) "Everything above your head is high voltage. Seven-feet up from ground level. If you lift the shovel to high, you're dead. If you raise your hands above your head, you're dead. If you touch any of these over here or those over there, you guessed it you're dead. You (pointing at me), what are you, six-four? Stand on your tip-toes, you're dead."

The job only lasted two weeks but the company had a new job in Arlington, up on the Columbia River. If I wanted to, I could come with them up to that job. I would have to get my own place and find my own ride, but I could go if I wanted. I said yes. Now where the hell is Arlington?

I rented a car to move. My mother used her credit card for the security but I paid for the seven-day rental in cash. I could use fifteen miles a day. Antelope was seventy-five miles from Bend and Arlington was way past that. Fifteen miles a day was only one trip, one way so I started to search for the speedometer cable when I found out that this model of car had a fuse for the speedometer/odometer. So I took it out. Now the car would only use as many miles as I wanted it too.

We moved from our little town. In the time we were there, the couple whom we had gotten to know the best were the ones who owned the car that had rescued me that night in the snow.

Sadly, they got a divorce in the time we were there. More sadly was that I couldn't trade my wife for the woman. She was quite an attractive thing and mine was mean as hell. Additionally, they had let us borrow the AMC Hornet for a couple of weeks for me to go to Bend. On one family outing in the Hornet, we were driving south on 97. just a mile from the Crooked River Gorge. A few cars ahead of us, someone slammed on their brakes. We were able to avoid tail ending the car in front of us by taking to the right shoulder of the road. A tractor trailer behind us could not stop. He told us later that his unfortunate decision was because he had seen our baby in the back when we had passed him on an incline. Instead of taking the chance of hitting us, he veered into oncoming traffic. He collided head on with a midsize Ford pick-up truck. The impact was so hard that it jackknifed the fully loaded semi and the pick-up flew tumbling through the air. The driver never stood a chance to avoid the accident.

My wife and I were first on the scene. I was already pulled over and the traffic was stopped. The driver's name was Mark. As I ran to his location off of the side of the road, his truck was on its top. He was half way out of the driver's side window and his left arm was nearly severed at the elbow. His head showed serious injury, and I was a little bit worried he might not make it. As I surveyed the scene, I saw other drivers coming to assist me. Many drivers were all about helping this guy. I've been on many scenes of injury and never have I had the amount of people in the same accident willing to help.

Someone said they saw a flicker of flame and although the movies exaggerate the explosive power of a car on fire, the situation required moving Mark. I know this is a risk better not taken but we had to do what seemed best at the time. I figured that any precaution was better than allowing avoidable risk. I had control of the scene. I directed a few of the drivers for blankets and one little lady even donated her pillow. My wife cradled his head, as I, and the truck driver who had hit him worked our arms under his body for a make believe stretcher. As we removed him to a spot several yards from the pick-up truck, observers were returning with a hospitals worth of blankets, first aid kits, and comfort items. Meanwhile, some others were working to put out the flames. I treated Mark in the best tradition of military field medicine. My wife continued to cradle his head. A nice 16-year-old teen looked after our sleeping child. I constantly asked Mark questions about himself and his family in an effort to keep him conscious. My wife combed her fingers through his hair and located all of his injuries for future use of the paramedics. People around us guided traffic to get through and someone went ahead to get a phone call through to 911. Until the ambulance arrived, we took care of him. As we closed in on an hour, Mark weakening under the pressure of his numerous cuts, scrapes, bruises and broken bones, the trucker cried, the ambulance, and fire rescue did arrive.

We visited him in the hospital a few days later but he had no clue who we were.

The move took two trips in the car I had rented. As we came for the second load, the store owner had a message for us. The car was finally fixed. I could pick it up at any time and I only owed him another $120. Only, I had given that old fool half of everything I had earned for months. I could not believe he would charge me for two engines that I had never even gotten to turn a key in and then ask me to pay $120 for the car now. When I got there, he told me it was money for new oil and gaskets, then asked my help to attach some of the hoses. For the money I paid him it should fasten its own hoses.

I returned my rental to Bend. I had put the fuse back in before returning it. The guy behind the counter seemed very impressed with how few miles I put on it. Then my mother drove me to get my car. She dropped me off in Madras. I picked up my car and, cursing under my breath at the old man who had held it captive for so long, proceeded to drive it to our new home a few hours away. That little wagon was so gutless that I couldn't have sped if I had wanted to. It smoked and drank two and a half quarts of oil on the drive. That would be its operational guideline for as long as I would have that little car, two and a half quarts to every five gallons of gas. It was like mixing the fuel for a dirt bike. Every job I would take with the Union required us to move.

Twelve acres. Thats what we had to do. Turn a power substation from two acres to twelve. The boss wanted me to run from place to place as well. He was paying and he wanted his laborers running. On the other hand, I was his only laborer. Lucky for him, I also have a knack. I can figure out and run any piece of equipment, tractor or vehicle so I was also his operator, dump truck driver, operator, form ripper, hod carrier, substitute iron worker, cement finisher, etc. I was a manual shovel operator and flame thrower/ snow removal guy as well. When we got there the fall was upon us and the wind whipped the sand and dirt into our faces until we were sandblasted. When the winter hit us, we worked through the wretched cold and hip deep snow. Not one of us was missing a day of work in eight months. No one called in sick. No one let the weather stop them: two carpenters, two iron workers, two bosses, sometimes four, two augers, an occasional earth moving equipment guy, and I, the sole labor for all of them. Our lunches constantly contained concrete lime from our clothes. We would form up a pour for the next day, pour in the morning, rip the pour forms from the last day, and leap frog the forms to the next. It was a rhythm that we all knew in our sleep. I was the only one to shovel, rip forms, and transport them. I was to go down into the fifteen foot deep holes and fill buckets with the left over dirt that the five to six foot augers would leave behind then climb out of the hole with a ladder then draw them to the surface by a rope attached to each handle. When the surface was covered between the holes that we were digging for footings, I would get the bobcat tractor, and clear the mess If it was too narrow I would shovel the dirt into the bobcat bucket. I would then move it across the twelve-acre yard to the pile. When the trucks of supplies had to be unloaded they would call me off of my duties to use the extended lift, six-foot-tire-fork lift to unload it. I would also use the lift to carry fifteen-foot rod iron "cages" we had prepared to where they belonged. Each morning, I would start early. I would clear the snow from our trenches with a propane weed burner. It was so cold that the propane would refuse to flow. I would spend as much time heating the tank with the flame from the burner as I would attempt to melt the snow.

My wife and I were not a happy couple. Her temper was sharp and unpredictable. I made an effort every day to leave for work early enough to be an hour early. I would unlock the gate for the crew and sit in my car drinking coffee outside the shack. I was always the first to arrive and the last to leave.

It was a Sunday. I woke up, and I couldn't move. I stood up and fell on my face. The doctor in the town was very open to coming in to her office for me. She took a culture and sent me home for some rest. I didn't know she actually ran it to the hospital herself. The next morning I got a call. She asked me to have someone drive me to her office. I was never one to have anyone do for me something if I was at all capable of it myself. Plus, she didn't know it but my wife never knew how to drive. "The test results came back. We need to get you into the hospital in The Dalles," she spoke quietly and resolute. I've called for an ambulance. "What? You don't think I can take care of my man?" My wife blew a gasket. I am not sure when this became about her but she must have read a script that I didn't. The doctor shot me a look of utter confusion. I shrugged my shoulders as best I could, trying to let her know I understood her dismay. "Listen…Lis…Listen to me." The doctor spoke as calmly as she had moments before. She was experiencing what I did on a daily basis. Nonsense never allows for a word in edgewise.

"Bronchitis"—she started in a low tone that would force my wife to listen—"tonsillitis, strep throat, pneumonia and Mononucleosis."

"Which one?" questioned my wife.

"All of them. And severe dehydration. He could die."

"Oh I doubt it." My wife crossed her arms, leaned her weight on one leg, cocking her other knee, and looked sideways out of squinted eyes at the doctor who had been so kind as to come in on a Sunday, run thirty miles to the hospital and escort my cultures thew a system of tests to insure expedience and accuracy because she feared for the outcome.

What happened next was a caving by me and the doctor to a woman with no compassion or medical expertise. I would go home to have my needs addressed by my wife. Her patience lasted all of about two days. Then I was a "lazy good for nothin…"

It was Monday. We had a late start that day so I had to go down to the boss's trailer rental before work. I told him how sorry I was and how I hated to be the only one to call in sick on this whole job. He in turn told me it was okay. I was going to get my pink slip today anyway. The job was finished. They could handle it. He then went back in his trailer and brought me the pre-filled out slip of termination to be returned to the laborer's union. The date was already filled. I was 175 miles from the laborers office. Side note: The doctor never charged me for any of her services or that of the lab.

BEND, OREGON: KINDNESS COMES IN MANY MASKS

In late '93 early '94, I separated from my first wife. Not the kind of legal separation you get when rich people file papers in court and all of that stuff. No, this was one of those times when she put my bag in front of the door with my clothes and guns in it and said, "If you can't see that I love you, just leave!" Well, after a couple of days of her screaming at me every waking hour, I didn't really feel the love so I just went.

I went shooting almost every day. I was laid off from work and on unemployment. So as long as the union wasn't calling, I had nothing but time. I love to shoot and it was a fine time to hone my skills to the utmost. In my opinion, 500 or more rounds an outing is a great morning. It is probably the best way to lose one's self and possibly to find one's self as well.

One day I went to the range for the umpteenth time in a row and there was another man there. He had an M-1 Garand rifle and a several clips of ammo. We spoke when I first arrived and he let me try a couple of shots. He was pretty impressed with my marksmanship as I hit the center of the target at about 150 yards. Each hole touched the other. The shots were perfect. He had no interest in trying any of my pistols so we stopped talking and went on to practicing separately.

A while later I had lost track of where he had gotten off to. He was shooting up the gravel pit. There was a path, so to speak, cut into the red lava rock. It was wide enough for a 4x4 to travel if you like to ride rough, which most of us do. His target was located up the hill on that trail. My targets were just about anything I could see. I don't need to bring more garbage out to the range. Many people in the past had left their targets behind: old TVs, car batteries, an old refrigerator, the hub cap to an old Cadillac, shotgun shells, and the cigarette butts from my own smokes. I love to set up the old used shells and casings along with a cigarette butt or two or three on the fridge and shoot them off as fast as I could from about fifteen yards. I would put two or three guns on, fully loaded, and a few speed loaders and magazines for the quick reload. I would set up enough targets on the old fridge to make it a challenge and then walk away. When I paced off a good distance I would spin and fire as fast as I could pick them off. I nearly never missed and it was a show for my inner child to see. I want him to know that all of those years of westerns and cap guns had not gone to waste. I would show off for my inner child and I know for sure he would smile.

This day I was loading up a couple of the clips that I had for my Jennings .22 pistol, a small gun I had purchased when it was all I could afford. I shoved a magazine in, chambered a round and started walking a 9mm casing away from me. Walking is when you shoot it many times in a row forcing it to get farther and farther from you with every hit. The point is to do this without hitting it. You just shoot under it causing it to jump away, but if you do hit it, no harm no foul. I made this game up one time when I had shot so much that I became bored. As I was reloading after the fourteenth shot in a row and having moved the 9mm casing nearly completely out of sight, the ground about ten feet behind me exploded. I heard the trailing ricochet as the sound of the rifle shot got to me. The human brain is a marvel in all the animal kingdom. Nothing in the known world can make adjustment to conditions, calculate intricate process or react with instinct faster than a human brain allowed to do its job. Less than a second passed as all of this took place. I drew my Target Bulldog .357 magnum pistol and without a thought fired in the direction of the shot. I could not have known if the shot was intended to hit of scare me, but I knew I was going to make sure there wasn't a second shot. After I fired the first round from the hip, I raised the gun to eye level and placed a shooting solution on my target at over one hundred and fifty yards away, up a hill. A very long distance for a pistol but if you have to make a shot like that it is best to have a .357 mag. loaded with 158 grain semi-jacketed soft tips traveling at over 1300 feet per second to do it with.

On the tip of my front bade site, elevated above the adjustable rear sites was the man I had been talking to earlier. I could see him in a kneeling position at the point where his target was located, his rifle not in his hands. If he had brought his aim a few inches to the right I would have been dead. I watched as he rose to his feet, back peddled a few steps and turned to run into the woods, out of site over the hill and out of my range.

I was very careful as I walked at a half jog, cautiously up the red lava trail. I had three pistols strapped to me and the .357 still in line of site shooting position, waiting for a shooting solution to present itself. I knew he would have plenty of time to go around me if he knew the terrain, but I also was aware that the only fire arm he had was the one he had attempted to end me with. Since I didn't know where that gun was, I was leery of being to open, but knew I had to do my best to get to the top of that hill before he realized how vulnerable I was.

When I got to the top of the hill, I found his rifle on the ground. The trigger assembly was mangled and blood was on the ground. It was obvious that I had succeeded in making an impossible shot. I had shot on the turn and managed a 150 yard pistol shot that literally took off his shooting finger. Parts of which were now parts of the rifle's trigger mechanism. I picked up the rifle and went hunting for the man who wanted me dead.

It took about ten minutes for me to catch him. He was lost and trying to find his way out of the woods when the pain was too much for the sissy, and he just sat at the base of a Ponderosa pine tree, weeping.

I approached him with caution even know I was pretty certain that he was unarmed. "What's up?" I asked him as casually as I could, aiming at his head. He sat with tears and fear in his eyes not answering me. "Dumb thing you did there." I said, calculating the effect.

"Are you gonna kill me?" he asked as I took up a seat next to him on the ground, still aiming the gun at him but a little more relaxed. "Nope," I said. "I don't think I will. But one day I am going to ask you for or to do something. When I do, don't even think about saying no. Just remember today and the kindness that I am showing you. I'm going to keep the rifle as a trophy."

"That was an unbelievable shot."

"Yes it was. Sometimes I amaze even myself." I said. "Maybe the reason I don't want to kill you right now is that you are the only witness I have that I made that shot. Or, perhaps I just needed the excitement in my life. Life gets pretty monotonous sometimes."

"Why'd you shoot at me anyways?"

"Life gets pretty monotonous at times," he said as he held his shattered hand with the two missing fingers. His mood a little lighter, he let out a small giggle at having answered with my words. I'm not sure if he was more relieved to be living another day, or if he had just forgotten his pain through the fear of the unknown. "Now you wait here until you hear a couple of shots. Don't try and follow me out or I might change my mind, but if you wait, I'm going to signal you when I get back to the car to leave. Just follow the sound back to your truck, and you can go. I'm going to take your license with me so I know where to find you if I want to collect on your debt." I held out my hand as he went for his wallet. First with the wounded hand, and then corrected himself by getting it with the left.

I left him there at the base of the tree while I made my way back to the base of the pit. I was pretty pleased with myself for making that shot. At the same time I wondered why I wasn't mad. Sure I had told him a good reason but the question still comes back to me sometimes. His rifle was in a storage unit I lost a while later. I kept it for a few years but a head injury, I'll tell you about soon caused me to lose track of some memories and the storage locker was one of them.

BEND OREGON: TREES MAKE BAD PARKING SPOTS

In 1994, I was separated from my first wife still when I saw a truck that I just had to have. I ignored my faux fear of suburbans but it took a great looking truck to get me to do so. I saw it in the parking lot of the Bend Cinemas where several cars have appeared for sale over the years. It was plastered with homemade signs that spelled out a brief description in barely legible scrawl. It was a 1969, two-wheel drive, suburban. It was jacked up like a 4x4 and had a bumper on it that weighed 300 pounds, had side bars that stood straight up just past the height of the hood, and the sixteen-inch-wide, one-fourth-inch-thick steel wrapped around the corners of the fender wells and instead of your normal flat bumper, came to a point in the very front. The truck was white and the bumper black. I had to have it. I was making enough on unemployment to get it in two weeks so I called the guy on the phone and got him to sell it to me for two payments equaling $500.

At first the truck ran pretty badly. I called up a buddy of mine that has the ability to fix any engine he can touch. His specialty is Chevy, so I knew he could do what was needed to fix this thing up. At the same time, I was a little concerned about the condition of the engine being that the guy I bought it from had claimed to have replaced it just before selling it.

The fix was pretty simple. A little timing and a few crossed wires later we were able to gap the points, and she ran like a raped ape. The only thing missing was a kickdown cable to allow it to shift down when the accelerator pedal is depressed to a certain level. I would get one in the future. For now, I could manually shift if I needed to.

I got a job flagging traffic in the southern part of the state soon after I bought the truck. A suburban makes for a great place to camp when you're broke. I read a book that my brother had given me in the day time. It was called *Job: A comedy of justice* by Robert Heinlein. (To this day it is my favorite book.) At night, I would stand out in the middle of the road with a sign waiting for cars to come while I was bathed in nine gazillion watts of light from a portable light source. Being that this took place near Crater Lake National Park, the traffic was very slow at night. I liked it that way.

I was near the boat launch, enjoying the sun and the cool sound of the water one afternoon on about the fourth day of the job when I went to start the truck to go to work after having just finished the book I had been reading. As the key turned, smoke and then fire came from under the hood. I leaped from my seat and out the door. As I opened the hood, I noticed that the fire was extinguishing itself. The wiring harness had been totally obliterated. There were very few wires left to use for patching it back together, and I had to get to work in half an hour. I immediately started yanking out speaker wires from the stereo system that I had installed prior to going on the job. I would have to follow each scorched wire from its point of origin to the point of ending, and I didn't have time to wait. Luckily, my supply of electrical tape was vast. I had left several rolls in the truck from me and the guys putting in the speakers. I was most worried about the wire to the starter which had most likely been the week point that started the frying wires in the first place. I had no choice. Besides that, it worked. No color coding or fancy connectors. No heat shrink wrap to make my work look good. Just clear, heavy gauge speaker wire and it worked. I made it to work on time and took up my position in the spotlight. I spent my free time standing there when cars were not present, to wrap all of the wires in tape. Bye the end of the night, I had a pretty good looking repair job.

Father's day came while I was on that job. I was able to go to Washington State to see my kids over the weekend. I had to call home and have my roommate deposit my check from unemployment the week before, and I would be able to drive up to see my boys. The first leg of the journey was to get to I-5. The road I had been on linked I-5 to hwy 97. I drove to I-5, turned north, and cruised. The oversized tires couples with a 400 turbo hydromatic transmission and a 350 cu engine made for a 70 mph cruising speed. Sure the limit was 55 mph but who am I to listen to the rules, right?

Around Roseburg, my alternator decided to stop charging the battery. There just so happened to be a grateful dead concert in Salem, so I limped the old beast up to there. Amazing enough, I had no trouble finding a nice place to park for the night, so I went into the crowds of "deadheads" looking for one of two things: "free sister," I said in an elevated voice, and GM alternator. I figured that one of these things would come to me in time. Incredibly enough it turned out to be the free sister. "I just need a place to sleep," she told me at first. "No problem. But we have to share the back of the truck,." I told her as we headed that way.

I think that it startled her a little when I took off my .357 which I had been wearing and placed it near my head for ease of access. She understood when I explained my work situation and the need for security when you're out in the woods all alone.

The morning came soon. She was young and sweet, so I bought us breakfast and found an auto parts store near the truck that just so happened to carry the alternator in stock. It only took a couple of minutes to replace the dead one and return it for the core deposit of about five bucks, that's when she asked if she could come with me and be my girl.

I didn't want to say no. I could have given her a pretty good time, and you never know what may have come of it but my ex was not one to accept me bringing another woman especially since she was still head over heels for me. I had to tell her no and tell her goodbye. I gave her a couple of bucks for the road. We hadn't done anything for her to feel cheap about, so the money was just a nice gesture and not a suggestion. I should have gotten her number. A few minutes later and I continued my trip, alone.

I returned to work after seeing my boys for the weekend. I was happy to be able to go. My boys were overjoyed to see me as well. The job lasted another week as the paving was completed. I returned to Bend and my apartment and friends and to the unemployment line.

A work associate of my roommate's had a lot of vehicles. Included was a Corvette. Believe it or not, this guy replaced the cam out of the Corvette for another hotter model. For whatever reason, he thought it a good idea to give the old one to me. He also gave me a set of tires that were new and a set of headers for the exhaust. I didn't ask for any of this but I tell you what, I appreciated it very much. I had to help another guy cut an Oldsmobile up into small pieces to take to the scrap yard. In the process, I took the front seat. It was high backed and bucketed yet it was a bench so we didn't lose the center seat. We took all the parts and put them on the very next day.

Remember the friend who fixed the timing and the wires? He was all for letting me and my brother get to work out of his garage at his house where we would find more than enough tools to get the job done. His name is Rob. (I have a lot of friends named Rob.) Rob helped with all of the finer tuning items. Timing is essential for a Corvette cam. But we still didn't have the kickdown cable, and we decided to wait on the tires because we had really done a lot for one day.

That truck was hot. I don't know if a suburban has ever had the love and care we put into that truck that day. I was dirty and tired when I got home that night so it figures that my brother would find out at the last minute that a party was going on out in the woods. Plus, we still weren't done for the day.

We had to take an old Volvo to the junk yard before it closed. I didn't have much time so we put on a tow strap and hooked it up. There were no doors so my roommate put on a pair of old motorcycle goggles (he was a Harley Davidson mechanic) and my brother put on swimming goggles. We had to take it down to the salvage yard the back way dirt roads that seldom crossed the pavement. As I pulled them in the car, they had smiles from ear to ear. Every bump was one that a Volvo was never meant to take. The bottom would grind on rocks and at one point we had to stop to put the exhaust into the trunk. Every pound is another few cents in our pockets, you know.

As we wound our way to the junkyard as fast as we could reasonably, or unreasonably go, we came to a road just before we got there, that we all knew well. My jacked up rig would sail over this jump and have us bouncing down the road every time. This time was a little different. The hump rose up to a mound in the middle of the road. From the direction that we were coming, you could not see the other side where it essentially fell out in a cliff- like fashion. I got near the top, down shifted to low one, pounded my foot to the floor (having forgotten about the new fix-up we had done to the engine), and began my leap, only to take the slack out of the tow strap which just about gave the guys whiplash in the car behind me that I was towing, drilled the nose of my truck, steel bumper and all, into the dirt on the other side, and bounced to a halt as I put on the breaks. The guys in the car didn't see me through their dirt covered goggles as they came over the drop off, dug the nose of the Volvo into the same spot I had hit, and nearly drove up my tail pipe before coming to a stop using the emergency break because the breaks don't work on a car that isn't running. Dirt flew, heads snapped, we all laughed, and I broke the bolt in the floor that held my seat belt in place. The same bolt kept the center and driver's belts secure. The guys tried to act mad at me for the attempted neck breaking, but it's pretty hard to be mad when your laughter gives you away.

When we returned to the apartment, my brother went on about the party. He begged and I said no. He pleaded and I said no. After all, I didn't owe him anything. He was living off of me. I fed him and his friend and that guy's girlfriend and put a roof over their heads. He offered to clean my truck before the party, and I said yes. Boy did he, too. He vacuumed it and everything so after a shower and some food, we headed out.

First, we stopped by a love interest of mine. She wasn't home. We headed to another guy's house who knew the location of the party we were headed to, and there was a full blown before-party going on. We already had a case of Heineken in the back of the truck so my brother though it prudent to get loaded in about fifteen minutes that we were there. This was great because he is such a fun drunk. I always love being with a short tempered ass that picks on the weakest target. A bully is too nice of a choice of words. We did, however, find out where we were going. At least as close to directions as you can get from a drunk party animal who is trying to direct you to a location on a dirt road with unmarked turns and forestry roads.

We were finally on our way to the party that I wasn't thrilled to be going to in the first place. As we drove, the alcohol began to fully act on my brother's personality. His charm and grace were in full bloom. Now, I am not really proud of this but there was a boy who was riding with us that night. He was fourteen and had latched on to me as a role model. He had come up from California with my brother and his friends. He was the son of the girl shacking up with my brother's best friend. A guy my brother called "brother" more than he did me. They used to let George, the boy, drive when they would get to drunk or high to drive.

Needless to say, George drove most of the way from California for them.

George was being George when my brother lost his cool and started in. I had to say something real fast or George wouldn't have come out of the situation very well. He was sitting in the middle between us and another guy was in the back seat. The guy in back wasn't a very good conversationalist, however, because he is deaf or at least, mostly. You have to yell to talk to him. My brother was just about to get foolish enough to question my resolve. George was on a roll with the smartly-sense-of-humor-born of a child raised in one of the drug capitols of the United States, when a roll of the tong brought out the words, "Let me drive."

"Nope, I'm not drunk and I haven't even gotten used to this thing yet," I told him with every intention of sticking to my guns. Just then, my brother chimed in. "Come on, man. You know you wanted to drive at his age."

Well this was a change. My brother was on his side so quickly that I might have gotten whiplash if I hadn't been in great shape. If it meant that they were going to get along then I had to do it. I pulled the truck over and gave a few words of warning to George, accepted the appreciative jibes from my brother, and we all peed. (Hey, it's a guys-in-the-woods thing.)

We were miles out in the woods. There was a full moon and the gravel road was a lonely one. Nobody would know about a fourteen-year-old kid taking the wheel. As he did, his foot was heavy. He punched the gas about halfway to the floor, the four-barrel carburetor opened up, gravel flew, and we were off like a shot. The only thing we could see was the trees and gravel roads. Our instructions included the twenty-one miles to the turn, and we were getting close.

George wasn't a bad driver. A couple of times I had to reach over and down shift with the column shifter, but hey, he didn't yet know how to handle this unique monster. My brother and I were talking and I was doing anything I could think of to keep his spirits up. I knew if I didn't then either he and someone else, or he and I, would be fighting by the end of the evening. As we were talking, I looked up at the windshield. The trees filled the glass. No gravel or dirt was within view. I knew this wasn't the way I remembered the road. As I looked at the speedometer, I saw eighty-five miles per hour and thought to myself, *I should probably intervene here.* We were sideways around a corner. George's eyes were wide and I could feel panic roll from him like an ocean wave. I reached up and grabbed the wheel with my left hand and gave it a jerk. I knew we had better straighten out, or we would not like the outcome. My efforts were rewarded temporarily. The truck seemed to want to drift the left turning corner. Unfortunately, fate had other plans. The front tire hooked the edge of the road. There wasn't a soft shoulder out here in the woods. A fact that I didn't know was about to become crystal clear. The gravel road we were on was once paved. The rocks and gravel worked as marbles on glass as we sped around that corner. When the front end hooked the edge, instead of spinning us as we would have preferred, because we had just about rounded the corner, the back end followed and slid down the embankment in a whipping motion. The rear end smashed up against a large rock, shattering the back axle. This swung the front straight into the tree line and the trees reappeared in the windshield.

If you've ever been in a life and death situation then you may recall that sometimes the world comes to a halt just long enough to realize what you are about to go through. When you trip, your mind tells you "this is going to hurt, put your hands down." If an object comes flying in your direction, you have a moment of utter clarity that allows you to move or stay and take it. Well, George had a moment like that. He trusted me to keep him safe and it most likely saved him.

As the rear axle was smashed, we all leaned rapidly to the left. The friend in the back seat scalped his head on the rear window frame. The window was open and so he didn't break any glass. His legs were crossed at the ankle under the front seat. Having his left over his right caused his left hip to be ripped out of the socket. That was the entire extent of his injuries. As painful as that sounds, he was lucky.

My brother was belted in the front seat on the passenger side. His first motion was to the left as all of ours was. He was cushioned by my body. His seat belt was the only one attached in the front due to the prior playful dirt dive.

George in that moment was driving. His grip on the steering wheel was tight with fear but not near enough to stop my two-hundred pounds from freeing it. George told me that when that happened he knew that if he grabbed around my neck he would be safe so he wrapped his arms around me and there he stayed, completely unaware that his ring finger on his left hand had been severed by my weight freeing his grip and was only held on by a thread of skin.

I came across George and gave him the chance to grab on, I guess. But the ride was not finished. We were all still in motion. The trees in the windshield were now coming on fast. Our angle changed, we were at eighty-five miles per hour with saplings passing the side windows, the sounds of mowing them down was a portent of things to come.

Just ahead was a full grown pine tree. It was immobile and unwavering. There was no chance of winning a contest with that adversary. The tree was large enough to take three quarters of the entire hood of my 1969 Chevy suburban without budging. At this point, the truck impacted with an enormous, metal-crushing thud that was heard over a mile away.

The friend in the back seat was thrown into the back of the front seat. He was lying down from the first impact. His injuries were at an end and he started to moan. A dark and silent world was now surrounding him. His hearing impairment must have made the fear overwhelming as the lights were now extinguished from the impact of the collision.

My brother was lying down at the point of impact. My body being pulled from under his head, his upper torso flew forward as the seat belt held his waist in place. As the impact completed, his chest was held in place on the floorboard of the truck. Because as he went forward, the big, newly finished 350cu inch engine came to meet him. Buffered only by the fire wall to protect him from the heat, we were all thankful for the steel body of that beast that night. Somewhere in the mix of it all, his only major injury took place. George was smart in the moment when it counted most. He held on. He was to get a small nick out of his forehead from glass on the windshield but that was a small price to pay to fly on Superman's back that night. Of all the things that could have happened, I am most thankful for the few that actually did.

With my passenger securely in place, I took to flight. First, however, I would have to free myself. As I mentioned earlier, the seat belt was broken so that was no point of contention. I would have to get that steering wheel out of the way though. It was a small racing style with three spoke styling. My first injury probably occurred when I took that in the chest. The wheel spanned from mid-sternum to hip. I bent it backward, completely inverting it with my weight. This exposed the three bolt heads, so just for good measure one of them took a chunk of me from the tip of my penis while I passed by. That left my legs under the metal dashboard. Thigh bones are strong but we all know what happens to a board when the proper force is put to them. The bones broke like wet pine branches. Not clean but rather flexed. All of this was happening as the tree was bringing the hood up to a folded peak. I was really eager to meet up with it I guess. Once freed from to the points that held me, I flew face first through the glass windshield, George protected from debris with the exception of his forehead getting cut by windshield glass as we passed. I met the hood as it rose up to greet me with my face. I had paint in my front tooth from the hood's old paint job until 2006. The angle allowed me to ricochet upwards as if taking to the sky. One problem, however, if I was to take flight, that tree was going to have to move. Since that wasn't likely to happen, I took great impact with my face once more. Heck, it had worked before and everything seemed to have moved—the windscreen, the hood. This caused me to bounce off of the tree and land on my feet at which time George fell off of my back and landed with a thud in the thick pine needles that covered the forest floor.

Laughing, George asked me, "What happened?" I answered him with a half giggle, half pissed off tone, "You wrecked my gawd-damned truck!" I was bent over slightly at the waste when I shook my head like a wet dog coming from a lake and did my Donald Duck impression. I looked down at George in the darkness and could make out what looked like blood covering his face. "Oh my!" "Don't worry," he said reassuringly while stifling a laugh, "It's yours." With this revelation, he rose to his feet and dusted himself off. "Fuck, my fingers torn off!" he then went over to the truck where the battery was still lighting the radio. Turning to me, George yelled out, "Marks dying!" I went to the side of the truck and looked through the window. A large flap of skin hung from his neck. We would find out later the rear-view mirror had freed itself in the impact and flown through the cab like a throwing star. It cut my brother from the corner of the mouth, downward in a U-shape and come back up behind his ear. Meanwhile, I could hear the friend in the back seat screaming out as he realized the pain and felt the fear of silence in the dark.

I thought for sure my brother had cut his jugular vein. It was a miracle I guess, that saved his life. The wound was skin deep, exposing the artery but not severing it. I didn't know that. I couldn't have. I just needed to be there in that truck to help him out. I leaped over the hood of the truck and back through the window. I cut my butt on the left over glass as I entered into our would-be grave. I gently took up his head as the radio played AC/DC in slow motion and the light was in the first stages of fading. It didn't take long to realize that he was securely stuck in position. That seat was placed in there to stay and stay it did.

We talked. George was right there. I sent him to the road to see what he could but the light was so low we were on our own. I reached in the back to help out our deaf comrade and this seemed to help. My brother and I discussed our childhoods and what our mother was going to say. We spoke of the things we should have done, and we spoke of the case of Heineken that had flown to the front of the cab and shattered all over him. The waste of the broken bottles and the beer drinkers curse we may have to face. We joked about me reaching back into the back seat and replacing the massive clump of scalp that had been scalped from our friend in the back seat. I wondered if I was going to lose him that night. No one knew where we were, and we were a long ways out.

It's not possible for me to tell you how it felt to have a small pick-up truck pull up on the side of the road near us. Two girls were out camping about a mile down the road when they heard the loud impact. They jumped into their little truck and came out to find us. I don't know who they were, but they were a welcome sight. I sent them on to get help. The nearest place was thirty miles out, Sunriver.

Time went pretty smooth from that point. About an hour in real time flew as though only minutes. I knew as the light died and the tape stopped playing, that my brother would live. He had stopped bleeding and the flap of skin in my hand was sticking to the wound. George had handled everything like a trooper. Our friend in the back had taken to minor whining. As far as I could tell, everyone would do just fine.

Search and rescue, two ambulances, and AirLife were scrambled to the scene. It took two "jaws of life" to free my brother form the seat. We had done a fine job of bolting that sucker in. George and the friend from the back seat took one ambulance. My brother and I shared the other. I sat while he was laid down. We drove up to a cross road intersection where the chopper could land. My brother was taken from the ambulance and flown in to the hospital. He was assumed to be the worst. I was sitting in the ambulance waiting for the EMT to return. When he did, he asked if I would like to lie down. "No thanks," I said as he looked at me confused. "I think the rules say that we have to have you lying down," he said as he signaled toward the gurney. "Well then," I said with a humor in my voice that covered my relief to have these people here taking the responsibility out of my hands.

It was a forty-five minute ride to the hospital. When I got there, our friend from the back seat was already in surgery. My brother was as well. George was smiling at me as I was wheeled in. "Wanna race?" I asked joining him in a grin.

The plastic surgeon was there soon after my arrival and walked straight over to me. "Go ahead and get him first." I gestured toward George, the fourteen-year-old boy with a bloody forehead and a severed finger. "He has a whole life ahead of him. Make him pretty," I said with a smile. She was gathering her implements of the craft.

"Have you seen yourself?"

"No?" I said with a little question in my tone. She gathered a mirror from another table and brought it over. She looked at me for a brief moment and sighed, then she handed me the mirror.

I had no idea that I was about to see the worst of us in the mirror. As I looked into the mirror I could see straight into my sinus. My nose had been severed both on the right outside nostril all the way to the bridge of the nose. The center of the nose, the part that separates the nose holes was completely severed, and my entire nose was swung open like a front door inviting the world to see inside. If I had sneezed I may have lost it. I had a split in my right eye brow from eye lid to the center of my forehead.

My right eyelid was severed and pinned with dried blood to the beginning of my ex-nose hole, where the nostril used to be. It was held on by a thread of skin in the inside corner of my eye. Two streaks were cut into my cheek bone, each of about two and a half to three inches horizontally. She started sewing.

All told, I had two stress fractures in my femurs: a well-broken nose, my sternum was cracked from top to bottom, a very good and strong concussion, dislocated clavicle, over 240 stitches to put my face back together, and I was up taking care of the rest. (Well, George and I were.) In a year, memory loss would cause me to go in for a CT scan that would reveal three separate places where my jaw was broken and eleven vertical fractures to my forehead.

Follow up to this is as follows:

The accident occurred at 12:00 a.m. July 1st, 1994. By eight that morning, I was helping my roommate take the engine out of his VW bus. Eight days later, I was called on a job to work with the final phase of the pipeline job that I had worked dynamite on earlier in the season. The first task was to rebuild all the fences around the pumping stations and haul off all of the cement. I must have looked quite the site with my bruised face and cast on my nose. I saw more than a little skepticism in the boss man's eyes when he first saw me. I still had the concussion and broken everything but I was not going to let that ruin my reputation. Everyone knew I was the go to guy for the jobs other guys couldn't handle. I spent my life proving that if to nobody else but to myself. By the end of the job, I was loading five ton trucks with hay that I would then feed into a mulching spreader that looked like a cannon and sprayed the hay like a water cannon. One guy would swivel that thing back and forth while I ran the seventy- five pound bails as fast as I could, cut the ties and fed them into the chute. The only other guy on the crew, the boss, would drive at the slowest, creeping speed the truck could manage. This all helped to hold the seed down that they had spread while I was driving to the farm to get the hay.

My brother was cooped up at his ex-girlfriend's house for a while. His spirit was pretty well-shattered. The death of a favorite dog of ours finally brought him out for the funeral. The friend from the back seat sued for the majority of the insurance money. He screwed the rest of the guys out of their ability to have something good come of their pain as insurers only split $50,000 between them and he took $25,000. I didn't expect anything. It was my insurance. George has turned out to be a pretty good guy, from what I hear. I wonder if he ever stops to think what a great decision it was to grab on to my neck like that. It probably saved his life.

BEFORE THE QUAKE

February 28, 2001 is a day that most people in the "Great (yeah right) Northwest" can tell you where they were. An earthquake with a magnitude of 6.8–7.0, depending on the source, occurred as the midday traffic was about to wind up. Many old buildings fell apart. Brick was the worst. I personally got a brick from the Seattle chocolate factory. Lights and power were down and cell phones were useless after the first couple of minutes as they were shut down to allow use by emergency services. I didn't even know it had happened.

I had been with my wife a few moments before the actual shaking started. I played hooky from an hour of work and met her at my son's "mommy and me" tumbling classes. We had a great time, and I was so happy to get to spend time with them that I was in a cloud when I got back into the nearly empty, old, decrepit, rattling linen delivery van, and drove off, oblivious of the shaking, rattling and rolling. There were empty racks made of wire and an empty plastic tub on wheels that I was trying to get down town to deliver, when I gladly found myself sidetracked by the family issue. To say that the noise in the vehicle was obnoxious is way too much of an understatement.

The night before was Mardi Gras. The city of Seattle had experienced several acts of vandalism. The news had shown riots that were national news. Bomb threats were called in to many business and the police were feckless in their protection. One scene had shown a wall of policemen in complete crowd control regalia, standing against the wall down town, as a black man chased another down the street, shooting at him. The police made no effort to catch him. Heck, they never even stepped away from their leaning post on the wall and that was on the news, live and in color.

As I entered the highway, I notice a slew of cars pulled over to the side of the road. Many were carrying out the same ridiculous routine that I swear, I have never had a reason to do myself. They were each shaking the front tires of their cars as if their tires had, some how, miraculously all loosened at the same time. I saw this display of spontaneous retardation and put my foot further toward the floor. All I could think of was a sniper shooting out tires and I was unarmed and a big target in the delivery van. I just wanted off of the road and away from the danger zone. I figured that the police could handle this one.

I entered the downtown area and drove toward the skyscraper forest that held the old-age home that I was to drop this roller bin at. I noted that many of the buildings had people outside looking up at them. "Oh my Gawd," I said to myself. "Some jerk is calling in bomb threats. These poor fools don't even know how silly they look."

My drive to the old fogy home was over an hour long. Normally, it would have taken about half of that. I did get there though. I range the buzzer and showed my credentials and was allowed in for my delivery. I placed the bin in its proper place and went in for the signature that I needed. "Hey, you guys might want to be careful. I think that someone is calling in bomb threats. Everyone is out looking at their buildings. You know how nuts it was down town here last night," I said, feeling as if I was passing the information that would save them time and hassle. "Or it could have been that earth quake," the manager said without looking up from the paper he was filling out on the table. *Or that,* I thought that he was joking. The radio in the truck was not working and had probably not been for several years. It wasn't for another half an hour that I heard from a friend through my cell phone, that there had actually been a real quake. I was well into traffic then. It was soon well-known how I had left my wife and baby in the middle of a quake and not even known it. I was teased about that for a long time. After all, I live for natural disaster and I seam to miss it every time.

My wife was in the gym. She kissed me goodbye and watched me walk out to the delivery van. I started the engines and she returned to speaking with the owner of the gym who was a friend of ours. She heard the noise and then the shaking began. She told me how the wooden building swayed and shimmied and the owner started screaming her head off and would not quit. Our youngest son just watched and looked for some kind of reason in what was going on. The owner continued to scream. The ground rolled under their feet and the building swayed and creaked. The owner continued to scream.

My wife at the time said she was waiting for me to return at any moment. I did not. I was on my way elsewhere. When the whole thing was over, she waited for me while she calmed the owner of the gym. I did not return. I sometimes wonder what percentage of our relationship was lost that day. It's terrible when the superhero flies away just before they are needed.

Today, for example, I have my days, boy do I have my days. Today is the perfect example for this book to tell what a day in the life of me is really like.

Let us start at the very beginning, 1:00 a.m.

With all of the kids out of school, my kids had a friend over. To call her a friend is an understatement as she has endeared herself to us so much that we consider her to be family. Erin is her name. She is eight years old as of this month and is the friend of my girlfriend's daughter, Nikki. She stays over more than once a week average and eats here more than four days a week on average. If dinner is done and she isn't here, don't get to comfortable because there is a strong chance that her little knuckles will be wrapping on the door in short order.

Connor is also eight and also my girlfriend's child. So at one in the morning, I hear a knock on the bedroom door. "Who is it?" I ask in my old man, grumpy-old-fart voice from a barely there grasp of reality.

"Connor."

"What?" I ask in the aforementioned voice.

"Nicole is taking the whole bed and Erin wants to go home," he says, knowing that waking me is taking his little life in his hands.

"Oh...Oh-kaaay?"

"What can I do?" I ask puzzled because this hasn't happened before. "She wants Piggy." Sure enough, I was baby sitting her ever present Piggy. I had him still tucked under my arm. He had eaten popcorn and watched the movie with me and Connor's mother. I then cuddled him as if he were my own stuffed animal and dozed off to sleep. So there he was and she wanted him back so she could go home.

"Come on in and get him," I said a little sad as the realization came to me that we had let down our near-daughter.

Connor opened the door and came in. He grabbed the little stuffed pig from under my arm and smiled as if it were silly to see a two hundred and fifteen pound, six-foot-four-inch man with a pink Piggy. So I laid my head back down on my pillow and almost let myself drift back off into the dream world. But I couldn't. I had to see if I could save the situation.

I dressed appropriately for the company and went out into the hallway and to the doorway of the kid's room. I saw Erin in the room. She was packing up to go. Nikki was already fast asleep. Once she falls asleep, a tornado would be but a lullaby to her. She and her family have a sleep disorder that makes them comatose until they choose to awaken. Connor wasn't in the room at the time but came to the room when he heard Erin and I talking. "Do you want me to make you a bed on the floor?" I asked in my sweet daddy voice.

"Naw, the carpet is infested with ants," she said. And she was right. We have a problem with ants in this complex of apartments. That and teens who break the globes off of the small sidewalk lights are about my only complaint with this place. Without further thought she plucked up the cell phone from the strap that she wears without fail, around her neck and dialed her house.

"My dad's coming to get me," she said.

"It's okay." My heart sunk as I said goodnight and returned to bed where my girlfriend was having dreams of kickboxing or something and I was positioned well as a punching bag.

At 5:30 a.m., the dog let me know that just because the kids had a couple of days off didn't mean that his schedule had changed. So I got up and took the dog out into the rain. I smoked a cigarette as the rain pelted me in my bathrobe. Coda, the doggy dude took way too long and was far less concerned about getting wet than I was. When he finished his business, I put my hand into the plastic grocery bag, flipped it inside out, and reached for the pile of doggy doody. Sleep still ravaging my brain, I scarcely noticed the moisture accompanying the warmth of a newly formed pile. "Moisture." More of a mental statement of fact. "Moisture?" Now becoming more of a question in my head. "*Moisture!*" A sudden acknowledgment that in order for the inside portion of the bag to be wet, there had to be a hole.

Coda and I deposited the bag of stuff into the dumpster and returned to the apartment. My swearing actually was leaving my face in the form of an incoherent mumbling. I swear that Coda was snickering at me in his doggy way as he watched me washing my hands in the kitchen sink. "Soap, lots of soap. Good dog. More soap." Now I couldn't return to bed. I was awake. Good news for me, however, was that the coffee pot had been placed on timer out of habit. Bad news was the coffee in the pot had brewed for a long time before being shut off so the timer was set but the coffee was old and burned. I grumbled as I sat at the computer and turned it on while sipping tar from my mug.

Everything went pretty well for the next hour until I had to wake my woman from her slumber. After the usual shaking and sweet talking, rolling and shaking, talking sweetly and rumbling, and the alarm sounding for the umpteenth time, she opened her eyes. I said something, she said something, then I said…She was asleep again so fast that I had not uttered a sentence. I continued the waking ritual.

She has to be to work this day at 8:00. At 7:20 (mind you I'm still in my robe and jammie bottoms), she comes out of the bathroom with a great idea. "You know what would be great?" she starts out. "If you ran over to Winco and got some doughnuts for my meeting this morning."

I said, "No it wouldn't," as I looked down myself in a gesture of 'are you kidding me?' "It's okay, you don't have to, I just thought that it would be great for me to bring something for the meeting, and you could get you and the kids some too." I went back to my seat in front of the computer where my daily dose of news and editorial was on and my e-mail was up waiting to be read. I thought to myself about how the kids would like to wake up to fresh doughnuts, and how I would be hearing about this for the next twenty years or so if I didn't change my mind.

I went to my room where she was getting ready for work. "Maybe you could get ready a bit faster and stop for them yourself," I said as if that plan would ever work.

"It's alright. You don't have to." (as I put on my pants) "I won't hold it against you in twenty years." She said this as a play on my own joke that she would hold things against me in twenty years. I begrudgingly got dressed and went for the doughnuts.

I arrived back at the apartment in time to catch her outside starting her truck to warm up. I watched her walk back into the house as I drove down the hill. I parked in the spot next to her truck and put the pastries on her passenger seat and went on into the house. My frustration with her was a little obvious so our goodbye kiss was much more brief than normal and she headed out to work.

Tonya (my girlfriend) works at a bank. She works with women and that in itself tells what kind of day she has, women gossiping and smearing one another in order to get some sort of unspoken recognition. E-mailing endlessly to someone out in the ether, every movement of the bowels, cigarette break, mistakenly black pen used where a blue should have been used, shredder malfunction, verbal gaff, hell, date of manufacture on every dime I guess from the amount of time one of the ladies (and I use the term lightly) spends on the e-mail.

The newest girl used to be a barista and can't make a pot of coffee, clean a pot, grind a bag for customers, fill little one-fourth pound bags for the customers, or any of the things that someone having nothing else to offer on their resume' would be capable of achieving. She can't open the store of do any of the tasks asked of her past immediate duties of cashier. She doesn't offer to help when someone is obviously in need of it, for instance, Tonya went to a school and got the children to start savings accounts for their future. In all, it looks as though it will be forty-eight to fifty-eight kids' accounts to open. (It turned out to be 72.) Each having the additional responsibility of having a parent cleared to be on the account as well. After two days, the e-mail woman offered and registered four of the accounts. The new girl did, wait for it…wait for it…zero. Not a single one to help her fellow worker. So on this day, Tonya had a misunderstanding with the e-mail monkey. The manager and her boss who does not work in the bank branch were there. The manager stepped into the situation, making it into a conflict where a minor miswording had taken place.

CUT BACK TO THE HOUSE

I sat in listening to my morning conservative talk show. My little girl and I were watching one of my TV shows together a little later when a knock on the door had us pause it. The upstairs neighbor was asking in her very limited English whether or not I have contacted the management to fix the leak that she has in her bathroom. You see, the night before, we had a fast drip occur in our master bath when the neighbor flushed her toilet. Tonya was sitting on the toilet smoking in the bathroom at the time. We were just minding our own business, smoking, and talking when the drip went right down the back of her neck. I rushed up the stairs and alerted my neighbor's two adult children, asking them to translate the emergency nature of the problem to her. So this morning, she wanted to know if I had contacted the management. I said yes, more or less because trying to explain my morning would require enlisting English to Russian dictionary, Google translator, and a lot of charades.

As soon as she left, my daughter and I went to the manager's office to report the problem. "I have an emergency maintenance problem," I told her. I was expecting a few hours to get the apartment cleaned up, vacuum up all the dog hair from the unreported beast of a dog, hide said beast, straighten my room, clean my bathroom, etc. But NOOoooo. She didn't even let me finish the explanation. Once I got the point out about a toilet leaking through the ceiling, she was on the radio to the head of maintenance. "Thank-you," I said trying to remain calm. Then Nikki and I were out the door and planning the frantic cleaning, vacuuming, hiding, etc., to take place. I figured we would still have a fifteen minute gap to fill. No such luck. As we came down the hill from the office, we witnessed the maintenance golf cart moving at high speed through the parking lot. He was headed straight to our place. It was a race to the wire.

We parked in the last space available to us. This left him to park a little out of view of us. We ran as fast as we could into our place. Nikki got the dog onto the back porch and closed the shades just as I heard the door. I answered the door and said, "Come with me, right into the master bath." It's the same spot as before. (I had a leak form a hole in the drywall a year earlier.) As we rushed up the hall to the master bedroom, I pushed him feverishly to the disaster while trying to avoid him seeing large, black hair balls on the floor that looked like mice in the darkness. I let him pass as we entered the room. I then turned to Nikki and whispered to pick up the hair of the floor. She disappeared briefly, as the man checked on the sight of the impending dribble. Nikki signaled me from the hallway, then came to me closer, as I was unable to make out what it was she was trying to tell me. "I can't!" she whisper yelled. "Look."

There in the hall was an enormous pile slash puddle of doggy poo. I then saw a couple of drips lead up the hall to another smeared mess in front of the kids door, eight or ten feet away. Apparently, the dog's tummy was not doing well. I must have walked within inches of it. After coming in to the dark hall from the lit room, my eyes had not adjusted well until we got past the nastiness. Once adjusted, my eyes then started to water from the strong stench. As I returned to the bathroom to check on our maintenance guy, he darted out past me on his way to the door. I sidestepped to place myself between the odiferous pile and him, "I have a sick kid." My excuse was thin but it would have to do.

As soon as the door closed, I sprang into action. I grabbed a bag, gripped as much as I could and went for the trash. I darted back into the hall with paper towels in hand. "Knock, knock!" a rapid knock on the door. He was back. I led him this time, not stopping as I dropped the paper towels over the piles. Nicole, at this time, went into the bathroom and pretended she was brushing her teeth.

"Nasty, yeach! My mouth tastes horrible after throwing up," she said in a perfect acting performance.

After he left, I cleaned the house vigorously. I steam cleaned the floor with my portable steam cleaner and mopped the floor in the front entryway where the dirt from muddy, rain drenched shoes had left it looking like we were a family of farmers. Then we scrambled to shut kids doors to hide the mess and vacuum the entire house. I cleaned out the steam cleaner and all of the nasty that it held. (Bleach smell over doo any time.) All the while the dog was on the back porch where we have no facing neighbors. I wasn't sure if or when the maintenance guy would come back.

Tonya came home for lunch during all of this cleaning and was in disbelief at the happenings. Her day was a miserable disaster as well, so we swapped stories in the master bath as we smoked together. After Tonya left to go back to work, we finished cleaning, let the dog in and I finally sat down.

Lucas was at the computer by this time. We talked and joked about how some things in life just have bad timing as well as how bad the house smelled. Squirt bottle air freshener made it slightly more bearable. We also had all of the windows open and were shivering from the less than friendly breeze. The dog had a few heaving spells over the next five or ten minutes and I had to clean spots of vomit off of the floor in the living room. Lucas then went to go to the bathroom. He entered the hallway and turned around. "I can't," he said with a "darn-it" look on his face. "Is someone in the bathroom?" I asked, puzzled. "Nope... He did it again."

"Are you serious or are you joking?" I asked this with the knowledge that it had happened but with the hope that it had not. I began to clean again. Oh what a mess. The poor guy couldn't help himself, I know, but oh how it smelled.

More air freshener, more steam cleaning, more air freshener, more scrubbing out of the machine. And more worries as to whether we would be reported and evicted. Oh-my, what-a day.

Tonya's day at work had gone just as bad. She had gotten into trouble for correcting a fellow employee in front of the boss's boss. When she came home, we talked about her day and what had transpired and how she had gotten back to work to find that she had been written up for the "conflict" that never really happened. They took her monthly bonus for the entire month when she had shown exceptional successes in her work life. Her accomplishments were now subject to a gray cloud. All of the joy from doing so well and bringing in so many new accounts and working so feverishly to accommodate school kids, teachers, networking groups, and regular customers who regularly wrote wonderful comment cards on her, now clouded by despair; any bonus for opening new accounts or bringing in customers, gone for the whole month; her manager, whom she has tried to talk with and tried to ask for assistance asked her why she hadn't come to her before with problems. "There is no feeling of confidentiality," she told her. And if you knew the whole story about the gossip in there, you would understand why. Tonya is an outcast for not being willing to gossip. Funny thing is, the manager as much as told her so in the one on one conference to discuss her write-up. Sometimes when it rains it pours. (Out the wrong end!)

THAT'S NOT NORMAL

In August of 2008, I was driving trucks for UPS freight. I would deliver products that were too big for the smaller delivery vans. Most of it was over 70 pounds and so would have to be sent through us. A lot of it was several hundred pounds. I had the route that serviced Bellevue, Washington. I spent my days weaving into receiving areas that commonly had me backing between Porsche, Mercedes, Lamborghini, Ferrari, and so on. Nobody wanted my route because it required a lift gate on the back of the trailer. Most of my route had no dock for semi-tractor trailers and the work required a substantial amount of lifting. Car parts, couches, Fricken Treadmills, Awnings, professional printers, even septic tanks and tractor parts; Buckets, extending arms, etc.

On the morning of August 30, I was forced to take a series of truck leaf springs off of the pallet and load them on the back, one by one. Each weighed about 185 pounds. They were to be delivered to another branch of the company as my first delivery.

Every day, we drivers would organize our loads as we saw our route requiring. It isn't as easy as just going in order like the regular household deliveries, although we had many of those as well. Some business won't take things until they are ready. Others want to be the first or even before the route starts. It is a talent just to get the truck loaded and each driver must know their area. Also, most drivers don't want to kill themselves and so they only take ten or eleven stops. Mine ran between sixteen and twenty two. I couldn't leave anything behind. I wasn't built to slack off.

I always make it known, wherever I have worked, that I am the guy that can be counted on in any situation. I would sometimes take a truck out with one or two deliveries that took up the whole trailer and then return for my own, even know it meant being behind on mine or going sixty miles round trip out of my way. I would, on occasion be singled out as the guy to take one delivery that was way out of my route, to a stubborn customer because nobody else could handle them as well. I always handled them very well and found ways to make most of them smile as I was leaving, with a joke or a smart alec comment back at them, but always with a modicum of respect. You want to know the strange thing though? I was almost always in to the terminal before anyone else. The other guys would say that I was working myself out of a job or giving away hours. No wonder they went union.

This morning, I arrived at the small package plant of UPS in plenty of time. I opened the sliding door on my trailer and out fell the first spring. I almost grabbed it when I remembered that it is covered with a film of oil to protect it from rusting. So I went into the warehouse to find one of the guys who could get a fork lift to come get it.

After twenty minutes or so, I was getting behind schedule. I had expected to be done in five minutes. It was like a ghost town in this place. Without a thought, I grabbed my gloves from inside the driver's door, beside my seat and went to the back of my truck. I knew where they went. It was a short twenty feet from where it sat. So, I picked it up in perfect form. Something that isn't often possible when actually lifting things out in the field, so to speak. As I straightened up with the spring in hand, I felt an electric zap and a sting in my lower back. "That's not normal," I said out loud to myself. I then squatted back down, let the piece slip from my hands and could not stand back up.

I did get back to my feet. I did finally find someone. The pain grew worse by the minute as I continued the delivery. I asked him, "You guy have all of those used hand truck and I am surely injured. Is there any way I could borrow one? Our boss won't even replace our hand trucks or pallet jacks and mine disappeared some time ago."

"Nope, you can't borrow one. See ya later." He was a bastard I'm sure. No woman who would give birth to a guy like that could find a man to marry her.

I used our little computer called a DIAD, to send a message for help. I then drove to the next of my deliveries. I messaged again and drove to the next, and the next and the next. I never got a message back. By early afternoon, the pick-ups were on and I was getting them too. All day, I just had the customers get their own stuff. All of them knew me and knew that I wouldn't ask if it weren't for real. My final home delivery was a fifty-pound box. It was about two-feet high and four-feet square. I cut it from the pallet on the back of the truck and attempted to carry it to the front door. Suddenly, a burn started at the point of the initial injury and burned its way to my upper spine. As I got to the door, I apologized to the lady for not bringing it further in. I told her of my injury and she understood.

It was humiliating for me to have to ask for the help from my customers all day. I worked the twelve hours before I called in and said, don't send me another pick-up, I'm coming in." The ride back to the terminal was thirty miles of hell in stop and go traffic. Every bump intensified my pain. Every push of the clutch required phenomenal courage. When I got back, I couldn't pick up my clip board. [and] I had to crawl up the stairs.

In dispatch, this was the verbatim conversation:

Me: "I'm hurt. I need a ride to the hospital."

Second boss in charge, Steve: "Knock it off." (All were friends of mine and still are. This was thoughtfully taken as a joke.)

Me: "Steve! I'm really hurt and I can't drive myself. I need to go to the hospital."

Steve: No time you goof. Busy. You'll have to die right here. (Looking my way really quickly and then back to what he was doing.) No blood. If you're hurt, where's the blood."

Dispatcher: Hi! What cha doin? (Tickity tickity on the type keys.)

Me: "Okay, Okay! Please...I am serious. I really hurt my back and I can't walk. I am barely able to stand. Could somebody please take me to the hospital?"

New boss and true dick: "Go out and unhook. Why you standing around?"

Me: "Gawd! Don't you hear me? You're standing right here. I need a ride to the ER."

New boss and true dick: "Okay then. I'll get my keys." He then took a long pause and looked into my eyes, turned and walked out shaking his head.

He dropped me at the ER, alright, out at the far end of the sloped parking lot. "Call me when you're finished," he told me. I got the diagnosis of torn muscles. I was given four days off of work. Each night you could hear me climb the stairs as every step I unintentionally let out a moan. Even after the doctors confirmed there was an injury, my new boss treated me as a fake. I had doctor appointments for ten weeks and was on light duty, running the night office work. All the while, my doctor insisted on the torn muscle idea. At my request the insurance finally asked for an MRI and found that my discs had been squished flat and were squeezing off the nerves in my back.

After treatment that consisted of "come back next week" and "does it still hurt?" I went in for an injection into my spine. I should say three. Because they give you shots into the area of soft skin at the tip of your tailbone. One for pain that hurt like hell, one for dye to see what they are doing under the x-ray, that hurt like crazy, (And shows that they were unable to see what they were doing to this point.) and the final one to stab into your main nerve and send you through the ceiling. I went back to work and eventually left the company and went to work for another. On February 12, of the following year, my spine gave way. The damage was too extensive and the discs to misshapen. I had essentially crushed my spine from too many years of hard labor. My vertebrae are damaged as well and the last one is in contact with the one above it.

The first month of the injury, my son, Brandon had to feed me coffee and my oldest had to drive me to the doctors. I got to work each night out of sheer willpower. Medications didn't help and the company was self insured so the money that I was already unable to live on, became less than a third of what we were used to. We were hungry and the rent was late and all of the fine trappings of the poor were the things that we wished that we had.

The last time I went into the ER in February, I asked the doctor how long it would take to get back to work. He said, "How long till you want to be paralyzed?"

I may never be able to do the things that I have done or be the person I was, but I teach my children my fighting skills and I am trying to pass on the work ethic that I have developed throughout my life. I want them to know who I was and why. Who I am now is still able to do what most men can't. But, I was able to bench press 550 pounds and did preacher curls with 200 pounds. I could out run any man (the older I got the faster I got) and fly with eagles. I jumped from planes and fought with giants and no one could tear me down. The only person to ever defeat me was me. I survived a heart attack and a mental break down and never missed a day of work. I played with them on the trampoline and chased them and the entire population of the park in a giant game of tag. I hung by my toes from a swing set pole just to be a goof. I carried my kids on my legs, held out straight, while swinging on the monkey bars, hand over hand for several minutes as they laughed with glee. I taught them to dive and swim and play like children, because I was one of them. I saved people and children and rescued people from fires. A few of these things I may do again, but for the most part, those days came to an end when I was 38 years old.

FLY TOYOTA, FLY!

While I was hurt the first time with the broken back, my children showed such great strength that I wanted to reward them. You see, money was hard and we missed Christmas and Easter and the birthdays. So, when I went back to work, the very day I went back to work, I got a call saying that the fourth time I had reapplied for my insurance, it was accepted. I had been rejected three times. So when the check arrived the next day, for $1200, I bought my two eldest, 14 and 16, new matching laptop computers. They were refurbished, but they had warranties and looked new. I even upgraded the ram to maximum. I also bought my youngest a game system that he was really wanting. At the same time, I had recently had two land rover vehicles die in the same day and was in the process of killing the last days of a Frankenbunny VW Rabbit. So when my taxes came in, I bought a Toyota Supra, turbo.

All was well with the car. It was fast as lightning. I had a race down the highway where an old man in a Porsche pulled along side and signaled me to go, so we stood on it and opened up the turbo.

The speeds climbed and the force sat me back in my seat. We were neck in neck when he suddenly fell back. I looked up and there was a wall of traffic a mile ahead, over the hill we had topped. I glanced down before applying break and we were passed the 155 mph speedometer reading where mine ended. So I know the car was fast to begin with. Stock, they are said to pull 160 mph. I believe it.

My car developed a head gasket leak and so I took it to the local shop to be fixed. I called on it a week and a half later to be told that they had done nothing to it. I was very angry. Just then, a friend and one of the mechanics at our shop said that he would do the job very cheep. So we made arrangements to pick up the car and take it to his house. I would buy the parts, and we would work together to get it on the road again.

I bought all of the best parts. Everything was top of the line. I even bought red hoses and a matching intake filter. The best gasket package, replacement belts, and even eight dollars and ninety-nine cents a piece spark plugs. It took some time, but it finally was ready for the road.

I drove it to work for a week as a test. If all went well, the badges would be put back on in the next weekend. So, I enjoyed having it back and driving my baby. But the low end was not where it should be so we tweaked it a little bit more and badged it and took out for a test drive.

There was a sputter in the engine after a high pressure hose was used to clean the engine. The best fix for that is to run it out until the water evaporates. We took it to the store with a friend's daughter in the back seat. She had washed it up for us and so deserved a ride. On the way back from the store, I was told to take a little side road. "Go!" my mechanic yelled. I stepped hard on the throttle.

"The corner!" yelled Haven from the back seat. I let up on the gas.

"It's a long way up here. Go for it!" says my mechanic friend. Gas on.

"The corner!" Haven was adamant.

Gas off. About now, we were topping the high point in the road and I could see the corner. I put my foot into the gas and we topped 100 mph from 30 mph in a blink. The car was smooth as glass at 120 mph. At 135 mph the corner was fast approaching. I took my foot off of the gas and applied the...Oh Gawd! "No Brakes!" I said it stern and loud enough that they new without question that I was not joking. I put my foot down two more times into the nothing that was supposed to resist.

We were on a straight road with a 10 mph corner at the end, a high dirt hill to the right, a dirt road that went out of sight ahead and three blood smears if I didn't do this right. I saw saplings on the corner and had decided in a blink to take the car into a drift and sideways into the saplings. The dirt road was an unknown that went downward out of sight. I later found out that a house sat directly in the path, and we would have gone through their living room, had we gone straight.

As I approached the corner, I angled the car for the most drift when, low and behold a wooden power pole. Well, I've had my face sewn back on and didn't enjoy it. I pulled the wheel a bit more, tires squealing into the turn.

BACKGROUND

The man who owned the site had found many wrecked cars on mornings after drinking binges. He took dirt from the property and built an angled ramp for these cars to be stopped by.

We hit the berm at an angle enough to ricochet off of the pole, only contacting with the front fender and drivers mirror and only enough to crack the mirror up and down. We then launched twelve feet in the air as evidenced by the berries on the lower part of the bumper and the lack of damage to the berries. We then flew forty feet. Our flight path took us over the bushes and, oh my goodness, a 1969 Chevy pick-up. Our tires skidded across the hood and brought the front end down. The front stopped in a pile of dirt, excavated while building the berm. So there we sat.

I opened the door, motor still running and looked out to see six feet of air between me and the ground as I sat directly over the trench the dirt came from. The only part of the car on the hood of the truck at this point was the twin tail pipe tips and they were barely damaged. The only injury was due to the initial ricochet, my mechanic bruised his butt cheek on the shifter and stuff flew from the back, all over Haven as she smacked her head on the back of the passenger seat to receive a goose egg.

All in all, not bad. No real injuries and Haven's dad took it well that we had flown his daughter without express written permission.

IN CLOSING

I hope that I have chosen the stories from my life that others find interesting. Each story that I write reminds me of three more. As I write these for the eyes of my children and the eyes of strangers as well, I have to keep in mind that some stories are best untold. All of the things written about here are true and part of my life. When I can't remember, I say that I can't and when I don't want too many eyes, I keep the location from being written, but the stories are true.

I have had experiences prior to my eighteenth birthday that most people can never equal in an eighty-year-life span. I am still sorting through the stories and my memories as I write the closer, so I have no idea if I will have mentioned the thirty-eight broken bones, hang gliding with eagles, five bullet holes or seven knife (well, stab) wounds. I am sure that snow storms are in the mix, getting sick trying to give my family food and shelter, because I want my kids to know the man and what it took to be their father. With any luck, I will tell of the other stories of fun and not just the ones of pain. The only problem is that in my life, the luck isn't always good, fun usually ends in some kind of pain but the stories are always worth telling.

Growing up was difficult, but I made the best of it. I was always the most optimistic person that I had ever known. It was indelibly linked to my psyche to get over it, around it, under it or through it without allowing the buggers on the other side to win.

As I write this tonight, I dream of the life that I had. When I was a young child, I said that I want to end my life on the front porch and I will never have to say, "I wish that I had done that." I have soared with eagles on a hang glider that I bought with my own money, before I was old enough to drive. I saw the hatch lings from the sky from so close that both mommy and daddy eagle gave me stern warning in the form of fly byes. I have lived through the toughest of battles and come out unscathed. When I did get hurt, I still won and came back with my head held high. Not for anybody else, but for myself. Because I lived my life alone for so much of it, that I learned that I was my biggest fan. I taught myself everything and did it better than anyone. I amaze professionals at their own professions and challenge champions at their own specialty.

Now, at forty-two, I may never dance with Scoobies again. I may never ride a roller coaster or run for miles or even yards for that matter. I can't ever do the things that I have done, again. But, I did it all. I did everything and did it with my own disastrous style. I gave hope to those without hope just by being me. They saw my misadventures and sour luck and were able to look at me and say "at least I'm not you." I saved lives, delivered babies, rescued people from fires, and wrecked cars. I wrecked cars myself as well. I have jumped from perfectly good airplanes, broken bones and broken other peoples bones. I've been a hero and, if you were a bad guy who didn't realize he was the bad guy, been a villain. I've lived my life giving the shirt off of my own back to the point of ruin. I never asked for help without exhausting every other avenue and when I did ask for help, rarely, if ever, received any.

I can fix anything. I fix cars, computers, bicycles, skateboards, and once fixed a balloon, but I can't fix me. I broke my back and know that it is just a matter of time before I lose even more. I broke my psyche a while back and came back after five years. I fixed that too, only to find that I was not the person that I was, yet the guy I became isn't bad either.

When the world seems against your every move, wash your face and hands and start again. The worst thing that can happen is to live to an old age having tried nothing, so get out and do what it is that you want; to make you who you want to be. The front porch will be waiting for you when you're ready.

But, if you are like me, you will sit there with your grand kids and their children, telling stories of how you became who you are and how not to do things.